U0446964

【英汉对照全译本】

AN INQUIRY INTO THE NATURE AND CAUSES OF THE WEALTH OF NATIONS
国民财富的性质与原理

[英]亚当·斯密 著

赵东旭 丁 毅 译

（二）

中国社会科学出版社

CHAPTER XI

Of The Rent Of Land

Rent is the produce which is over what is necessary to pay the farmer ordinary profit.
Rent, considered as the price paid for the use of land, is naturally the highest which the tenant can afford to pay in the actual circumstances of the land. In adjusting the terms of the lease, the landlord endeavours to leave him no greater share of the produce than what is sufficient to keep up the stock from which he furnishes the seed, pays the labour, and purchases and maintains the cattle and other instruments of husbandry, together with the ordinary profits of farming stock in the neighbourhood This is evidently the smallest share with which the tenant can content himself without being a loser, and the landlord seldom means to leave him any more. Whatever part of the produce, or, what is the same thing, whatever part of its price, is over and above this share, he naturally endeavours to reserve to himself as the rent of his land, which is evidently the highest the tenant can afford to pay in the actual circumstances of the land. Sometimes, indeed, the liberality, more frequently the ignorance, of the landlord, makes him accept of somewhat less than this portion; and sometimes too, though more rarely, the ignorance of the tenant makes him undertake to pay somewhat more, or to content himself with somewhat less, than the ordinary profits of farming stock in the neighbourhood. This portion, however, may still be considered as the natural rent of land, or the rent for which it is naturally meant that land should for the most part be let.

It is not merely interest on stock laid out in improvements,
The rent of land, it may be thought, is frequently no more than a reasonable profit or interest for the stock laid out by the landlord upon its improvement. This, no doubt, may be partly the case upon some occasions; for it can scarce ever be more than partly the ease. The landlord demands a rent even for unimproved land, and the supposed interest or profit upon the expence of improvement is generally

第十一章 论地租

地租,作为使用土地的代价,自然是承租者根据土地的实际情状所能支付的最高价格。在确定租约条件时,地主总是试图使留给承租者的土地生产物的份额,只够用来补偿其购买种子、支付劳动工资、购置和维持牲畜及与其他农具的费用再加上当地农业资本的平均利润。这显然是租地者在不亏本的条件下所能接受的最低限额,而地主也根本不想再给他更多了。多于这个数额的生产物部分或者换句话说,也即这部分产物的价格,地主都自然地想设法将其据为己有。地租,显然就是承租者根据土地的实际情况所能支付的最高限额。当然了,有时候由于地主的慷慨大方,更多是由于地主的无知,地主接受了比这一数额稍低的地租;同样的道理,尽管比较少见,但有时候承租者也由于无知支付比这一数额稍高的地租,即满足于接受比当地农业资本平均利润稍低的利润。但这个数额仍然可以视为自然地租,也即可以自然使大部分土地出租出去应得的租金。

地租或许被认为只不过是回报地主改良土地资本的合理利润或利息。当然,在某些场合情况下部分情况的确如此,但这仅仅是部分而已。因为对于那些没有改良的土地,地主也索取地租。而所谓改良费用的利息或利润,通常只是这种原始地租的附

地租是支付农场普通利润以外的那部分产物

地租不仅仅是改良土地的资本利息

an addition to this original rent. Those improvements, besides, are not always made by the stock of the landlord, but sometimes by that of the tenant. When the lease comes to be renewed, however, the landlord commonly demands the same augmentation of rent, as if they had been all made by his own.

<small>and is sometimes obtained for land incapable of improvement, such as rocks where kelp grows;</small>
He sometimes demands rent for what is altogether incapable of human improvement. Kelp is a species of sea-weed, which, when burnt, yields an alkaline salt, useful for making glass, soap, and for several other purposes. It grows in several parts of Great Britain, particularly in Scotland, upon such rocks only as lie within the high water mark, which are twice every day covered with the sea, and of which the produce, therefore, was never augmented by human industry. The landlord, however, whose estate is bounded by a kelp shore of this kind, demands a rent for it as much as for his corn fields.

<small>and for the opportunity to fish.</small>
The sea in the neighbourhood of the islands of Shetland is more than commonly abundant in fish, which make a great part of the subsistence of their inhabitants. But in order to profit by the produce of the water, they must have a habitation upon the neighbouring land. The rent of the landlord is in proportion, not to what the farmer can make by the land, but to what he can make both by the land and by the water. It is partly paid in sea-fish; and one of the very few instances in which rent makes a part of the price of that commodity, is to be found in that country.

<small>It is therefore a monopoly price.</small>
The rent of land, therefore, considered as the price paid for the use of the land, is naturally a monopoly price. It is not at all proportioned to what the landlord may have laid out upon the improvement of the land, or to what he can afford to take; but to what the farmer can afford to give.

<small>Whether particular parts of produce fetch a price sufficient to yield a rent depends on the demand.</small>
Such parts only of the produce of land can commonly be brought to market of which, the ordinary price is sufficient to replace the stock which must be employed in bringing them thither, together with its ordinary profits. If the ordinary price is more than this, the surplus part of it will naturally go to the rent of the land. If it is not more, though the commodity may be brought to market, it can afford no rent to the landlord. Whether the price is, or is not more, depends upon the demand.

加额。况且并不总是由地主出资来改良土地,有些时候是由承租土地者出资改良的。然而,当续签租约时,地主往往都要求增加地租,仿佛所有的改良都是由他出资进行的。

有时地主对于人力完全无法改良的土地也索取地租。比如说海藻(kelp),它是海草的一种,当经过燃烧后,就可以产生一种用于制造玻璃、肥皂和其他用途的碱盐。不列颠的几个地方,尤其是在苏格兰,都生产这种海藻。它生长于高水位、一天能被海水淹没两次的岩石上。所以,这些海藻根本不可能通过人力来增加数量的。但是,地主对于这种由产生这种海藻的海岸线为界围成的地产,也像对他们的谷田一样征收地租。

> 有时候地主对于根本无法改良的土地也征收地租,如有助于生长海藻的岩石;

设得兰群岛附近海域渔产极为丰富。鱼就构成了当地居民的大部分生活资料。但是,居民要想从这些水产物中获利,必须居住在附近的陆地上。这时当地地主所征收的地租,就不是与农夫从土地上所能获得的收益成比例,而是与他从土地和海上这两方面所能获得的收益成比例。这种地租的一部分是用海鱼来支付的。这种地租构成商品价格的一部分的例子比较少见,此处我们可以看到一例。

> 以及从捕鱼的机会中获得地租。

所以,地租作为使用土地支付的代价,自然就是一种垄断价格。它完全不与地主改良土地的资金或者地主所能收取的数额成比例,而与农夫所能支付的数额成比例。

> 所以,地租是一种垄断价格。

只有平均价格足以补偿将其送往市场所需的资本加上这种资本的平均利润的那部分土地生产物,才能经常送往市场进行销售。如果平均价格超过了这个限度,其剩余部分自然就归作土地地租了。如果没有超过这个限度,尽管货物仍可运往市场销售,但却并不能给地主支付地租。价格是否高于这个限度取决于需求。

> 部分产物的价格是否足以提供地租,取决于需求。

<small>Some parts are always in sufficient demand; others sometimes are and sometimes are not.</small>   There are some parts of the produce of land for which the demand must always be such as to afford a greater price than what is sufficient to bring them to market; and there are others for which it either may or may not be such as to afford this greater price. The former must always afford a rent to that landlord. The latter sometimes may, and sometimes may not, according to different circumstances.

<small>Wages and profit are causes of price; rent is an effect.</small>   Rent, it is to be observed, therefore, enters into the composition of the price of commodities in a different way from wages and profit. High or low wages and profit, are the causes of high or low price; high or low rent is the effect of it. It is because high or low wages and profit must be paid, in order to bring a particular commodity to market, that its price is high or low. But it is because its price is high or low; a great deal more, or very little more, or no more, than what is sufficient to pay those wages and profit, that it affords a high rent, or a low rent, or no rent at all.

<small>The chapter is divided into three parts.</small>   The particular consideration, first, of those parts of the produce of land which always afford some rent; secondly, of those which sometimes may and sometimes may not afford rent; and, thirdly, of the variations which, in the different periods of improvement, naturally take place, in the relative value of those two different sorts of rude produce, when compared both with one another and with manufactured commodities, will divide this chapter into three parts.

PART I   *Of the Produce of Land which always affords Rent*

<small>Food can always purchase as much labour as it can maintain.</small>   As men, like all other animals, naturally multiply in proportion to the means of their subsistence, food is always, more or less, in demand. It can always purchase or command a greater or smaller quantity of labour, and somebody can always be found who is willing to do something in order to obtain it. The quantity of labour, indeed, which it can purchase, is not always equal to what it could maintain, if managed in the most economical manner, on account of the high wages which are sometimes given to labour. But it can always purchase such a quantity of labour as it can maintain, according

对于土地生产物中的部分产物的需求,总是可以使其以超过运往市场原价的价格销售出去;而有些产物则或者可能或者不可能卖出这样的高价。那么前者就总能够给地主提供地租;而后者就会根据情况的不同,有时能够提供地租,有时不能够提供地租。

> 部分产品总是能够满足需求,而其他部分则有时有有时没有这样的需求。

因此,应当看到,地租是以不同于工资和利润的方式进入商品的价格构成的。工资和利润的高低是价格高低的原因,而地租的高低则是价格高低的结果。因为一个特定商品送往市场销售所需支付的工资与利润有高有低,所以商品的价格也有高有低。这个商品的价格有些远远高于、有些远远低于或者不高于支付工资和利润的额度,正是这个价格的有高有低造成了有些商品能够提供高地租、低地租或者不能提供地租。

> 工资和利润是价格的原因,地租是价格的结果。

本章分为三部分专门研究:第一,总能提供地租的土地生产物;第二,有时能提供、有时不能提供地租的土地生产物;第三,在不同的改良时期,这两种不同的天然生产物彼此之间相比较或者与制造品相比较时,所产生的相对价值的自然变化。

> 本章分为三部分。

第一部分 论总能提供地租的土地生产物

与所有其他动物一样,人类的繁衍自然而然地与其生活资料成比例。因此,食物总是或多或少地为人所需求。食物总可以购买或者支配或多或少的劳动力,而且也总可以找到愿意为获得食物而做事的人。当然,由于有时为劳动支付的工资很高,食物所能购得的劳动量并不总与以最节约的方式进行管理时所能维持的劳动量相等。不过食物总能根据附近地区劳动者的平均生活

> 食物总能购得它所能维持的劳动数量。

to the rate at which that sort of labour is commonly maintained in the neighbourhood.

<small>Almost all land produces more than enough food to maintain the labour and pay the profits, and therefore yields rent.</small> But land, in almost any situation, produces a greater quantity of food than what is sufficient to maintain all the labour necessary for bringing it to market, in the most liberal way in which that labour is ever maintained. The surplus too is always more than sufficient to replace the stock which employed that labour, together with its profits. Something, therefore, always remains for a rent to the landlord.

The most desart moors in Norway and Scotland produce some sort of pasture for cattle, of which the milk and the increase are always more than sufficient, not only to maintain all the labour necessary for tending them, and to pay the ordinary profit to the farmer or owner of the herd or flock; but to afford some small rent to the landlord. The rent increases in proportion to the goodness of the pasture. The same extent of ground not only maintains a greater number of cattle, but as they are brought within a smaller compass, less labour becomes requisite to tend them, and to collect their produce. The landlord gains both ways; by the increase of the produce, and by the diminution of the labour which must be maintained out of it.

<small>The rent varies with situation as well as with fertility.</small> The rent of land not only varies with its fertility, whatever be its produce, but with its situation, whatever be its fertility. Land in the neighbourhood of a town gives a greater rent than land equally fertile in a distant part of the country. Though it may cost no more labour to cultivate the one than the other, it must always cost more to bring the produce of the distant land to market. A greater quantity of labour, therefore, must be maintained out of it; and the surplus, from which are drawn both the profit of the farmer and the rent of the landlord, must be diminished. But in remote parts of the country the rate of profits, as has already been shown, is generally higher than in the neighbourhood of a large town. A smaller proportion of this diminished surplus, therefore, must belong to the landlord.

<small>Good roads, etc., diminish differences of rent.</small> Good roads, canals, and navigable rivers, by diminishing the expence of carriage, put the remote parts of the country more nearly upon a level with those in the neighbourhood of the town.

水平购到得以维持下去的劳动数量。

但是,几乎所有的情况下,土地上生产的食物扣除维持将食物送往市场进行销售所需的劳动者的食物之外,还存在着多余的部分。这个多余的部分,也总是在扣除补偿雇用劳动所支付的资本和利润之外,还存在剩余可留作地主的地租。

> 所有土地的生产物比劳动支付和利润要多,因此可以提供地租。

在挪威和苏格兰荒芜的旷野上,生长着一种牧草。用这种牧草饲养出来的牲畜的奶和繁殖出来的牲畜,扣除维持饲养牧畜所必需的全部劳动力和支付给畜牧人或者畜群所有者的平均利润之外,还存在少量的剩余可作为地主的地租。牧场地租随着牧场优良程度而增加。优良的土地要比同样面积的劣等土地能饲养更多的牲畜,而且还由于牲畜可以集中在较小的地区来饲养和收集他们的产品,这样就需要较少的劳动力。这样,从增加土地生产物的数量和维持费用的减少这两个方面地主都可以获得利益。

不管土地的生产物是什么,土地的地租是随着土地的肥沃程度不同而不同的;不管土地的肥沃程度如何,土地的地租又是随着土地的位置的不同而不同的。那些靠近城市的土地就要比同样肥沃但却位于偏僻地方的土地,可以提供更高的地租。尽管耕种后者所用的劳动量并不比耕种前者所花用的劳动量多,但将生产物从偏僻地区运到市场上却需要更多的劳动量。因此,偏僻地区必须需要更多数量的劳动,农场主的利润和地主的地租所得的剩余部分也就必然减少了。但在前面我们已经提到,通常情况下偏僻地区的利润率要比城市邻近地区的利润率高,因此,在这个减少了的剩余中,属于地土的那一部分必然会更少了。

> 土地肥沃程度和位置的地租不相同也不同。

由于良好的道路、运河和通航的河道可以降低运输费用,就使得偏僻地区与临近城市的地区更加接近于同一水平。因此在

> 良好的道路等减租差地可以少地异。

They are upon that account the greatest of all improvements. They encourage the cultivation of the remote, which must always be the most extensive circle of the country. They are advantageous to the town, by breaking down the monopoly of the country in its neighbourhood. They are advantageous even to that part of the country. Though they introduce some rival commodities into the old market, they open many new markets to its produce. Monopoly, besides, is a great enemy to good management, which can never be universally established but in consequence of that free and universal competition which forces everybody to have recourse to it for the sake of self-defence. It is not more than fifty years ago, that some of the counties in the neighbourhood of London petitioned the parliament against the extension of the turnpike roads into the remoter counties. Those remoter counties, they pretended, from the cheapness of labour, would be able to sell their grass and corn cheaper in the London market than themselves, and would thereby reduce their rents, and ruin their cultivation. Their rents, however, have risen, and their cultivation has been improved since that time.

<small>Corn land yields a larger supply of food after maintaining labour than pasture.</small>   A corn field of moderate fertility produces a much greater quantity of food for man, than the best pasture of equal extent. Though its cultivation requires much more labour, yet the surplus which remains after replacing the seed and maintaining all that labour, is likewise much greater. If a pound of butcher's-meat, therefore, was never supposed to be worth more than a pound of bread, this greater surplus would every-where be of greater value, and constitute a greater fund both for the profit of the farmer and the rent of the landlord. It seems to have done so universally in the rude beginnings of agriculture.

<small>In early times meat is cheaper than bread.</small>   But the relative values of those two different species of food, bread, and butcher's meat, are very different in the different periods of agriculture. In its rude beginnings, the unimproved wilds, which then occupy the far greater part of the country, are all abandoned to cattle. There is more butcher's-meat than bread, and bread, therefore, is the food for which there is the greatest competition, and which

所有的改良中改善交通是最有效的改良。偏僻地区必定是一个国家幅员最为辽阔的地方，交通的改善促进了这些地区的开发。由于这样打破了城市附近乡村的垄断，所以对城市是有利的。即便对这些农村来说交通改良也是有益的，尽管它们会给那些旧市场带来一些竞争性的商品，但它们同时也会为农村的农产品打开许多新的市场。再者，垄断是良好经营的大敌，只有通过自由竞争和普遍的竞争，来迫使每个人为了自卫不得不采取良好经营的方法，才能建立起良好的经营。大约五十年前，伦敦近郊的一些州郡曾经向国会申诉，反对把征收通行税的道路扩展到偏僻的州郡。他们认为由于那些偏僻州郡的劳动力便宜，那些地区的牧草和谷物也会以相对于临近伦敦的州郡较低的价格在伦敦市场出售，这样一来就会减少靠近伦敦的州郡的地租，破坏了他们的耕种。然而实际上自那个时候起，他们的地租却提高了，而他们的耕种也改善了。

　　一块中等肥沃程度的谷田比同样大小的最好的草地所能为人类生产出的食物多得多。虽然耕种谷田需要花费更多的劳动量，但在扣除对种子的补偿和维持所有劳动的费用之后还会存在大得多的剩余。因此如果一磅鲜肉的价格从来都没有超过一磅面包的价格，那么这种较大的剩余到处都具有较大的价值，就构成了为农场主提供利润和为地主提供地租的较大资源。在农业的原始阶段，情况看来通常如此。

　　但在不同的农业发展时期，面包与鲜肉的相对价值是大不相同的。在农业原始初期，占据着绝大部分国土面积的未开垦的土地都用来饲养牲畜。由于鲜肉数量多于面包，面包就成了竞争性最大的食物，也因此可卖得最高的价格。乌洛阿告诉我们，在布

consequently brings the greatest price. At Buenos Ayres, we are told by Ulloa, four reals, one-and-twenty pence halfpenny sterling, was, forty or fifty years ago, the ordinary price of an ox, chosen from a herd of two or three hundred. ①He says nothing of the price of bread, probably because he found nothing remarkable about it. An ox there, he says, costs little more than the labour of catching him. But corn can no-where be raised without a great deal of labour, and in a country which lies upon the river Plate, at that time the direct road from Europe to the silver mines of Potosi, the money price of labour could not be very cheap. It is otherwise when cultivation is extended over the greater part of the country. There is then more bread than butcher s-meat. The competition changes its direction, and the price of butcher's-meat becomes greater than the price of bread.

<small>but later on it becomes dearer,</small>   By the extension besides of cultivation the unimproved wilds become insufficient to supply the demand for butcher's-meat. A great part of the cultivated lands must be employed in rearing and fattening cattle, of which the price, therefore, must be sufficient to pay, not only the labour necessary for tending them, but the rent which the landlord and the profit which the farmer could have drawn from such land employed in tillage. The cattle bred upon the most uncultivated moors, when brought to the same market, are, in proportion to their weight or goodness, sold at the same price as those which are reared upon the most improved land. The proprietors of those moors profit by it, and raise the rent of their land in proportion to the price of their cattle. It is not more than a century ago that in many parts of the highlands of Scotland, butcher's-meat was as cheap or cheaper than even bread made of oat-meal. The union opened the market of England to the highland cattle. Their ordinary price is at present about three times greater than at the

---

① [Vol. i., p. 532, in the French translation of Juan and Ulloa's work, *Voyage historique de l'Amérique méridionale par don George Juan et don Antoine de Ulloa*, 1752. The statement is repeated in almost the same words, substituting 'three or four hundred' for 'two or three hundred', below.]

宜诺斯艾利斯,在四五十年以前一头牛的平均价格是 4 雷阿尔(real)[1],即 21 个半便士,而且在购买时还可以在二三百头的牛群中随意挑选①。他没有谈到面包的价格,或许他认为面包的价格没有什么值得提到的地方吧。他说在那边一头牛的价格不超过捕捉一头牛所耗费的劳动的价格。然而无论在何处,种植谷物都需要大量的劳动力,对于这样一个处在当时欧洲直通波托西银矿的普拉特河流域的国家来说,劳动力的货币价格肯定不会很便宜的。然而当耕种扩展到国内大部分地区时,情形就截然不同了。面包变得比鲜肉要多,竞争的方向转变了,鲜肉价格反而变得比面包高了。

另外,随着耕种的扩展,尚未开垦的荒野已经不足以满足鲜肉的需求了。一大部分耕地都必须用来饲养和催肥牲畜,因此鲜肉的价格必须要足以支付饲养牲畜所花费的劳动、地主的地租和农场主将土地用于耕种时所能收到的利润。但是,完全没有开垦的荒野上所饲养出的牲畜和改良最好的土地上所饲养出的牲畜,比照品质和重量,它们在同一市场可以按照同样的价格出售。这样荒野土地的所有者就获利了,由于牲畜的价格提高,就提高了他们土地的地租。不到一个世纪以前,在苏格兰高地许多地区的鲜肉的价格与燕麦面包的价格相等,甚至还会更为便宜。后来英格兰和苏格兰统一后,就打开了苏格兰高地牲畜在英格兰的市场。现在它们的平均价格大概是本世纪初的三倍,而且在此期间

① 见居安(Juan)和乌洛阿(Ulloa)的法文译本。《唐·乔治·居安和唐·安东·德·乌洛阿南美航海史》第 1 卷第 532 页,1752 年。后面讲述了差不多同样的内容,只是将二三百改为三四百。

[1] 雷阿尔:西班牙和拉丁美洲旧时曾使用过的一种银币。

beginning of the century, and the rents of many highland estates have been tripled and quadrupled in the same time. In almost every part of Great Britain a pound of the best butcher's-meat is, in the present times, generally worth more than two pounds of the best white bread; and in plentiful years it is sometimes worth three or four pounds.

<small>and pasture yields as good a rent as corn land,</small>
It is thus that in the progress of improvement the rent and profit of unimproved pasture come to be regulated in some measure by the rent and profit of what is improved, and these again by the rent and profit of corn. Corn is an annual crop. Butcher's-meat, a crop which requires four or five years to grow. As an acre of land, therefore, will produce a much smaller quantity of the one species of food than of the other, the inferiority of the quantity must be compensated by the superiority of the price. If it was more than compensated, more corn land would be turned into pasture; and if it was not compensated, part of what was in pasture would be brought back into corn.

<small>and sometimes a greater one,</small>
This equality, however, between the rent and profit of grass and those of corn; of the land of which the immediate produce is food for cattle, and of that of which the immediate produce is food for men; must be understood to take place only through the greater part of the improved lands of a great country. In some particular local situations it is quite otherwise, and the rent and profit of grass are much superior to what can be made by corn.

<small>as in the neighbourhood of a great town,</small>
Thus in the neighbourhood of a great town, the demand for milk and for forage to horses, frequently contribute, together with the high price of butcher's-meat, to raise the value of grass above what may be called its natural proportion to that of corn. This local advantage, it is evident, cannot be communicated to the lands at a distance.

<small>or all over a populous country which imports corn,</small>
Particular circumstances have sometimes rendered some countries so populous, that the whole territory, like the lands in the neighbourhood of a great town, has not been sufficient to produce both the grass and the corn necessary for the subsistence of their inhabitants. Their lands, therefore, have been principally employed in the production of grass, the more bulky commodity, and which cannot be so easily brought from a great distance; and corn, the food of the great body

苏格兰高地的许多土地的地租也增加三四倍。如今几乎在不列颠的各处,一磅最好的鲜肉的价值约是两磅最好的白面包的价值的两倍以上,尤其在丰收的年月,有时甚至会值三磅到四磅。

因此,在改良的过程中,那些没有经过改良的牧场的地租与利润,在一定程度上会受到改良了的牧场的地租与利润的调节,而改良了的牧场的地租与利润,又会受到谷田的地租与利润的调节。谷物一年只收割一次,而取得鲜肉却需要四五年的时间。所以同样的一亩地生产的鲜肉的数量要比生产的谷物的数量少得多,这样数量少的必须以较高的价格来获得补偿。如果一旦价格补偿的程度超过了这个限度,就会有更多的谷田改作牧场;而如果价格的补偿程度没有超过这个限度,就会有一部分已经用作牧场的土地又重新转回种植谷物。_{牧场提供地租和谷田一样多,}

不过,牧草和谷物在地租和利润上的这种均等,直接生产牲畜食物和直接生产人类食物在土地的地租和利润上的这种均等,只能说当在一个国家大部分的土地都已经经过改良时才会发生。而在某些个别地方,情形却截然不同,牧场的地租和利润要比谷田的地租和利润高得多。_{有时牧场提供的地租要比谷田提供的地租高,}

所以,靠近大城市的地方,对牛奶和马料的需求伴随着鲜肉的高价,经常使牧草的价格也提高到超过它对谷物价格的自然比例。显然,这种地方性利益是不可能扩展到偏僻地区。_{如在靠近大城市的地区,}

特殊的情况有时会使一个国家的人口非常的密集,以至于这个国家的所有土地都如同是大城市的邻近地区一样,这样生产出的牧草和谷物就不足以满足居民生活的需要。所以这个国家的土地就主要用来生产牧草,因为它们体积较大且不易从远方运来,而大多数人民所消费的谷物则由外国进口。现在的荷兰即是_{或进口谷物的人口众多的国家,}

such as Holland and ancient Italy, of the people, has been chiefly imported from foreign countries. Holland is at present in this situation, and a considerable part of ancient Italy seems to have been so during the prosperity of the Romans. To feed well, old Cato said, as we are told by Cicero, was the first and most profitable thing in the management of a private estate; to feed tolerably well, the second; and to feed ill, the third. To plough, he ranked only in the fourth place of profit and advantage. ① Tillage, indeed, in that part of ancient Italy which lay in the neighbourhood of Rome, must have been very much discouraged by the distributions of corn which were frequently made to the people, either gratuitously, or at a very low price. This corn was brought from the conquered provinces, of which several, instead of taxes, were obliged to furnish a tenth part of their produce at a stated price, about sixpence a peck, to the republic. The low price at which this corn was distributed to the people, must necessarily have sunk the price of what could be brought to the Roman market from Latium, or the ancient territory of Rome, and must have discouraged its cultivation in that country.

and occasionally in a country where enclosure is unusual. In an open country too, of which the principal produce is corn, a well-enclosed piece of grass will frequently rent higher than any corn field in its neighbourhood. It is convenient for the maintenance of the cattle employed in the cultivation of the corn, and its high rent is, in this case, not so properly paid from the value of its own produce, as from that of the corn lands which are cultivated by means of it. It is likely to fall, if ever the neighbouring lands are completely enclosed. The present high rent of enclosed land in Scotland seems owing to the scarcity of enclosure, and will probably last no longer than that scarcity. The advantage of enclosure is greater for pasture

---

① [Cicero, *De officiis*, lib. ii. ad fin. Quoted in *Lectures*, p. 229.]

如此。在罗马繁荣时代,古意大利情况似乎也是如此。西塞罗告诉我们,老加图[1]曾说过:"在私有土地的经营中,善于饲养牲畜是头等有利可图的事情;饲养的还算可以是次等的;饲养的不好是三等获利。"他把耕种仅仅列为利得和好处的第四位①。确实,在意大利邻近的古罗马,谷物常常被无偿地或低价地分配给人民,那么该地区的耕种大大受到阻碍。这些被分配的谷物,来自被征服省份。其中有的不纳赋税,但须将产物 1/10 按规定的每配克 6 便士的法定价格提供给罗马共和国。共和国把这些谷物低价地分配给人民,这必然降低罗马旧领土的谷物在罗马市场上的价格,因而必然阻碍该国的耕种。

如意大利和荷兰,

在一些开阔的地区,那里以谷物为主要产物,一片圈围得很好的草地,其地租往往比附近谷地的地租高。圈围更便于维持饲养耕畜,而圈围地这样高的地租,并不是由于草地生产物的价值,而是由于利用耕畜耕种的谷田生产物的价值。若邻近土地全都被圈围,那高地租很可能就会跌落。现在苏格兰圈围地的高价地租似乎归因于圈围地太少,如果圈围地扩大,其地租大概就会不会这样高。圈围土地对草地比对谷物更有好处,它节省看守牲畜

圈不的也如有时地常国家是此,

---

① 西塞罗:《论责任》,第 2 篇全篇,引自《关于法律、警察、岁入及军备的演讲》第 229 页。

[1] 马库斯·波希乌斯[老加图(Marcus Porcius)前 234 年~前 149 年]:罗马政治家和将军,著有罗马的第一部历史。在任监察期间,他试图恢复罗马社会生活的简朴作风。

马库斯·波希乌斯[小加图(Marcus Porcius)前 95 年~前 46 年]:罗马斯多噶派哲学家、政治家,老加图的曾孙。他是尤里乌斯·恺撒政治野心的保守派对手,他支持庞贝并在内战中反对恺撒,并在恺撒在塞浦路斯取得决定性胜利后自杀。

than for corn. It saves the labour of guarding the cattle, which feed better too when they are not liable to be disturbed by their keeper or his dog.

<small>Ordinarily the rent of corn land regulates that of pasture.</small>　But where there is no local advantage of this kind, the rent and profit of corn, or whatever else is the common vegetable food of the people, must naturally regulate, upon the land which is fit for producing it, the rent and profit of pasture.

<small>Improved methods of feeding cattle lower meat in proportion to bread.</small>　The use of the artificial grasses, of turnips, carrots, cabbages, and the other expedients which have been fallen upon to make an equal quantity of land feed a greater number of cattle than when in natural grass, should somewhat reduce, it might be expected, the superiority which, in an improved country, the price of butcher's-meat naturally has over that of bread. It seems accordingly to have done so; and there is some reason for believing that, at least in the London market, the price of butcher's-meat in proportion to the price of bread, is a good deal lower in the present times than it was in the beginning of the last century.

<small>The price of meat was higher at the beginning of the seventeenth rentury [sic] Inan in 1763-4;</small>　In the appendix to the Life of Prince Henry, Doctor Birch has given us an account of the prices of butcher's-meat as commonly paid by that prince. It is there said that the four quarters of an ox weighing six hundred pounds usually cost him nine pounds ten shillings, or thereabouts; that is, thirty-one shillings and eight pence per hundred pounds weight. ①Prince Henry died on the 6th of November 1612, in the nineteenth year of his age. ②

In March 1764, there was a parliamentary inquiry into the causes of the high price of provisions at that time. It was then, among other proof to the same purpose, given in evidence by a Virginia merchant, that in March 1763, he had victualled his ships for twenty-four or twenty-five shillings the hundred weight of beef, which he considered as the ordinary price; whereas, in that dear year, he had paid twenty-seven shillings for the same weight and sort. ③This high price in 1764 is, however, four shillings and eight pence cheaper than the ordinary price paid by prince Henry; and it is the best beef only, it must be observed, which is fit to be salted for those distant voyages.

---

①　[*The Life of Henry Prince of Wales*, by Thomas Birch, D. D., 1760, p. 346.]

②　[*Ibid.*, p. 271.]

③　[*A Report from the Committee who, upon the 8th day of February, 1764, were appointed to inquire into the Causes of the High Price of Provisions with the proceedings of the House thereupon*. Published by order of the House of Commons, 1764, paragraph 4.]

的劳动,使牲畜不受守护人或他的狗的惊扰,也吃得更好。

但在没有这种地方性利益的地方,谷物或其他人普通蔬菜事物的地租和利润,在其适应生长的地方,必须自动根据草地的利润和地租来调整。

一般谷物的地租调节草地的地租。

人工牧草的使用,例如芜青、胡萝卜、包菜,与使用天然牧草相比,同样面积的耕地能饲养更多的牲畜。这样就可以期望能降低进步国家中鲜肉高于面包价格的幅度。而且,事实上似乎也是如此;至少在伦敦市场上鲜肉对面包的相对价格,现今比上世纪初要低得多。

饲养牲畜方法的改良降低鲜肉与面包价格的比例。

伯奇博士在他所著《亨利亲王传》的附录中记录了这位亲王日常购买的鲜肉的价格。重 600 磅的牛一头通常花费他 9 镑 10 先令,即每 100 磅 31 先令 8 便士①。亨利亲王是在 1612 年 11 月 6 日死的,当时他 19 岁②。

17 世纪初肉价比 1763—1764 年高

1764 年 3 月,议会曾对当时食品价格高昂的原因进行了调查,在这次搜集的许多证据中,有一个弗吉尼亚商人提供的证词:他于 1763 年 3 月备办船上食物,支付每百磅牛肉 24 先令至 25 先令的价格,他认为这是普通价格,而在物价高的 1764 年,对于同质同量的牛肉,他却支付 27 先令③。但是,1764 年这样高的价格,却比亨利亲王所付的日常价格还便宜 4 先令 8 便士;同时还应当指出,只有最好的牛肉才适于腌藏,供远道航海之用。

---

① 托马斯·伯奇:《威尔士亨利亲王传》,1760 年,第 346 页。
② 同上书,第 271 页。
③ 《下议院就食物价格高昂原因于 1764 年 2 月 8 日任命的委员会调查报告》,由英国国会下议院指示出版,1764 年,第 4 段。

The price paid by prince Henry amounts to $3\frac{4}{5}d.$ per pound weight of the whole carcase, coarse and choice pieces taken together; and at that rate the choice pieces could not have been sold by retail for less than $4\frac{1}{2}d.$ or $5d.$ the pound.

In the parliamentary inquiry in 1764, the witnesses stated the price of the choice pieces of the best beef to be to the consumer $4d.$ and $4\frac{1}{4}d.$ the pound; and the coarse pieces in general to be from seven farthings to $2\frac{1}{2}d.$ and $2\frac{3}{4}d.$; and this they said was in general one half-penny dearer than the same sort of pieces had usually been sold in the month of March. ① But even this high price is still a good deal cheaper than what we can well suppose the ordinary retail price to have been in the time of prince Henry.

<small>whereas wheat was cheaper</small> During the twelve first years of the last century, the average price of the best wheat at the Windsor market was $1l.$ $18s.$ $3\frac{1}{6}d.$ the quarter of nine Winchester bushels.

But in the twelve years preceding 1764, including that year, the average price of the same measure of the best wheat at the same market was $2l.$ $1s.$ $9\frac{1}{2}d.$ ②

In the twelve first years of the last century, therefore, wheat

---

① [*Report from the Committee*, paragraph 3 almost *verbatim*. The Committee resolved 'that the high price of provisions of late has been occasioned partly by circumstances peculiar to the season and the year, and partly by the defect of the laws in force for convicting and punishing all persons concerned in forestalling cattle in their passage to market. ']

② [These prices are deduced from the tables at the end of the chapter.]

亨利亲王所支付的价格,那是包括整个牛身、次等肉和上等肉合在一起的价格,等于每磅 $3\frac{4}{5}$ 便士。按照这种推算下来,当时零售的上等肉,每磅不可能少于 4 便士半或 5 便士。

在 1764 年议会作调查时,作证人都说,当时上等牛肉的上好肉块的零售价格每磅为 4 便士到 $4\frac{1}{4}$ 便士,而下等肉块的价格,每磅由 7 法新到 $2\frac{1}{2}$ 便士或 $2\frac{3}{4}$ 便士。他们说,一般地说,此种价格比三月间的普通市价,每磅约高 $\frac{1}{2}$ 便士①。但是,连这样高的价格,也比亨利亲王时代的普通零售价低廉得多。

上世纪开始 12 年间,温莎[1]市场上等小麦的平均价格是每夸特[2]为 1 镑 18 先令 $3\frac{1}{6}$ 便士,合 9 温彻斯特蒲式耳[3]。小麦则价格较低。

然而,在 1764 年之前的 12 年(包括 1764 年)内,同一市场上上等小麦的平均价格则为 2 镑 1 先令 $9\frac{1}{2}$ 便士②。

因此,在上世纪头 12 年内,小麦价格比在 1764 年前的 12

---

① 《下议院就食物价格高昂原因于 1764 年 2 月 8 日任命的委员会调查报告》,第 3 段完全是逐字照搬。该委员会认为,"最近食物价格昂贵的原因部分是由于当年的特殊天气,部分是由于惩罚、垄断牲畜上市以及有关人员法律实施后的负面效应"。

② 这些价格从本章末所附表格中推算得出。

〔1〕温莎(Windsor),英格兰中南部自治区,位于伦敦西南的泰晤士河上。温莎堡自从征服者威廉时期以来一直是王室住所。

〔2〕夸特(Quarter),一种谷物容量单位。

〔3〕蒲式耳(Bushel),英国法定体积或容量单位,用于度量干燥固体和液体。

appears cheaper, and butcher's-meat a good deal dearer, than in the twelve years preceding 1764, including that year.

<small>The rent and profit of corn land and pasture regulate those of all other land.</small> In all great countries the greater part of the cultivated lands are employed in producing either food for men or food for cattle. The rent and profit of these regulate the rent and profit of all other cultivated land. If any particular produce afforded less, the land would soon be turned into corn or pasture; and if any afforded more, some part of the lands in corn or pasture would soon be turned to that produce.

<small>The apparently greater rent or profit of some other kinds is only interest on greater expense,</small> Those productions, indeed, which require either a greater original expence of improvement, or a greater annual expence of cultivation, in order to fit the land for them, appear commonly to afford, the one a greater rent, the other a greater profit than corn or pasture. This superiority, however, will seldom be found to amount to more than a reasonable interest or compensation for this superior expence.

<small>as in hop, and fruit gardensi,</small> In a hop garden, a fruit garden, a kitchen garden, both the rent of the landlord, and the profit of the farmer, are generally greater than in a corn or grass field. But to bring the ground into this condition requires more expence. Hence a greater rent becomes due to the landlord. It requires too a more attentive and skilful management. Hence a greater profit becomes due to the farmer. The crop too, at least in the hop and fruit garden, is more precarious. Its price, therefore, besides compensating all occasional losses, must afford something like the profit of insurance. ① The circumstances of gardeners, generally mean, and always moderate, may satisfy us that their great ingenuity is not commonly over-recompenced. Their delightful art is practised by so many rich people for amusement, that little advantage is to be made by those who practise it for profit;

---

① [Only if the extra risk deters people from entering the business, and according to pp. 112, 113 above it would not.]

（包括1764年在内）内低廉得多，而鲜肉价格却高得多。

在一切大国中，大部分耕地都用来生产人类的粮食或牲畜的食物。这些耕地的地租和利润调节着其余所有耕地的地租和利润。假若生产任何特殊生产物的土地，提供的地租和利润比上述少，那种土地很快就会改作谷物或牧场。如果能提供的地租和利润更多，那么原来用于谷田或牧草的部分土地很快就会改用来生产那种特殊的生产物。

谷物或牧场的地租调节其他所有土地的地租和利润。

为了使土地适合于那特殊生产物的生产，有的需要花费比谷田或收场所要花的更多改良支出，或每年要花更多的耕种支出。这些产品与谷物或牧草相比，前者似乎能提供更多的地租，后者能提供更多的利润。不过，这种较高的收入很少发现能超过较高支出的合理利息或补偿。

作其他用途的土地表面的地租和利润较高只是较高支出的利息。

在啤酒花园、果树园和蔬菜园，地主的地租和农场主的利润一般比谷田或草地大。但是将土地改变成适合这种栽植的状况需要更多的开支，所以地主应得到更多的地租。此外，这还需要更精心、更专业的管理，所以农场主应得到更多的利润。而且这些作物，至少是啤酒花园和果树园的收成，很不确定，所以这些产品的价格除了补偿所有的意外损失外，还必须提供类似保险的利润的某种东西①。种园者的境遇一般是很平常的，最多是中等水平。我们可以相信，他们的聪明才智并未得到超额的补偿。许多有钱的人从种植园者从事的技巧得到愉快的满足。以至于以种园谋生得不到很大利益，因为那

如在啤酒园和果树园；

---

① 只有在额外风险阻挡人们进入这一行业时才是如此，否则不会这样。

because the persons who should naturally be their best customers, supply themselves with all their most precious productions.

<small>kitchen-gardens;</small>　　The advantage which the landlord derives from such improvements seems at no time to have been greater than what was sufficient to compensate the original expence of making them. In the ancient husbandry, after the vineyard, a well-watered kitchen garden seems to have been the part of the farm which was supposed to yield the most valuable produce. But Democritus, who wrote upon husbandry about two thousand years ago, and who was regarded by the ancients as one of the fathers of the art, thought they did not act wisely who enclosed a kitchen garden. The profit, he said, would not compensate the expence of a stone wall; and bricks (he meant, I suppose, bricks baked in the sun) mouldered with the rain, and the winter storm, and required continual repairs. Columella, who reports this judgment of Democritus, does not controvert it, but proposes a very frugal method of enclosing with a hedge of bramblesand briars, which, he says, he had found by experience to be both a lasting and an impenetrable fence[①]; but which, it seems, was not commonly known in the time of Democritus. Pal. ladius adopts the opinion of Columella, which had before been recommended by Varro. In the judgment of those ancient improvers, the produce of a kitchen garden had, it seems, been little more than sufficient to pay the extraordinary culture and the expence of watering; for in countries so near the sun, it was thought proper, in those times as in the present, to have the command of a stream of water, which could be conducted to every bed in the garden. Through the greater part of Europe, a kitchen garden is not at present supposed to deserve a better enclosure than that recommended by Columella. In Great Britain, and some other northern countries, the finer fruits cannot be brought to perfection but by the assistance of a wall. Their price, therefore, in such countries, must be sufficient to pay the expence of building and maintaining what they cannot be had without. The fruitwall frequently surrounds the

---

① [Columella, Dererustica, xi. ,3.]

些应该成为他们的最佳顾客都自己种植他们所能提供的所有珍贵产品。

地主从这种改良所得到的利益,似乎都没有超过补偿原始的^{菜园}支出。在古代的耕种中,除了葡萄园外,一个浇灌很好的蔬菜园似乎成为生产最有价值的产品的那部分农场。但是古希腊哲学家德谟克利特[1],被古代人认为是耕种技艺之父,早在两千年前就这方面写了相关的著述。他认为把蔬菜园围起来是不聪明的行为,他给出的理由是菜园的利润不足以补偿砌墙的费用;而砖块(我想他说的那种砖块是指由太阳晒干的那种)被风雨和冬季风雪毁坏,就需要修补。科卢梅拉在提到德谟克利特的论断时并没有反驳他的意见,但是提出了一个省钱的办法:用由荆棘和石楠做成的篱笆。他说根据他的经验,那是持久不易侵入的栅栏①;然而在德谟克利特时代,这一点似乎还不为众人所知晓。瓦罗(Varro)首先采纳科卢梅拉的意见,后来又为帕拉第尤斯(Palladius)采用。根据这些古代农事改良者的意见,蔬菜园生产的产品价值,似乎仅仅足以支付特殊栽培和灌溉的费用。在那时和现在都认为靠近太阳的国家应控制水源,并将它引导至蔬菜园中的每一片地中。当今的欧洲大部分地区,没有找到比由科卢梅拉提出的更好的圈围方法,仍然沿用他的提法。在不列颠及其他一些北方国家,不借助于围墙,优良的水果就不能成熟。因此在这些国家优良水果的价格,必须偿付必不可少的围墙建筑费和维持费。

---

① 科卢梅拉(Columella):《论乡间事》第 11 章第 3 节。
[1] 德谟克利特(Democritus),约公元前 460~前 370 年,古希腊哲学家,他发展了宇宙原子论,并拥护以自制和安乐为人生目标的学说。

国民财富的性质与原理

kitchen garden, which thus enjoys the benefit of an enclosure which its own produce could seldom pay for.

and ri-neyards. That the vineyard, when properly planted and brought to perfection, was the most valuable part of the farm, seems to have been an undoubted maxim in the ancient agriculture, as it is in the modern through all the wine countries. But whether it was advantageous to plant a new vineyard, was a matter of dispute among the ancient Italian husbandmen, as we learn from Columella. He decides, like a true lover of all curious cultivation, in favour of the vineyard, and endeavours to show, by a comparison of the profit and expence, that it was a most advantageous improvement. ①Such comparisons, however, between the profit and expence of new projects, are commonly very fallacious; and in nothing more so than in agriculture. Had the gain actually made by such plantations been commonly as great as he imagined it might have been, there could have been no dispute about it. The same point is frequently at this day a matter of controversy in the wine countries. Their writers on agriculture, indeed, the lovers and promoters of high cultivation, seem generally disposed to decide with Columella in favour of the vineyard. In France the anxiety of the proprietors of the old vineyards to prevent the planting of any new ones, seems to favour their opinion, and to indicate a consciousness in those who must have the experience, that this species of cultivation is at present in that country more profitable than any other. It seems at the same time, however, to indicate another opinion, that this superior profit can last no longer than the laws which at present restrain the free cultivation of the vine. In 1731, they obtained an order of council, prohibiting both the planting of new vineyards, and the renewal of those old ones, of which the cultivation had been interrupted for two years, without a particular permission from the king, to be granted only in consequence of an information from the intendant of the province, certifying that he had examined the land, and that it was incapable of any other culture. The pretence of this order was the scarcity of corn and pasture, and the super-abundance of wine. But had this

---

① [De re rustica,ii. ,3.]

果树围墙往往围绕着蔬菜园,这样蔬菜园就能享受自身产品很难支付的圈围了。

　　葡萄园如果种植适当并且被培养成熟的话将会是农场中最有价值的部分,这似乎成为古代农业以及现代所有葡萄酒产国毋庸置疑的基本原理了。然而从科卢梅拉那里知道在古代意大利的商人中,种植新葡萄园是否有利,却是一件有争议的事情。他是一个热爱新奇植物的人,赞同种植新葡萄园,并通过利润与成本的比较来试图证明这是一种最有利益的改良①。然而这种新项目的利润与成本的比较通常是靠不住的,并且在农业中尤其是这样。如果这种种植的所得普遍地与他所想象的那么大,那么就不会有关于这问题的争论。今天的葡萄酒产国中这一点还经常是一个争论纷纭的问题。事实上和科卢梅拉一样,他们的农业作家、高级种植的爱好者和提倡者都很赞同栽种新葡萄园。在法国的旧葡萄园所有者希望阻止种植新葡萄园的一种焦虑心情,似乎赞同了他们的意见,而且那些有经验的人表明都觉得目前在那个国家种植葡萄比栽种其他任何植物更有利可图。可是,同时似乎也表示出另一方面的意见,葡萄园的高利润必须受到限制,葡萄自由种植的那些法律的保护才能持续下去。1731年旧葡萄园主收到了官方的法令:除非得到国王的许可,否则禁止新葡萄园的种植,两年未耕的葡萄园的复垦也是不被允许的。国王在州长检验过这片土地,并且证明这土地不适宜于任何其他耕种之后才可能颁发许可证。这部法令发布的理由是谷物和牧草的缺乏和葡萄酒的过剩。不过如果葡萄酒的过剩的确是事实的话,即使没有政

和葡萄园。

---

① 《论乡间事》,第2章第3节。

super-abundance been real, it would, without any order of council, have effectually prevented the plantation of new vineyards, by reducing the profits of this species of cultivation below their natural proportion to those of corn and pasture. With regard to the supposed scarcity of corn occasioned by the multiplication of vineyards, corn is nowhere in France more carefully cultivated than in the wine provinces, where the land is fit for producing it; as in Burgundy, Guienne, and the Upper Languedoc. The numerous hands employed in the one species of cultivation necessarily encourage the other, by affording a ready market for its produce. To diminish the number of those who are capable of paying for it, is surely a most unpromising expedient for encouraging the cultivation of corn. It is like the policy which would promote agriculture by discouraging manufactures.

<small>Land fitted for a particular produce may have a monopoly.</small>   The rent and profit of those productions, therefore, which require either a greater original expence of improvement in order to fit the land for them, or a greater annual expence of cultivation, though often much superior to those of corn and pasture, yet when they do no more than compensate such extraordinary expence, are in reality regulated by the rent and profit of those common crops.

It sometimes happens, indeed, that the quantity of land which can be fitted for some particular produce, is too small to supply the effectual demand. The whole produce can be disposed of to those who are willing to give somewhat more than what is sufficient to pay the

府的这种法令,它的种植的利润自然会降到和牧草以及谷物利润的自然比例之下,这样也会有效地阻止新葡萄园的种植。关于所谓由于葡萄园过多导致了谷物的稀少,大家都知道法国在生产葡萄酒的产区,那里的土地适于栽种谷物,并且其栽培比其他各州更精细,在勃艮第、吉耶讷和上郎格多克[1]也是如此。一种耕种事业雇用很多劳动者,必然给另一种耕种事业的产品提供充分的市场,从而鼓励另一种耕种事业。减少能购买葡萄酒的人数绝不是最行之有效的奖励谷物耕种事业的权宜之计。这种权宜之计就像是等于通过阻碍制造业来鼓励农业发展的政策。

因此,那些产品的地租和利润或许需要有较大土地改良费用使土地适合于栽种,或需要有较大的每年耕种费用,尽管它往往大大超过谷物或牧草的地租和利润,然而它们如果仅仅对其超额费用进行补偿时,它们实际上是受普通作物的地租和利润的调控。

适于生产特殊产品的土地可能有垄断性,

的确,有时也发生这样的情况,适于栽种某特殊产品的土地数量过小,不足以满足有效需求。生产出来的全部产物出售给那些愿意支付略高于他们所出的价格,稍稍超过这作物生产以至上

---

〔1〕 勃艮第(Burgundy),法国东部一个历史上的地区,盛产红葡萄酒。从前是法国的一个省。公元 5 世纪该地区首先由勃艮第建立王国。在 14 世纪和 15 世纪,勃艮第势力达到顶峰的时期,它曾控制了现在的荷兰、比利时和法国东北部的广大区域。在 1477 年被路易十一并入法国皇家领地。

吉耶讷(Guienne),历史上法国西南部的地区,曾为法国一省。自 1152 年亚奎丹的爱丽诺与亨利二世结婚后成为英国的一部分,1453 年被法国收回。

朗格多克:历史上的一个地区和法国中南部的以前的一个省,位于罗讷河西部地中海海湾处。得名于当地居民所讲的罗曼语,它于 8 世纪被法兰克人征服并于 1271 年并入法兰西王室统治范围。

whole rent, wages and profit necessary for raising and bringing it to market, according to their natural rates, or according to the rates at which they are paid in the greater part of other cultivated land. The surplus part of the price which remains after defraying the whole expence of improvement and cultivation may commonly, in this case, and in this case only, bear no regular proportion to the like surplus in corn or pasture, but may exceed it in almost any degree; and the greater part of this excess naturally goes to the rent of the landlord.

<small>such as that which produces wine of a particular flavour,</small>   The usual and natural proportion, for example, between the rent and profit of wine and those of corn and pasture, must be understood to take place only with regard to those vineyards which produce nothing but good common wine, such as can be raised almost any-where, upon any light, gravelly, or sandy soil, and which has nothing to recommend it but its strength and wholesomeness. It is with such vineyards only that the common land of the country can be brought into competition; for with those of a peculiar quality it is evident that it cannot.

The vine is more affected by the difference of soils than any other fruit tree. From some it derives a flavour which no culture or management can equal, it is supposed, upon any other. This flavour, real or imaginary, is sometimes peculiar to the produce of a few vineyards; sometimes it extends through the greater part of a small district, and sometimes through a considerable part of a large province. The whole quantity of such wines that is brought to market falls short of the effectual demand, or the demand of those who would be willing to pay the whole rent, profit and wages necessary for preparing and bringing them thither, according to the ordinary rate, or according to the rate at which they are paid in common vineyards. The whole quantity, therefore, can be disposed of to those who are willing to pay more, which necessarily raises the price above that of common wine. The difference is greater or less, according as the fashionableness and scarcity of the wine render the competition of the buyers more or less eager. Whatever it be, the greater part of it goes to the rent of the landlord. For though such vineyards are in general more

市所必需的大部分耕地的地租、工资和利润,按它们的自然比率或按大部分其他耕地支付的比率计算。在这种情况下,而且只在这种情况下,在这种价格中除去改良及耕种的全部费用后所剩余的部分,同谷物或牧草的类似剩余部分不保持一定的比例,而且可在任何程度上超过。这种剩余的大部分,自然归于地主。

比如葡萄酒的地租利润对谷物牧草的地租利润的普通和自然比例,必须理解为只对某类葡萄园才会适用。这种葡萄园生产的只不过是土壤松软、含有沙砾或含有沙的土壤上才能生产的优良普通的葡萄酒。而所产葡萄酒,除浓度与有益健康外,又无可以称道的特色。一个国家的普通土地只能和这种普通葡萄园进行竞争,而与有特殊品质的葡萄园,那显然无法与之竞争了。

例如生产特殊味道的葡萄酒的土地,

葡萄树在一切果树中最易受到土壤差异的影响。有这样的看法,葡萄从某种土壤中获得一种特殊的美味,任何其他的培育和管理办法都是不能做到的。这种美味无论是现实上还是想象中的,有时仅为少数几个葡萄园产物所特有,有时扩大到一个小区域中的绝大部分,有时扩大到一个省的很大部分地区。进入市场的葡萄酒的全部出售量,不足以满足这些人的有效需求,即满足不了那些人的需求:愿支付为产制和运输这种葡萄酒的一般地租、工资和利润率,这些地租、利润和工资按普通葡萄园所支付的地租、工资和利润率支付的价格计算。因此,所有的酒卖给愿支付更高价格的人,这必然就抬高了这种葡萄酒的价格,使其超过普通葡萄酒的价格。两种价格相差的大小决定于这种葡萄酒的流行性与稀少性所激起的购买者竞争程度的大小。但不管相差多少,其大部分都归于地主。虽然这种葡萄园一般都比其他葡萄园的栽培更为谨慎精细,但葡萄酒的价格,似乎成为了慎重栽培

carefully cultivated than most others, the high price of the wine seems to be, not so much the effect, as the cause of this careful cultivation. In so valuable a produce the loss occasioned by negligence is so great as to force even the most careless to attention. A small part of this high price, therefore, is sufficient to pay the wages of the extraordinary labour bestowed upon their cultivation, and the profits of the extraordinary stock which puts that labour into motion.

<small>or the West Indian sugar colonies.</small> The sugar colonies possessed by the European nations in the West Indies, may be compared to those precious vineyards. Their whole produce falls short of the effectual demand of Europe, and can be disposed of to those who are willing to give more than what is sufficient to pay the whole rent, profit and wages necessary for preparing and bringing it to market, according to the rate at which they are commonly paid by any other produce. In Cochin-china the finest white sugar commonly sells for three piastres the quintal, about thirteen shillings and sixpence of our money, as we are told by Mr. Poivre, a very careful observer of the agriculture of that country. What is there called the quintal weighs from a hundred and fifty to two hundred Paris pounds, or a hundred and seventy-five Paris pounds at a medium, which reduces the price of the hundred weight English to about eight shillings sterling, not a fourth part of what is commonly paid for the brown or muskavada sugars imported from our colonies, and not a sixth part of what is paid for the finest white sugar. The greater part of the cultivated lands in Cochinchina are employed in producing corn and rice, the food of the great body of the people. The respective prices of corn, rice, and sugar, are there probably in the natural proportion, or in that which naturally takes place in the different crops of the greater part of cultivated land, and which recompences the landlord and farmer, as nearly as can be computed, according to what is usually the original expence of improvement and the annual expence of cultivation. But in our sugar colonies the price of sugar bears no such proportion to that of the produce of a rice or corn field either in Europe or in

的原因,而不是慎重栽培的结果。对这种高价的产物而言,粗心大意产生的损失将会非常的大,迫使最粗心的人也不得不多加注意。因此,这高价中的一小部分,就足够支付生产上额外劳动的工资以及推动这种劳动的额外资本的利润。

欧洲各国在西印度占有的产糖殖民地可与这贵重的葡萄园相比较。产糖殖民地的全部产量不够满足欧洲人的有效需求,所以,这全部产量只能卖给这样一些人:他们愿意支付高价,价格超过了这产品生产和上市按其他任何产品通常支付的地租、工资和利润率,这些所必须支付的地租、工资和利润的价格按它们的一般价格支付。据柏伏尔(Poivre)先生告诉我们说在交趾支那[1]最上等的精制白糖价格,通常为每公担(quintal)三比索,约合英币13先令6便士,柏伏尔先生对这个国家的农业作过非常仔细地观察。这里所称的公担,合150到200巴黎镑,平均相当于巴黎175镑。按100英镑折合约八先令来计算,这还不到我们从我们殖民地进口的红糖或粗砂糖通常支付的价格的1/4,价格也不及最上等精制白糖的1/6。交趾支那大部分耕地是用来生产人民大众所食的小麦和大米。在那里,大米、小麦和砂糖的价格也许成自然的比例,即大部分耕地的各种作物之间自然而然地发生比例,尽可能按通常最初改良费用和每年耕种支出计算的报酬支付给各地主和各农场主。但在我国产糖殖民地,砂糖价格同欧美稻田或麦田的产品的价格并不保持这种的比例。一般而言,砂糖植物的

西印度的食糖殖民地,

---

〔1〕 交趾支那(Cochin - China),今天以西贡为首府越南南部。法国占领越南后,将越南由北至南分为三部分:东京(Tonkin,即北圻,首府河内)、安南(Annam,即中圻,首府顺化)和交趾支那(Cochin - China,即南圻,首府西贡)。

America. It is commonly said, that a sugar planter expects that the rum and the molasses should defray the whole exprience of his cultivation, and that his sugar should be all clear profit. If this be true, for I pretend not to affirm it, it is as if a corn farmer expected to defray the expence of his cultivation with the chaff and the straw, and that the grain should be all clear profit. We see frequently societies of merchants in London and other trading towns, purchase waste lands in our sugar colonies, which they expect to improve and cultivate with profit by means of factors and agents; notwithstanding the great distance and the uncertain returns, from the defective administration of justice in those countries. Nobody will attempt to improve and cultivate in the same manner the most fertile lands of Scotland, Ireland, or the corn provinces of North America, though from the more exact administration of justice in these countries, more regular returns might be expected.

and in a less degree the tobacco plantations of Virginia and Maryland.

In Virginia and Maryland the cultivation of tobacco is preferred, as more profitable, to that of corn. Tobacco might be cultivated with advantage through the greater part of Europe; but in almost every part of Europe it has become a principal subject of taxation, and to collect a tax from every different farm in the country where this plant might happen to be cultivated, would be more difficult, it has been supposed, than to levy one upon its importation at the custom-house. The cultivation of tobacco has upon this account been most absurdly prohibited through the greater part of Europe, which necessarily gives a sort of monopoly to the countries where it is allowed; and as Virginia and Maryland produce the greatest quantity of it, they share largely, though with some competitors, in the advantage of this monopoly. The cultivation of tobacco, however, seems not to be so advantageous as that of sugar. I have never even heard of any tobacco plantation that was improved and cultivated by the capital of merchants who resided in Great Britain, and our tobacco colonies send us home no such wealthy planters as we see frequently arrive from our sugar islands. Though from the preference given in those colonies to the cultivation of tobacco above that of corn, it would appear that the effectual demand of Europe for tobacco is not completely supplied, it probably is more nearly so than that for sugar: And though the present price of tobacco is probably more than sufficient to pay the whole rent, wages and profit necessary

栽培者通常希望糖酒和糖蜜能补偿其所有的栽培费,而纯利润全部从砂糖中获得。如果这属于事实(但我不敢确认),如同谷物耕种者希望以麦糠和麦秆二项补偿其所有的耕种费用,而纯利润以期从全部谷粒中获得。我常常看见伦敦及其他城市的商人协会在我们的食糖殖民地收买产糖殖民地的荒地;虽然距离遥远,这些国家地区的司法行政又不健全,其收入不确定,但他们仍然托代办人或代理人从事改良和耕种,希望能获利润。但是同样的方法在苏格兰、爱尔兰或北美产谷区域的最肥沃土地却没有人来尝试,虽然这些地方的司法行政制度更完善,他们也许可能得到正规的收入。

在北美的弗吉尼亚和马里兰,人们认为种植烟草比种植谷物更加有利可图,所以他们选择种植烟草而不是谷物。在欧洲大部分栽种烟草也是有利可图的,但是欧洲几乎所有地区的烟草都已成为主要课税对象,而人们认为从国内栽种的烟草地区来征税,要比对从进口烟草征收关税更为麻烦。因此在欧洲大多数地方禁止栽种烟草是一件最荒谬的事情,这样就赋予那些允许栽种烟草的地区一种垄断权力,由于弗吉尼亚和马里兰种植了大量的烟草,于是他们就享受到了这种垄断的大部分好处。虽然也存在一些人与其竞争,但似乎种植烟草不如种植食糖那么有利。我从来没有听说过任何烟草园是由居住不列颠的商人去投资改良和培植的,也没听说我们产烟草的殖民地把我们常看到的来自我们产食糖的殖民地那样富裕的种植者送回国。殖民地居民更爱栽种烟草而不愿栽种谷物,这样看来似乎欧洲对烟草的有效需求没有全部得到供给,但烟草的供给或许比砂糖的供给更接近于有效需求。现行烟草的价格也许超过了烟草生产和上市所必须支付

^{弗吉尼亚和马里兰的烟草园种植程度较轻。}

for preparing and bringing it to market, according to the rate at which they are commonly paid in corn land; it must not be so much more as the present price of sugar. Our tobacco planters, accordingly, have shewn the same fear of the super-abundance of tobacco, which the proprietors of the old vineyards in France have of the super-abundance of wine. By act of assembly they have restrained its cultivation to six thousand plants, supposed to yield a thousand weight of tobacco, for every negro between sixteen and sixty years of age. ①Such a negro, over and above this quantity of tobacco, can manage, they reckon, four acres of Indian corn. To prevent the market from being overstocked too, they have sometimes, in plentiful years, we are told by Dr. Douglas, (I suspect he has been ill informed) burnt a certain quantity of tobacco for every negro, in the same manner as the Dutch are said to do of spices. If such violent methods are necessary to keep up the present price of tobacco, the superior advantage of its culture over that of corn, if it still has any, will not probably be of long continuance.

It is in this manner that the rent of the cultivated land, of which the produce is human food, regulates the rent of the greater part of other cultivated land. No particular produce can long afford less; because the land would immediately be turned to another use: And if any particular produce commonly affords more, it is because the quantity of land which can be fitted for it is too small to supply the effectual demand.

In Europe corn is the principal produce of land which serves immediately for human food. Except in particular situations, therefore, the rent of corn land regulates in Europe that of all other cultivated land. Britain need envy neither the vineyards of France nor the olive

---

① [William Douglass, M. D. , *A Summary, Historical and Political, of the First Planting, Progressive Improvements and Present State of the British Settlements in North America*, 1760, vol. ii. , pp. 359, 360 and 373.]

的全部地租、工资与利润，按谷田一般支付的地租、工资和利润率来计算，但其超过的那部分必定要小于现行食糖价格中的超过部分。因此，我们的殖民地烟草种植者害怕烟草供应过剩，就像法国旧葡萄园所有者担心葡萄酒供应过剩一样。通过议会立法，规定年龄16岁到60岁的黑奴每人只得栽培烟草6000本，他们假定6000本可产烟草1000磅①。他们计算这样一个黑奴，除生产这个数量的烟草外，还能种植4亩地的玉蜀黍。道格拉斯博士告诉我们（我不确定他的这个消息），为了防止在丰年的时候市场上烟草供给过剩，有时按每个黑奴计算焚烧所生产的一定数量的烟草，就像荷兰人焚烧他们所生产的香料一样。如果需要采用这种过激的办法来维持现今烟草的价格，那么，种植烟草优于栽种种植谷物的好处，即使目前仍然存在，但也不会长久维持下去。

正是通过这种方式，生产人类粮食的耕地的地租决定着其他大部分耕地的地租。因此，除了特殊情况，谷物地租决定大部分其他耕地的地租，任何特殊产物所提供的地租，不会长久低于大部分耕地的地租，因为这块土地立即转为其他用途；要是任何特殊产物所提供的地租，通常高于大部分耕地的地租，那是因为适合耕种的土地数量过少，不能满足有效需求。

在欧洲，谷物直接充作人类粮食的土地生产物。所以，除了在特殊情况下，谷田的地租在欧洲决定着所有其他耕地的地租。所以大不列颠无须羡慕法国的葡萄园，也无须羡慕意大利的橄榄园。除了在特殊情况下，葡萄与橄榄这些果园的价格是须由谷物

---

① 威廉·道格拉斯：《不列颠北美殖民地的最初种植、后续改良和现状的历史和政治概述》，1760年，第2卷，第359、360、373页。

plantations of Italy. Except in particular situations, the value of these is regulated by that of corn, in which the fertility of Britain is not much inferior to that of either of those two countries.

<small>If the common food was such as to produce a greater surplus, rent would be higher:</small> If in any country the common and favourite vegetable food of the people should be drawn from a plant of which the most common land, with the same or nearly the same culture, produced a much greater quantity than the most fertile does of corn, the rent of the landlord, or the surplus quantity of food which would remain to him, after paying the labour and replacing the stock of the farmer together with its ordinary profits, would necessarily be much greater. Whatever was the rate at which labour was commonly maintained in that country, this greater surplus could always maintain a greater quantity of it, and consequently enable the landlord to purchase or command a greater quantity of it. The real value of his rent, his real power and authority, his command of the necessaries and conveniencies of life with which the labour of other people could supply him, would necessarily be much greater.

<small>for example, rice,</small> A rice field produces a much greater quantity of food than the most fertile corn field. Two crops in the year from thirty to sixty bushels each, are said to be the ordinary produce of an acre. Though its cultivation, therefore, requires more labour, a much greater surplus remains after maintaining all that labour. In those rice countries, therefore, where rice is the commo and favourite vegetable food of the people, and where the cultivators are chiefly maintained with it, a greater share of this greater surplus should belong to the landlord than in corn countries. In Carolina, where the planters, as in other British colonies, are generally both farmers and landlords, and where rent consequently is confounded with profit, the cultivation of rice is found to be more profitable than that of corn, though their fields produce only one crop in the year, and though, from the prevalence of the customs of Europe, rice is not there the common and favourite vegetable food of the people.

A good rice field is a bog at all seasons, and at one season a bog covered with water. It is unfit either for corn, or pasture, or vineyard, or, indeed, for any other vegetable produce that is

价值规定,而在谷物种植方面,英国土地的肥沃程度并不比这两国土地差。

如果在任何一个国家,人们普遍喜爱的植物粮食是谷物之外的另一种植物,并这种植物在这国家的普通土地上,用与谷田耕种相同或差不多的方法耕种,所能产出的比最肥沃谷田所生产的谷物要多得多,那么,地主的地租,也就是说,在支付劳动工资和补偿农场主资本连同其普通利润后的剩余食物数量,必然会大得多。不管这个国家维持一般劳动的价格是多少,这一较大的剩余量总能维持较大的劳动量,因而使地主也就能购买或支配更大数量的劳动。他的地租的真实价值,也就是他的真实权力和权威,对于他人劳动所提供的生活必需品和便利品的支配权,必定大得多。_{如果普通食物生产能较大的剩余,地租就会高一些;}

稻田比最肥沃的麦地所产的食物量大得多。据说,每亩稻田的普通产量为每年收获两次,每次为 30 蒲式耳到 60 蒲式耳。尽管耕种稻田需要更多的劳动,但维持这种劳动以后的剩余还有更多。因此,在那些产米的国家,大米成为大家普通爱好的食物,而耕种者主要也是靠大米维持生活,那么地主所获得的剩余比产麦国地主所得的剩余要多得多。在卡罗来纳,也像英属其他殖民地一样,耕种者一般兼有农场主和地主的身份,因此,地租与利润混在一起;尽管当地稻田每年只收获一次,尽管当地人民根据欧洲普通习惯,不以米为普通爱好的植物性食物,但都认为耕种大米,比耕种小麦更为有利。_{例如大米,}

块好的稻田,在一年季节都是泥泞的沼泽地,而且还有一个季节田里是充满着水的。这样的稻田既不适合种麦,也不适合作牧场或者作葡萄园,确切地说,除了种稻以外,它不适合栽种其

国民财富的性质与原理

very useful to men: And the lands which are fit for those purposes, are not fit for rice. Even in the rice countries, therefore, the rent of rice lands cannot regulate the rent of the other cultivated land which can never be turned to that produce.

<small>or potatoes.</small>   The food produced by a field of potatoes is not inferior in quantity to that produced by a field of rice, and much superior to what is produced by a field of wheat. Twelve thousand weight of potatoes from an acre of land is not a greater produce than two thousand weight of wheat. The food or solid nourishment, indeed, which can be drawn from each of those two plants, is not altogether in proportion to their weight, on account of the watery nature of potatoes. Allowing, however, half the weight of this root to go to water, a very large allowance, such an acre of potatoes will still produce six thousand weight of solid nourishment, three times, the quantity produced by the acre of wheat. An acre of potatoes is cultivated with less expence than an acre of wheat; the fallow, which generally precedes the sowing of wheat, more than compensating the hoeing and other extraordinary culture which is always given to potatoes. Should this root ever become in any part of Europe, like rice in some rice countries, the common and favourite vegetable food of the people, so as to occupy the same proportion of the lands in tillage which wheat and other sorts of grain for human food do at present, the same quantity of cultivated land would maintain a much greater number of people, and the labourers being generally fed with potatoes, a greater surplus would remain after replacing all the stock and maintaining all the labour employed in cultivation. A greater share of this surplus too would belong to the landlord. Population would increase, and rents would rise much beyond what they are at present.

    The land which is fit for potatoes, is fit for almost every other

他任何对人类有用的农作物。而适合种植小麦、牧草或者葡萄的土地,又不适合种稻。所以,即使在产稻的国家里,种植其他作物的耕地的地租也不能由稻田的地租来决定,因为其他耕地是不可能改做稻田的。

种植马铃薯的土地上产出的产量,不仅不会少于稻田产出的产量,而且与麦田的产量相比还要大得多。每亩土地生产出 12000 磅马铃薯,并不能算做很高的产量,而每亩土地生产小麦 2000 磅,却可以算是不错的产量。诚然,因为马铃薯所含水分较多,从马铃薯和小麦中所获取的固体营养与其重量是不成比例的。但是,即使假设马铃薯这种块根食物的重量中有一半是水分(这应该是很大的扣除),每亩土地所产的马铃薯,仍然有 6000 磅的固体营养,相当于一亩麦地三倍的产量。而且,耕种一亩马铃薯的费用要少于耕种一亩麦地的费用。就小麦在播种前通常需要的休耕而言,所需要的费用就要超过栽种马铃薯所需要的锄草及其他各种特殊费用。所以,假如马铃薯这种块根食物,在将来能够像米在一些产米国家那样成为欧洲某个地区人民普遍喜爱的植物性食物,因而种植马铃薯的土地面积在全部耕地中所占的比例提高到等于耕种小麦及其他谷物的土地面积在全部耕地中所占的比例,那么相同面积的耕地就能养活更多的人民。而且,如果劳动者一般都以马铃薯为主要食物,那么在总产出中,补偿了资本投资和雇佣劳动投资后,就会有更多的剩余。这些剩余的大部分,都将属于地主。到那时人口就会增长,而地租也会提高,远远高于现在的地租。

凡是适合种植马铃薯的土地,几乎都适合种植其他一切有用

> 或者马铃薯。

useful vegetable. If they occupied the same proportion of cultivated land which corn does at present, they would regulate, in the same manner, the rent of the greater part of other cultivated land.

<small>Wheat is probably a better food than oats, but not than potatoes.</small>　In some parts of Lancashire it is pretended, I have been told, that bread of oatmeal is a heartier food for labouring people than wheaten bread, and I have frequently heard the same doctrine held in Scotland. I am, however, somewhat doubtful of the truth of it. The common people in Scotland, who are fed with oatmeal, are in general neither so strong nor so handsome as the same rank of people in England, who are fed with wheaten bread. They neither work so well, nor look so well; and as there is not the same difference between the people of fashion in the two countries, experience would seem to show, that the food of the common people in Scotland is not so suitable to the human constitution as that of their neighbours of the same rank in England. But it seems to be otherwise with potatoes. The chairmen, porters, and coalheavers in London, and those unfortunate women who live by prostitution, the strongest men and the most beautiful women perhaps in the British dominions, are said to be, the greater part of them, from the lowest rank of people in Ireland, who are generally fed with this root. No food can afford a more decisive proof of its nourishing quality, or of its being peculiarly suitable to the health of the human constitution.

<small>Potatoes, however, are perishable.</small>　It is difficult to preserve potatoes through the year, and impossible to store them like corn, for two or three years together. The fear of not being able to sell them before they rot, discourages their cultivation, and is, perhaps, the chief obstacle to their ever becoming in any great country, like bread, the principal vegetable food of all the different ranks of the people.

的植物。如果马铃薯耕地在全部耕地中所占比例等于目前谷田在全部耕地中所占比例,那么马铃薯耕地的地租就会决定其他大部分耕地的地租,正如今天谷田的地租决定其他地租的情况一样。

我听说,在兰开夏(Lancashire)[1]的某些地方,认为劳动人民吃燕麦面包会比吃小麦面包更有营养。而在苏格兰,我也听到类似的说法。不过我对于此种传闻是持怀疑态度的。一般说来,吃燕麦面包的苏格兰普通人民不如吃小麦面包英格兰普通人民那么健壮而俊美;他们工作不如英格兰人出色,身体状况也比不上英格兰人。而两国的上层人民则没有这种差异,由此我们似乎可以推断,苏格兰普通人民的食物不如英格兰普通人民的食物那么适合于人类的体质。但就马铃薯而言,情形却似乎有很大的差异。据说伦敦的轿夫、挑夫和煤炭搬运工,以及那些靠卖淫为生的不幸女子大多数来自于以马铃薯为主要食物的爱尔兰最下层人民,而这些人也许可以算作是英国最健壮的男子和最美丽的女子。这是马铃薯提供的证明它含有特别适合于人类体质的营养的最明确的证据,任何其他植物都不能提供这样的证明。

> 小麦比燕麦更有营养,但却不一定比马铃薯更有营养。

马铃薯很难储存超过一年而不会变质,更不可能像谷物那样贮藏二三年。对于它能否在腐烂以前全部卖出的担心,阻止了人们栽种马铃薯,使得马铃薯不能像面包那样在任何大国,成为各阶层人民的主要植物性食品。

> 然而马铃薯易腐烂。

----

〔1〕 兰开夏郡(Lancashire),英格兰西北部的一个历史地区,位于爱尔兰海沿岸。它是盎格鲁·撒克逊时代诺森布里亚五国的一部分,在1351年成为巴拉丁领地。它的纺织业久负盛名,在产业革命后该地区迅猛发展起来。

PART II

Of the Produce of Land which sometimes does, and sometimes does not, afford Rent

Human food seems to be the only produce of land which always and necessarily affords some rent to the landlord. Other sorts of produce sometimes may and sometimes may not, according to different circumstances.

After food, cloathing and lodging are the two great wants of mankind.

<small>The materials of cloathing and lodging, at first superabundant, come in time to afford a rent.</small> Land in its original rude state can afford the materials of cloathing and lodging to a much greater number of people than it can feed. In its improved state it can sometimes feed a greater number of people than it can supply with those materials; at least in the way in which they require them, and are willing to pay for them. In the one state, therefore, there is always a super-abundance of those materials, which are frequently, upon that account, of little or no value. In the other there is often a scarcity, which necessarily augments their value. In the one state a great part of them is thrown away as useless, and the price of what is used is considered as equal only to the labour and expence of fitting it for use, and can, therefore, afford no rent to the landlord. In the other they are all made use of, and there is frequently a demand for more than can be had. Somebody is always willing to give more for every part of them than what is sufficient to pay the expence of bringing them to market. Their price, therefore, can always afford some rent to the landlord.

<small>For example, hides and wool,</small> The skins of the larger animals were the original materials of cloathing. Among nations of hunters and shepherds, therefore, whose food consists chiefly in the flesh of those animals, every man, by providing himself with food, provides himself with the materials of more cloathing than he can wear. If there was no foreign commerce, the greater part of them would be thrown away as things of no value. This was probably the case among the hunting nations of North America,

第二节 论有时能、有时不能提供地租的土地产品

人类的食物似乎是各种土地生产物中必然能够为地主提供地租的,其他产物则不一定。其他生产物,或能提供地租,或不能提供地租,依具体情况而定。

除了食物以外,人类最需要的产物就是衣服和住宅。

在原始自然状态下,土地能够为较多的人提供衣服和住宅材料,而只能为少的多得人提供食物。但是经过改良的土地,却能够为较多的人提供食物,而只能为少的多得人提供衣服和住宅材料,至少在人们需要这些材料并愿意支付代价时情况是这样的。所以,前一种状态下,衣服和住宅材料是有剩余的,因而价值很低,甚至完全没有价值。在后一种状态下,这些材料变得稀缺,因而价值增大。在前一状态下,大部分衣服和住宅材料因为没有价值而丢弃,使用部分的价格也只是勉强能够弥补改造这些材料使其适合人们使用所耗费的劳动与费用。因此,不能为地主提供地租。然而在后一状态下,这些材料全部被利用,而且经常出现供不应求。于是,对于这些材料的所有部分总是会有人愿意购买,且价格超过其生产和运到市场的费用。所以,这些材料的价格,总是能够为地主提供地租。

〔衣服和住宅材料最初的时候非常丰富,后来才能为地主提供地租。〕

在原始自然状态下,衣服材料来自较大动物的毛皮。所以,〔例如皮革和羊毛,〕那些以动物的肉为主要食物的狩猎和牧畜民族,在获得食物的同时,也获得了超过他们自身需求的衣服材料。如果没有对外贸易,那么这些剩余的材料,就被当作无价值东西而被抛弃。北美狩猎民族在未被欧洲人发现以前,就是这种情况。现在,他们把

before their country was discovered by the Europeans, with whom they now exchange their surplus peltry, for blankets, fire-arms, and brandy, which gives it some value. In the present commercial state of the known world, the most barbarous nations, I believe, among whom land property is established, have some foreign commerce of this kind, and find among their wealthier neighbours such a demand for all the materials of cloathing, which their land produces, and which can neither be wrought up nor consumed at home, as raises their price above what it costs to send them to those wealthier neighbours. It affords, therefore, some rent to the landlord. When the greater part of the highland cattle were consumed on their own hills, the exportation of their hides made the most considerable article of the commerce of that country, and what they were exchanged for afforded some addition to the rent of the highland estates. The wool of England, which in old times could neither be consumed nor wrought up at home, found a market in the then wealthier and more industrious country of Flanders, and its price afforded something to the rent of the land which produced it. In countries not better cultivated than England was then, or than the highlands of Scotland are now, and which had no foreign commerce, the materials of cloathing would evidently be so super-abundant, that a great part of them would be thrown away as useless, and no part could afford any rent to the landlord.

<small>stone and timber.</small>   The materials of lodging cannot always be transported to so great a distance as those of cloathing, and do not so readily become an object of foreign commerce. When they are super-abundant in the country which produces them, it frequently happens, even in the present commercial state of the world, that they are of no value to the landlord. A good stone quarry in the neighbourhood of London would afford a considerable rent. In many parts of Scotland and Wales

剩余的毛皮拿来交换欧洲人的毛毯、火器和白兰地酒,这样就使他们的毛皮具有了某些价值。我相信,在当今世界的商业发展状况下,只要建立了土地私有制,即使是最野蛮不开化的民族也在一定程度上进行了这种对外贸易,他们在较富裕的邻国中为那些本国土地生产、但不能在国内加工或消费的衣服材料找到了市场,并且以高于其运输费用的价格在这些市场上销售。于是,这些材料的价格,就能够给地主提供一些地租。当苏格兰高地的大部分牲畜在本地山区消费的时候,兽皮成为能够交换其他物品的最主要的出口商品,这无疑会增加高地土地的地租。以前,在英格兰本国不能加工或消费的羊毛,被销往当时更富裕和更勤劳的佛兰德斯人[1]的国家,其售价对生产羊毛的土地也提供了一些地租。然而,那些耕种水平比不上当时的英格兰,也比不上今天的苏格兰,又没有对外贸易的国家,衣服材料仍然有较多的剩余,仍然有一大部分由于无用而被丢弃,这一部分就不能给地主带来地租。

　　住宅材料,不能都能像衣服材料那样方便地运往遥远的地方,因而,也不容易成为对外贸易的对象。在住宅材料生产过剩的国家,即使在今天的商业发展状态下,这些过剩的住宅材料,也不能给地主带来什么收益。伦敦附近的一个较为优良的采石场,能够为地主提供大量的地租,而苏格兰和威尔士许多地方的采石

石材和木料。

---

[1] 佛兰德斯(Flanders),欧洲西北部一块历史上有名的地区,包括法国北部的部分地区、比利时西部地区和北海沿岸荷兰西南部的部分地带。几个世纪以来,作为一个服装业中心,它一直享有实际的独立权并且十分繁荣。低地国家的哈布斯堡战争导致了这一地区的最终分裂,并在两次世界大战中都遭受严重损失。

it affords none. Barren timber for building is of great value in a populous and well-cultivated country, and the land which produces it affords a considerable rent. But in many parts of North America the landlord would be much obliged to any body who would carry away the greater part of his large trees. In some parts of the highlands of Scotland the bark is the only part of the wood which, for want of roads and water-carriage, can be sent to market. The timber is left to rot upon the ground. When the materials of lodging are so superabundant, the part made use of is worth only the labour and expence of fitting it for that use. It affords no rent to the landlord, who generally grants the use of it to whoever takes the trouble of asking it. The demand of wealthier nations, however, sometimes enables him to get a rent for it. The paving of the streets of London has enabled the owners of some barren rocks on the coast of Scotland to draw a rent from what never afforded any before. The woods of Norway and of the coasts of the Baltic, find a market in many parts of Great Britain which they could not find at home, and thereby afford some rent to their proprietors.

<small>Population depends on food</small> Countries are populous, not in proportion to the number of people whom their produce can cloath and lodge, but in proportion to that of those whom it can feed. When food is provided, it is easy to find the necessary cloathing and lodging. But though these are at hand, it may often be difficult to find food. In some parts even of the British dominions what is called A House, may be built by one day's labour of one man. The simplest species of cloathing, the skins of animals, require somewhat more labour to dress and prepare them for use. They do not, however, require a great deal. Among savage and barbarous nations, a hundredth or little more than a hundredth part of the labour of the whole year, will be sufficient to provide them with such cloathing and lodging as satisfy the greater part of the people. All the other ninety-nine parts are frequently no more than enough to provide them with food.

But when by the improvement and cultivation of land the labour of one family can provide food for two, the labour of half the society becomes sufficient to provide food for the whole. The other half,

场,却不提供任何地租。在人口密度较大而且农业进步的国家里,作为住宅材料的无果树木,具有很高的价值,能够为其产地提供相当可观的地租。而在北美的许多地方,树木产地的所有者,却不仅得不到任何回报,而且对于任何愿意砍伐并运走他的大部分树木的人还会心存感谢。苏格兰高地有些地方,由于缺乏水、陆运输条件,所以只能将树皮运往石场,而木材则任其随地腐烂。当住宅材料大量剩余时,实际上被利用的那一部分的价值,也仅仅等于对木材进行加工时所耗费的劳动和其他支出。这一部分,由于不能为地主提供地租,常常被地主随意的送给需要他们的人。当然,如果邻近富裕国家需要这些住宅材料的时候,地主就会从中获得一些地租。例如,伦敦街道铺设石面时,就曾给苏格兰海岸一些光秃的岩石的所有者,带来了一点前所未有的地租。又如,在国内找不到的市场的挪威及波罗的海沿岸的树木,因在不列颠许多地方找到了市场,而给其所有者提供了一些地租。

　　一个国家的人口数量,是同本国食物所能养活的人数成比例,而不是同本国的衣服以及住宅材料所能供养的人数成比例。在食物供给充足的情况下,衣服及住宅材料就很容易得到。但是,如果住宅和衣服材料得到了供给,要找到食物却并非易事。在不列颠的很多地方,有些简单的住宅只需要一人一日的劳动就可以完成。而把兽皮制成最简单的衣服,尽管需要较多的劳动来修饰,但也不需要很多的劳动。即便是野蛮或未开化民族,只需全年劳动的1%就足以满足全部居民的住宅和衣服需求。而其余99%的劳动,往往只勉强够用来获取食物。

<small>人口数量取决于食物数量,</small>

　　但是在土地改良和耕种水平提高的情况下,一个家庭的劳动产出,能满足两个家庭的所需,也就是说只需要一半的社会劳动

国民财富的性质与原理

so the demand for the materials of clothing and lodging is increased by greater ease of obtaining food,

therefore, or at least the greater part of them, can be employed in providing other things, or in satisfying the other wants and fancies of mankind. Cloathing and lodging, houshold furniture, and what is called Equipage, are the principal objects of the greater part of those wants and fancies. The rich man consumes no more food than his poor neighbour. In quality it may be very different, and to select and prepare it may require more labour and art; but in quantity it is very nearly the same. But compare the spacious palace and great wardrobe of the one, with the hovel and the few rags of the other, and you will be sensible that the difference between their cloathing, lodging, and houshold furniture, is almost as great in quantity as it is in quality. The desire of food is limited in every man by the narrow capacity of the human stomach; but the desire of the conveniencies and ornaments of building, dress, equipage, and houshold furniture, seems to have no limit or certain boundary. Those, therefore, who have the command of more food than they themselves can consume, are always willing to exchange the surplus, or, what is the same thing, the price of it, for gratifications of this other kind. What is over and above satisfying the limited desire, is given for the amusement of those desires which cannot be satisfied, but seem to be altogether endless. The poor, in order to obtain food, exert themselves to gratify those fancies of the rich, and to obtain it more certainly, they vie with one another in the cheapness and perfection of their work. The number of workmen increases with the increasing quantity of food, or with the growing improvement and cultivation of the lands; and as the nature of their business admits of the utmost subdivisions of labour, the quantity of materials which they can work up, increases in a much greater proportion than their numbers. Hence arises a demand for every sort of material which human invention can employ, either usefully or ornamentally, in building, dress, equipage, or houshold furniture; for the fossils and minerals contained in the bowels of the earth, the precious metals, and the precious stones.

which thus makes them afford rent.

Food is in this manner, not only the original source of rent, but every other part of the produce of land which afterwards affords rent, derives that part of its value from the improvement of the powers

力便可以生产全社会所需要的食物,所以其余的一半劳动力,至少其中的大部分劳动力,就可以用来生产其他的物品,以满足人类其他需求和爱好。大部分这些需求和爱好的主要对象,包括衣服,住宅,家具以及成套的饰品。富人所消费的粮食与他的贫穷的邻居相比数量上并不见得多。在质量上,也许有很大的差别,因为选择和制作富人的粮食,可能需要更多的劳动和更高的技术,而在数量上,却是相差无几的。但是当我们把富人宽敞的住宅,巨大的衣柜,与穷人简陋的小屋和破旧的衣服相比较时,就会发现这两者在数量和质量上都存在巨大的差异。每个人对食物的欲望,会受到胃的容量的限制,而对于住宅、衣服、家具及便利品的欲望,却是没有限度的。所以,那些拥有自己所消费不了的食物的人,一定愿意把剩余的食物或其价值拿来交换其他自己所需要的其他东西。满足了有限欲望以后的剩余物品,被拿来换取能够满足无限欲望的物品。穷人为了获取食物,总是会努力工作,以满足富人的这些爱好;而穷人为了能够获得确定的食物,往往相互竞争,使其产品价格越来越低,质量越来越完善。随土地的改良及耕种水平的提高,食物的供应量逐渐增加,而劳动者的人数也随之增加。由于劳动者的工作性质是允许极大限度的分工,所以他们能够使用的原材料数量的增加比他们人数的增加比例大。因此,才有了人类对于建筑物、衣服、各种物品或家具等的需求,甚至对那些埋在地下的化石、矿产、贵金属和宝石,也都产生了需求。

> 因为对食物的欲求容易得到满足,所以人们对于衣服和住宅材料的需求就大。

  因此,食物不仅仅是地租的最初来源,而且后来能够提供地租的土地的其他生产物,其价值中相当于地租的部分,也是来自生产食物的劳动生产力的提高,而土地改良和耕种水平的提高导

> 它能够使它们支付地租。

of labour in producing food by means of the improvement and cultivation of land.

Those other pares of the produce of land, however, which afterwards afford rent, do not afford it always. Even in improved and cultivated countries, the demand for them is not always such as to afford a greater price than what is sufficient to pay the labour, and replace, together with its ordinary profits, the stock which must be employed in bringing them to market. Whether it is or is not such, depends upon different circumstances.

<small>They do not, however, even then always afford rent:</small>

Whether a coal-mine, for example, can afford any rent, depends partly upon its fertility, and partly upon its situation.

<small>for example, some coalmines are too barren to afford rent,</small>

A mine of any kind may be said to be either fertile or barren, according as the quantity of mineral which can be brought from it by a certain quantity of labour, is greater or less than what can be brought by an equal quantity from the greater part of other mines of the same kind.

Some coal-mines advantageously situated, cannot be wrought on account of their barrenness. The produce does not pay the expence. They can afford neither profit nor rent.

There are some of which the produce is barely sufficient to pay the labour,①and replace, together with its ordinary profits, the stock employed in working them. They afford some profit to the undertaker of the work, but no rent to the landlord. They can be wrought advantageously by nobody but the landlord, who being himself undertaker of the work, gets the ordinary profit of the capital which he employs in it. Many coal-mines in Scotland are wrought in this manner, and can be wrought in no other. The landlord will allow nobody else to work them without paying some rent, and nobody can afford to pay any.

---

① [This and the two preceding paragraphs appear to be based on the dissertation on the natural wants of mankind in *Lectures*, pp. 157-161; cp. *Moral Sentiments*, 1759, p. 349.]

致了劳动生产力这样的提高①。

但是,那些到后来才能提供地租的土地的其他产物,并不总是能够提供地租。即使在土地已经改良且开始耕种的国家,对这类土地产物的需求,也不能使得其价格高到支付工资、投资和运输费之后还有利润和剩余的程度。这类产物是否能提供地租,要看具体情况而定。_{即使在当时,这些产物也不一定能够提供地租:}

例如,煤矿能否提供地租,一方面要看它的丰富程度,另一方面还要看它地理位置的好坏。_{有的煤矿因贫乏过而能提供地租,}

矿山的丰富程度如何,是由使用一定数量的劳动、从这座矿山所能开采的矿物量是多于还是少于使用等量劳动从其地同类矿山所能开采出的矿物量而定。

有些煤矿,地理位置十分方便,但由于矿藏不够丰富,所以不适合开采。因为它的产出,不足以偿还费用。这样的煤矿,既不能提供利润,也不能提供地租。

有些煤矿的产量,仅仅可以用来支付劳动者的工资,补偿开矿所投入的资本,并提供平均利润。这种煤矿能够为开采者提供一些利润,而地主却不能从中得到任何地租。所以,像这类煤矿,只有地主自己开采,投入的资本才可能得到平均利润,其他任何人如果进行投资开采都不会获得利润。苏格兰有许多煤矿,就是这样由地主自己来经营的。这些煤矿因为没有地租,地主是不允许其他人开采的,而其他任何人即便开采,也是支付不起地租的。

---

① 这段以及前面两段是建立在《关于法律、警察、岁入及军备的演讲》第157~161页、《道德情操论》(1759年)第349页中人类的自然需求的论断基础之上。

or too disadvantageously situated.
Other coal-mines in the same country sufficiently fertile, cannot be wrought on account of their situation. A quantity of mineral sufficient to defray the expence of working, could be brought from the mine by the ordinary, or even less than the ordinary quantity of labour: But in an inland country, thinly inhabited, and without either good roads or water-carriage, this quantity could not be sold.

The price of coal is kept down by that of wood,
Coals are a less agreeable fewel than wood: they are said too to be less wholesome. The expence of coals, therefore, at the place where they are consumed, must generally be somewhat less than that of wood. The price of wood again varies with the state of agriculture, nearly in the same manner, and exactly for the same reason, as the price of cattle. In its rude beginnings the greater part of every country is covered with wood, which is then a mere incumbrance of no value to the landlord, who would gladly give it to any body for the

which varies with the state of agriculture.
cutting. As agriculture advances, the woods are partly cleared by the progress of tillage, and partly go to decay in consequence of the increased number of cattle. These, though they do not increase in the same proportion as corn, which is altogether the acquisition of human industry, yet multiply under the care and protection of men; who store up in the season of plenty what may maintain them in that of scarcity, who through the whole year furnish them with a greater quantity of food than uncultivated nature provides for them, and who by destroying and extirpating their enemies, secure them in the free enjoyment of all that she provides. Numerous herds of cattle, when allowed to wander through the woods, though they do not destroy the old trees, hinder any young ones from coming up, so that in the course of a century or two the whole forest goes to ruin. The scarcity of wood then raises its price. It affords a good rent, and the landlord sometimes finds that he can scarce employ his best lands more advantageously than in growing barren timber, of which the greatness of the profit often compensates the lateness of the returns. This seems in the present times to be nearly the state of things in several parts of Great Britain, where the profit of planting is found to be equal to that of either corn or pasture. The advantage which the landlord derives from planting, can no-where

苏格兰还有其他一些煤矿,矿藏虽然很丰富,但由于所处的地理位置不方便而无法开采。这些煤矿的产量虽然足够支付开采费用,而且使用的劳动也仅仅是平均的劳动量或者更少,但由于所处内地国家人口稀少而且水、陆运输不发达,这些开采出的煤矿无法销售出去。

> 有时候地理位置方便,因为理不便。

煤炭和木柴相比较,是不太受欢迎的燃料,据说,它也是一种不太符合卫生要求的燃料。所以在消费煤炭的地方,它的价格要低于木柴的价格。木柴的价格,会随着农业发展状况的变化而变化,就像牲畜价格随着农业发展状况的变化而变化一样,而且两者变动的原因也完全相同。在农业欠发达的状态下,各国大部分土地都生长着树木。在当时地主的眼中,这些树木都是毫无价值的,因而愿意让人随意砍伐。后来,随着农业的进步,那些树木,有的由于耕地的扩张而被砍去,有的由于牲畜的增加而遭到破坏。牲畜数量的增加同人类种植谷物的增加虽然不成比例,但在人类的保护和照顾下,牲畜也繁殖得很快。人类在丰收的季节给牲畜贮备饲料,以便在歉收的季节使用,这样人类就能够给牲畜提供比原始自然状态下所提供的多的食物。人类为牲畜消灭天敌,使它们能安全自由地享受大自然的赏赐。无数的牲畜群在森林中随意放牧,虽然不会对森林中的老树造成多大的伤害,但却严重地影响树木幼苗的生长。那么在一两个世纪以后,整个森林就会被毁灭。木柴的不足,抬高了自身的价格。因而就可以给地主提供很可观的地租。地主有时会认为,在最好的土地上种植无果树木,往往更有利可图,足以抵消其获利周期长这一缺陷。不列颠境内的许多地方,似乎都存在着类似的情况。在这些地方,人们认为种植树木的利润,与种植谷田或牧草的利润相

> 煤炭价格木材价格变低,材料随着农业状况变化。

exceed, at least for any considerable time, the rent which these could afford him; and in an inland country which is highly cultivated, it will frequently not fall much short of this rent. Upon the sea-coast of a well-improved country, indeed, if coals can conveniently be had for fewel, it may sometimes be cheaper to bring barren timber for building from less cultivated foreign countries, than to raise it at home. In the new town of Edinburgh, built within these few years, ① there is not, perhaps, a single stick of Scotch timber

But in the coal countries coal is everywhere much below this price.   Whatever may be the price of wood, if that of coals is such that the expence of a coal-fire is nearly equal to that of a wood one, we may be assured, that at that place, and in these circumstances, the price of coals is as high as it can be. It seems to be so in some of the inland parts of England, particularly in Oxfordshire, where it is usual, even in the fires of the common people, to mix coals and wood together, and where the difference in the expence of those two sorts of fewel cannot, therefore, be very great.

Coals, in the coal countries, are every-where much below this highest price. If they were not, they could not bear the expence of a distant carriage, either by land or by water. A small quantity only could be sold, and the coal masters and coal proprietors find it more for their interest to sell a great quantity at a price somewhat above the lowest, than a small quantity at the highest. The most fertile coal-mine too, regulates the price of coals at all the other mines in its neighbourhood. ②

---

① [The North Bridge was only made passable in 1772: in 1778 the buildings along Princes Street had run to a considerable length, and St. Andrew's Square and the streets connected with it were almost complete. A plan of that date shows the whole block between Queen Street and Princes Street (Arnot, *History of Edinburgh*, 1779).]

② [Buchanan (ed. of *Wealth of Nations*, vol. i. , p. 279), commenting on this passage, remarks judiciously: ' It is not by the produce of one coal mine, however fertile, but by the joint produce of all the coal mines that can be worked, that the price of coals is fixed. A certain quantity of coals only can be consumed at a certain price. If the mines that can be worked produce more than this quantity the price will fall; if they produce less it will rise. ']

等。不过,地主种植树木所获得的利润,至少在相当长的时间内,不能超过谷田或牧场所能提供的地租,而在农业发达的内地,种植树木的好处往往与这个地租相差更多。在土地改良得很好的沿海地区,用煤炭作为燃料比较方便,那么从农业欠发达的外国进口建筑所用的木材,往往比本国自己生产更合算。最近几年在爱丁堡新建筑的一些城市①,或许没有一根木料是苏格兰生产的。

不管木柴的价格是高是低,如果一个地方烧煤炭的费用接近于烧木柴的费用,那么我们可以认为,在这种情况下,煤炭在这里的价格就达到最高了。英格兰的一些内陆地区,特别是牛津郡,情况就是这样。牛津郡的普通百姓的火炉里,通常都是混烧木柴与煤炭,可见这两种燃料的费用不可能差别很大。

但在产煤的国家里,煤炭的价格总是低的。

在产煤的国家里,各地的煤炭价格,都远远低于这个最高价格。否则,这些国家就担负不起将煤炭由陆路或水路送往遥远地方的运输费用。这样,煤炭就只能够卖出很少一部分。煤矿的所有者以及采矿者就会发现,用略高于最低价格出售较多的煤炭比以最高的价格出售少量的煤炭更为有利。矿藏最丰富的煤矿决定附近所有煤矿的煤炭价格②。那些矿藏最丰富的煤矿的所有者

---

① 在1772年,North Bridge 开始通行;1778年沿着 Prince Street 的建筑物已经很长了;圣·安德鲁广场以及与其相连的街道也快要完工。那时的一个规划给我们显示了皇后街和 Prince Street 之间的整个街区(阿诺特,《爱丁堡史》,1779)。

② 布坎南(《国家财富》,第1卷,第279页)对该段作了评述。他明智地评价道:"不管一个煤矿储量有多么的丰富,但不是由该煤矿的产量,而是由所有正在开采的煤矿来一起决定煤的价格。一定的价格决定煤的消费量。如果煤矿的产量超过了这个消费量,其价格就会下降,如果产量低于这个消费量,价格就会上升。"

Both the proprietor and the undertaker of the work find, the one that he can get a greater rent, the other that he can get a greater profit, by somewhat underselling all their neighbours. Their neighbours are soon obliged to sell at the same price, though they cannot so well afford it, and though it always diminishes, and sometimes takes away altogether both their rent and their profit. Some works are abandoned altogether; others can afford no rent, and can be wrought only by the proprietor.

<small>The lowest possible price is that which only replaces stock with profits.</small> The lowest price at which coals can be sold for any considerable time, is, like that of all other commodities, the price which is barely sufficient to replace, together with its ordinary profits, the stock which must be employed in bringing them to market. At a coal-mine for which the landlord can get no rent, but which he must either work himself or let it alone altogether, the price of coals must generally be nearly about this price.

<small>Rent forms a smaller proportion of the price of coal than of that of most other rude produce.</small> Rent, even where coals afford one, has generally a smaller share in their price than in that of most other parts of the rude produce of land. The rent of an estate above ground, commonly amounts to what is supposed to be a third of the gross produce; and it is generally a rent certain and independent of the occasional variations in the crop. In coal-mines a fifth of the gross produce is a very great rent; a tenth the common rent, and it is seldom a rent certain, but depends upon the occasional variations in the produce. These are so great, that in a country where thirty years purchase is considered as a moderate price for the property for a landed estate, ten years purchase is regarded as a good price for that of a coal-mine.

<small>The situation of a metallic mine is less important than that of a coal mine,</small> The value of a coal-mine to the proprietor frequently depends as much upon its situation as upon its fertility. That of a metallic mine depends more upon its fertility, and less upon its situation. The coarse, and still more the precious metals, when separated from the ore, are so valuable that they can generally bear the expence of a very long land, and of the most distant sea carriage. Their

及经营者发现,只要以略低于附近煤矿的价格出售煤炭,就能使得地租和利润都大大增加。这样一来,对附近的煤矿来说,尽管这么低的价格不足以抵偿其费用,而且这价格总是要降低,有时甚至完全夺走他们的地租与利润,不久他们也不得不以同样低的价格出售煤炭。于是有些煤矿无法继续经营,被迫停产,其他煤矿因为不能提供地租而只好由其所有者自己来经营。

像所有的其他商品一样,煤炭在长期内能够卖得出去的最低价格,也就是仅仅足够补偿把它运送到市场去所需用的资本以及普通利润的价格。那些由于不能为地主提供地租,而必须由地主自己来经营,否则就不得不被遗弃的煤矿,其所产煤炭的价格,一般来说是接近这个最低价格的。

> 最低价格用以支付普通的利润。也许价格够来资本。

即使在煤炭能够提供地租的地方,地租在煤炭价格中所占比例,一般也比其在其他大多数土地原生产物价格中所占的比例小。一块土地的地租,一般说来等于其总生产值的1/3。这个比例,通常是确定的,不受收成好坏偶然变化的影响。然而对某一煤矿来说,如果能获得总产值的1/5作为地租就是非常高的了,而得到生产值的1/10作地租也算得上是较为常见的。而且,这个地租数额还是很不稳定的,要看产量是否有偶然变动而定。这种偶然变动的几率还是很大的,以至于在一个购买地产的价格为30倍的年租金还是中等价格的国家里,10倍的年租金就被认为是购买一个煤矿的好价钱了。

> 地租在煤炭价格中所占比例,小于其在大多数土地原生产价格中所占比例。

煤矿的价值对其所有者来说,取决于煤矿储藏量的丰富程度,同时也取决于煤矿的地理位置。而金属矿山的价值,则更多地取决于其矿藏的丰富,较少取决于地理位置的好坏。从矿石中提取出的普通金属,尤其是贵金属,具有很高的价值,因此一般说来都负担得起长途的陆运和更遥远的水运的费用。这种贵金属

> 金属矿的地理位置不如煤矿地理位置重要。

— 393 —

| 国民财富的性质与原理

market is not confined to the countries in the neighbourhood of the mine, but extends to the whole world. The copper of Japan makes an article of commerce in Europe ; the iron of Spain in that of Chili and Peru. The silver of Peru finds its way, not only to Europe, but from Europe to China.

<small>metals from all parts of the world being brought into competition.</small> The price of coals in Westmorland or Shropshire can have little effect on their price at Newcastle; and their price in the Lionnois can have none at all. The productions of such distant coal-mines can never be brought into competition with one another. But the productions of the most distant metallic mines frequently may, and in fact commonly are. The price, therefore, of the coarse, and still more that of the precious metals, at the most fertile mines in the world, must necessarily more or less affect their price at every other in it. The price of copper in Japan must have some influence upon its price at the copper mines in Europe. The price of silver in Peru, or the quantity either of labour or of other goods which it will purchase there, must have some influence on its price, not only at the silver mines of Europe, but at those of China. After the discovery of the mines of Peru, the silver mines of Europe were, the greater part of them, abandoned. The value of silver was so much reduced that their produce could no longer pay the expence of working them, or replace, with a profit, the food, cloaths, lodging and other necessaries which were consumed in that operation. This was the case too with the mines of Cuba and St. Domingo, and even with the ancient mines of Peru, after the discovery of those of Potosi.

<small>Rent has therefore a small share in the price of metals.</small> The price of every metal at every mine, therefore, being regulated in some measure by its price at the most fertile mine in the world that is actually wrought, it can at the greater part of mines do very little more than pay the expence of working, and can seldom afford a very high rent to the landlord. Rent, accordingly, seems at the greater part of mines to have but a small share in the price of the coarse, and a still smaller in that of the precious metals. Labour and profit make up the greater part of both.

的市场不仅仅局限于矿藏附近的国家,而是扩大到全世界。例如日本的铜,能够在欧洲市场上贸易;西班牙的铁,是智利及秘鲁市场上的商品;秘鲁的银,不仅在欧洲找到了销路,而且通过欧洲,远销到了中国。

威斯特摩兰郡或什罗普郡的煤炭价格,对纽卡斯尔的煤炭价格不会产生很大影响;而利奥诺斯的煤炭价格,对纽卡斯尔的煤炭价格,则完全没有影响。这些相距遥远的煤矿所产的煤炭,无论如何不会互相竞争。但金属矿产品则不然,即使是距离很远,却往往有可能产生竞争,而事实上也经常这样。因此,世界上金属矿藏最丰富的地方,其金属价格,尤其是贵金属的价格,总能够或多或少地影响世界各地矿山的金属价格。日本的铜价,必然会影响欧洲铜矿所生产的铜的价格。秘鲁的银价,或者说秘鲁的银在当地所能购买的劳动量或其他商品的数量,不但对欧洲银矿上的银价有影响,而且对中国银矿上的银的价格,也会产生某些影响。秘鲁银矿发现以后,欧洲大部分银矿被废弃了。因为银价降得太低,以至于这些银矿的产物,不足以补偿其开采费用,或者说,除补偿开采时所耗费的衣服、食物、住宅以及其他生活必需品以外,不能提供任何利润。波托西银矿被发现后,古巴和圣多明戈的银矿,甚至连原来秘鲁的矿山,也出现了这种情况。

因此,在一定程度上,每一座矿山所产的每一种金属的价格,都受世界当时开采量最大的矿山所产金属价格的支配,所以大部分矿山所产的金属价格,仅够补偿开采所需的费用,因而,不能给地主提供很高的地租。在大多数矿山所产的廉价金属价格中,地租只能占很小的部分,而在贵金属的价格中,地租所占的比例更小。劳动成本和利润,构成了这两种金属价格的大部分。

<small>Tin and lead mines pay a sixth in Cornwall and Scotland.</small>   A sixth part of the gross produce may be reckoned the average rent of the tin mines of Cornwall, the most fertile that are known in the world, as we are told by the Rev. Mr. Borlace, vice-warden of the stannaries. Some, he says, afford more, and some do not afford so much. ①A sixth part of the gross produce is the rent too of several very fertile lead mines in Scotland.

<small>The silver mines of Peru formerly paid a fifth, and now only a tenth.</small>   In the silver mines of Peru, we are told by Frezier and Ulloa, the proprietor frequently exacts no other acknowledgment from the undertaker of the mine, but that he will grind the ore at his mill, paying him the ordinary multure or price of grinding. ②Till 1736, indeed, the tax of the king of Spain amounted to one-fifth of the standard silver, which till then might be considered as the real rent of the greater part of the silver mines of Peru, the richest which have been known in the world. If there had been no tax, this fifth would naturally have belonged to the landlord, and many mines might have been wrought which could not then be wrought, because they could not afford this tax. The tax of the duke of Cornwall upon tin is supposed to amount to more than five per cent. or one-twentieth part of the value; and whatever may be his proportion, it would naturally too belong to the proprietor of the mine, if tin was duty free. But if you add one-twentieth to one-sixth, you will find that the whole average rent of the tin mines of Cornwall, was to the whole average rent of the silver mines of Peru, as thirteen to twelve. But the silver mines of Peru are not now able to pay even this low rent, and the tax upon silver was, in 1736, reduced from one-fifth to one-tenth. Even this tax upon silver too gives more temptation to smuggling than the tax of one-twentieth upon tin;

---

① [*Natural History of Cornwall*, by William Borlase, 1758, p. 175, but nothing is there said as to the landlord sometimes receiving more than one-sixth.]

② [' Those who are willing to labour themselves easily obtain of the miner a vein to work on; what they get out of it is their own, paying him the King's duty and the hire of the mill, which is so considerable that some are satisfied with the profit it yields without employing any to work for them in the mines. '—Frezier, *Voyage to the South Sea and along the Coasts of Chili and Peru in the Years* 1712, 1713 *and* 1714, with a Postscript by Dr. Edmund Halley, 1717, p. 109.]

尊敬的副监督波勒斯告诉我们,以产量丰富闻名于世的康沃尔[1]锡矿的平均地租,可以达到总产量的1/6。他还告诉我们,有些矿山能够提供的地租多一些,有些矿山少一些①。苏格兰许多产量很丰富的铅矿,也能够提供相当于总产量的1/6的地租。

<small>康沃尔锡矿和苏格兰铅矿能够提供相当于总产量的1/6的地租。</small>

佛雷泽和乌洛阿告诉我们,在秘鲁,银矿的所有者,往往只要求银矿的经营者,在他建造的磨坊中磨碎矿石,只收取一部分磨碎的矿石或碾磨费用②。直到1736年,西班牙国王才开始对这些银矿征税,税额为标准银产量的1/5;这可以当作到那时为止大部分秘鲁银矿——当时是世界最丰富的银矿的真实地租。如果不对矿山征税,这1/5当然属于地主,而当时有许多矿山由于负担不起这种赋税而没有开采的,也必定会开采。据说康沃尔公爵所征的锡税,超过整个价值的5%,也即超过1/20;不管它的税率是多少,如果锡矿是免税的,这些当然属于矿山所有者。如果把1/20与1/6相加就可发现,康沃尔锡矿的全部平均地租与秘鲁银矿的全部平均地租的比例,是13/12。然而,秘鲁银矿如今连这么少的地租也负担不起,而银税也在1736年从1/5减到了1/10。银税虽然如此之低,但是比1/20的锡税更能刺激人们去走私,因为

<small>秘鲁银矿以前提供的地租是其产量的1/5,现在只有1/10,</small>

---

① 威廉·波勒斯:《康沃尔自然史》,1758年,第175页。但是没有提到关于地主收入会多于1/6的地租。

② 那些不怕麻烦的人很容易就可以从地主那里得到矿脉,除了上缴给国王的税赋和支付磨坊工人的工资,其余的产出全部归自己所有。这个产量很大,有些人对这样的利润很满意而不再雇人在矿上为他们工作。见佛雷泽《1712年、1713年和1714年沿智利和秘海岸到南部海域航海记》(1717年,埃德蒙·哈雷博士做的后记),第109页。

[1] 康沃尔(Cornwall),英格兰西南端的一个地区,位于一座由大西洋和英吉利海峡环绕的半岛上。此地的锡和铜在古希腊商人中很有名。

and smuggling must be much easier in the precious than in the bulky commodity. The tax of the king of Spain accordingly is said to be very ill paid, and that of the duke of Cornwall very well. Rent, therefore, it is probable, makes a greater part of the price of tin at the most fertile tin mines, than it does of silver at the most fertile silver mines in the world. After replacing the stock employed in working those different mines, together with its ordinary profits, the residue which remains to the proprietor, is greater it seems in the coarse, than in the precious metal.

while profits are small. Neither are the profits of the undertakers of silver mines commonly very great in Peru. The same most respectable and well informed authors acquaint us, that when any person undertakes to work a new mine in Peru, he is universally looked upon as a man destined to bankruptcy and ruin, and is upon that account shunned and avoided by every body. Mining, it seems, is considered there in the same light as here, as a lottery, in which the prizes do not compensate the blanks, though the greatness of some tempts many adventurers to throw away their fortunes in such unprosperous projects.

Mining is encouraged in Peru by the interest of the sovereign. As the sovereign, however, derives a considerable part of his revenue from the produce of silver mines, the law in Peru gives every possible encouragement to the discovery and working of new ones. Whoever discovers a new mine, is entitled to measure off two hundred and forty-six feet in length, according to what he supposes to be the direction of the vein, and half as much in breadth. He becomes proprietor of this portion of the mine, and can work it without paying any acknowledgment to the landlord. The interest of the duke of Cornwall has given occasion to a regulation nearly of the same kind in that ancient dutchy. In waste and uninclosed lands any person who discovers a tin mine, may mark out its limits to a certain extent, which is called bounding a mine. The bounder becomes the real proprietor of the mine, and may either work it himself, or give it in lease to another, without the consent of the owner of the land, to whom, however, a very small acknowledgment must be paid upon working it. ①

---

① [Borlase, *Natural History of Cornwall*, pp. 167, 175. If the land was ' bounded' (bounding could only take place on ' wastrel or common ') the lord of the soil received only a fifteenth.]

贵重的物品必然比容积大的物品更加容易走私。所以有人说,西班牙国王的银税收得很少,而康沃尔公爵却能够得到很多的锡税。所以,在世界上含量最丰富锡矿生产的锡的价格中地租所占的部分,可能比其在世界上最丰富的银矿所产银的价格中所占的比率还大,因此廉价金属在补偿采矿所用的资本以及提供普通利润以后,留给矿山所有者的部分要大于贵金属。

秘鲁银矿开采者的利润,通常也不算很多。上述那两位作者最熟悉当地情形并最受人敬佩,据他们说,如果有人准备在秘鲁着于开采新的银矿,那是注定要倾家荡产的,所以大家都远离他。看来,采矿业在秘鲁和在这里一样都被看作一种彩票,中彩的少而不中彩的多,虽然少数大奖引诱许多愿意冒险的人把财产投入到这种注定会失败的项目中,所中的奖金也不足以补偿其所耗费的财产。银矿的利润很小。

可是,由于秘鲁国王每年的收入有很大一部分来自银矿,所以秘鲁法律总是对新矿藏的发现及开采给予各种奖励。不论是谁发现了新矿山,一律按照他推测的矿脉的方向,划出一块246英尺长、123英尺宽的矿区归他所有,他可以自由开采,而不必给地主支付任何地租。为了自己的利益,康沃尔公爵也在自己的国土内,制订了类似的法律。任何人在荒地或还没有被圈的土地内发现了锡矿,都有权在一定范围内,划出锡矿的边界,叫作矿山定界。而这位划定边界的人,就是该矿区的所有者。他可以自行开采而不必获得原地主的许可,也可以租给他人开采,不过在开采时要给地主一点小小的回报①。在以上那两个法规中,神圣的秘鲁国王的利益鼓励了采矿业。

---

① 《康沃尔自然史》,第167、175页,如果土地被界定,地主只能得到1/15。

In both regulations the sacred rights of private property are sacrificed to the supposed interests of public revenue.

The gold mines of Pevu now pay only a twentieth in rent.
The same encouragement is given in Peru to the discovery and working of new gold mines; and in gold the king's tax amounts only to a twentieth part of the standard metal. It was once a fifth, and afterwards a tenth, as in silver; but it was found that the work could not bear even the lowest of these two taxes. ①If it is rare, however, say the same authors, Frezier and Ulloa, to find a person who has made his fortune by a silver, it is still much rarer to find one who has done so by a gold mine. This twentieth part seems to be the whole rent which is paid by the greater part of the gold mines in Chili and Peru. Gold too is much more liable to be smuggled than even silver: not only on account of the superior value of the metal in proportion to its bulk, but on account of the peculiar way in which nature produces it. Silver is very seldom found virgin, but, like most other metals, is generally mineralized with some other body, from which it is impossible to separate it in such quantities as will pay for the expence, but by a very laborious and tedious operation, which cannot well be carried on but in workhouses erected for the purpose, and therefore exposed to the inspection of the king's officers. Gold, on the contrary, is almost always found virgin. It is sometimes found in pieces of some bulk; and even when mixed in small and almost insensible particles with sand, earth, and other extraneous bodies, it can be separated from them by a very short and simple operation, which can be carried on in any private house by any body who is possessed of a small quantity of mercury. If the king's tax, therefore, is but ill paid upon silver, it is likely to be much worse paid upon gold; and rent must make a much smaller part of the price ol gold, than even of that of silver.

---

① ['It is more rare to see a gold miner rich than a silver miner or of any other metal.'—Frezier, *Voyage*, p. 108. There seems nothing in either Frezier or Ulloa to indicate that they took the gloomy view of the prospects of the gold and silver miner which is ascribed to them in the text. From this and the curious way in which they are coupled together, here and above (pp. 169, 170), and also the fact that no mention is made of the title of either of their books, it seems probable that Smith is quoting from memory or from notes which had become mixed. It is possible that he confused Frezier with Ulloa's collaborator, Don George Juan, but Ulloa is quoted without Frezier above, p. 149, and below, p. 186.]

私有财产权都由于想象中的国家公共收入权利而被侵犯了。

在秘鲁,新金矿的发现与开采同样受到奖励,而国王的金税只占标准金产量的 1/20。金税与银税本来的税率都是 1/5,后来都减到 1/10,但是就开采的情况来看,即便 1/10 的税率也是太高。上面提到的两个作者佛雷泽和乌洛阿曾说过,通过开采银矿发财的人是很少见的,而通过开采金矿发财的就更少见了①。这 1/20 似乎是智利、秘鲁大部分地区的金矿所能支付的全部地租。走私黄金比走私白银要容易得多,这不仅仅由于从相对体积来说,金的价值高于银的价值,而且还由于金的特殊的生产方式。银在被发现时很少是纯的,一般都会像大多数其他金属那样掺杂着一些矿物质,只有经过极困难和极烦琐的操作才能把银从这些矿物质中分解出来,而这种操作,必须在专门的工场进行,这样就很容易受到国王官吏的监督。与此不同,金在被发现时几乎都是纯的,有时发现相当大的纯金块,即使掺杂有少量的砂土及其他杂质,只需要通过很简单的操作就可以把纯金从中分离出来。任何人都可在自己的住宅中进行这种操作,所需要的只是少量水银。所以,如果国王从白银只能取得很少的税收,那么他从金税所得的收入可能就更少了,因而地租在金价中所占的份额,一定小于它在银价中所占的份额。

秘鲁的现金矿在只支付产的 1/20 为地租作

---

① "很少见到金矿的所有者比银矿或其他金属矿的所有者富裕",佛雷泽《航海记》第 108 页;佛雷泽和乌洛阿似乎都从来没有像文章中说的那样对金银矿主的前景表示悲观。从这里以及他们被联系在一起的奇怪的方式,此处以及前面,以及没有人提及他们的著述这一事实,看来似乎斯密先生的引用是根据记忆或某些被混淆的资料。他有可能混淆了佛雷泽和乌洛阿的合作者董·乔治·胡安,但是引用乌洛阿并没有提及佛雷泽,见前面第 149 页和后面第 186 页。

The lowest price of the precious metals must replace stock with ordinary profits.   The lowest price at which the precious metals can be sold, or the smallest quantity of other goods for which they can be exchanged during any considerable time, is regulated by the same principles which must fix the lowest ordinary price of all other goods. The stock which must commonly be employed, the food, cloaths, and lodging which must commonly be consumed in bringing them from the mine to the market, determine it. It must at least be sufficient to replace that stock, with the ordinary profits.

but their highest price is determined by their scarcity.   Their highest price, however, seems not to be necessarily determined by any thing but the actual scarcity or plenty of those metals themselves. It is not determined by that of any other commodity, in the same manner as the price of coals is by that of wood, beyond which no scarcity can ever raise it. Increase the scarcity of gold to a certain degree, and the smallest bit of it may become more precious than a diamond, and exchange for a greater quantity of other goods.

The demand for them arises from their utility and beauty: The demand for those metals arises partly from their utility, and partly from their beauty. If you except iron, they are more useful than, perhaps, any other metal. As they are less liable to rust and impurity, they can more easily be kept clean; and the utensils either of the table or the kitchen are often upon that account more agreeable when made of them. A silver boiler is more cleanly that a lead, copper, or tin one; and the same quality would render a gold boiler still better than a silver one. Their principal merit, however, arises from their beauty, which renders them peculiarly fit for the ornaments of dress and furniture. No paint or dye can give so splendid a colour as gilding. The merit of their beauty is greatly enhanced by their scarcity. With the greater part of rich people, the chief enjoyment of riches consists in the parade of riches, which in their eye is never so complete as when they appear to possess those decisive marks of opulence which nobody can possess but themselves. **and the merit of beauty is enhanced by their scarcity.** In their eyes the merit of an object which is in any degree either useful or beautiful, is greatly enhanced by its scarcity, or by the great labour which it requires to collect any considerable

贵金属在市场上出售的最低价格,或者说,长期内贵金属在市场上所能交换的其他货物的最少数量,是由决定一切其他货物普通最低价格的原理所决定的。这种最低价格,是由将贵金属从矿山运往市场所需投入的资本,即由在这一过程中通常所需消费的衣服、食物和住宅决定的。最低价格必须足够补偿所投入的资本并提供一些一般利润。_{贵金属的最低价格必须足够补偿所投入的资本并提供一些一般利润。}

但贵金属的最高价格只取决于贵金属本身的实际供给是不是足够丰裕,而不取决于任何其他物品。这个最高价格,不由任何其他物品的最高价格决定,不像煤炭那样,其价格取决于木柴的价格。如果金的稀缺性提高到一定程度,很小的一块金可能变得比金刚钻还昂贵,并可能换来更多的其他物品。_{贵金属的最高价格由它的稀缺性决定的。}

人们对贵金属的需求,一部分是由于它的效用,一部分是由于它的美观。贵金属也许比除了铁以外的其他任何金属都有用。贵金属不容易生锈,因而更容易保持清洁,所以用金银来制作餐桌上和厨房里的器皿,更加讨人喜欢。银制的锅或壶要比铝制、铜制或锡制的更为清洁。同样的性质又使得金制的器具比银制的更受欢迎。贵金属的主要价值来源于它们的美观,这一特点使贵金属特别适合做衣服和家具的装饰品。没有任何一种颜料或染料,能够产生像镀金那样华丽的色彩。贵金属的稀缺性又大大增加了这种美观的特点。对大多数富人来说,富有的最大的快乐,在于炫耀他们的财富,而当自己拥有别人都没有的代表富裕的最主要的标志时,这炫耀就达到了极致。在他们眼里,一件稍微有点用处或较为美观的物品,会由于稀缺性而使其价值大大增加,或者可以说,只有花费很大的劳动量才能够收集相当数量的这种物品,除了他们以外任何别人都支付不起这么大的劳动量的_{对贵金属的需求是由它们的效用和美观;}_{稀缺性又增加了其美观的优点。}

quantity of it, a labour which nobody can afford to pay but themselves. Such objects they are willing to purchase at a higher price than things much more beautiful and useful, but more common. These qualities of utility, beauty, and scarcity, are the original foundation of the high price of those metals, or of the great quantity of other goods for which they can every-where be exchanged. This value was antecedent to and independent of their being employed as coin, and was the quality which fitted them for that employment. That employment, however, by occasioning a new demand, and by diminishing the quantity which could be employed in any other way, may have afterwards contributed to keep up or increase their value.

<small>The demand for precious stones arises altogether from their beauty enhanced by their scarcity.</small> The demand for the precious stones arises altogether from their beauty. They are of no use, but as ornaments; and the merit of their beauty is greatly enhanced by their scarcity, or by the difficulty and expence of getting them from the mine. Wages and profit accordingly make up, upon most occasions, almost the whole of their high price. Rent comes in but for a very small share; frequently for no share; and the most fertile mines only afford any considerable rent. When Tavernier, a jeweller, visited the diamond mines of Golconda and Visiapour, he was informed that the sovereign of the country, for whose benefit they were wrought, had ordered all of them to be shut up, except those which yielded the largest and finest stones. ①The others, it seems, were to the proprietor not worth the working.

As the price both of the precious metals and of the precious stones is regulated all over the world by their price at the most fertile

---

① [*The Six Voyages of John Baptista Tavernier, a noble man of France now living , through Turkey into Persia and the East Indies*, translated by J. P. , 1678, does not appear to contain any such statement. Possibly it is merely founded on Tavernier's remark that 'there was a mine discovered between Coulour and Raolconda, which the King caused to be shut up again by reason of some cheats that were used there; for they found therein that sort of stones which had this green outside, fair and transparent, and which appeared more fair than the others, but when they came to the mill they crumbled to pieces' (pt. ii. , p. 138).]

代价,因而物品的价值更加突出了。对于这些物品,他们情愿支付比那些更美观、更有用但比较普通的物品更高的价格。效用、美观和稀缺性这些特点,是贵金属价格昂贵的基础,也是它们到处都能交换大量其他货物的根本原因。贵金属在被用作货币以前就已经具有了高价值,并不是由于用作货币才赋予它们较高的价值,贵金属本身的高价值使它适合用作货币。由于这种用途,引起了对贵金属的新需求,同时减少了其他用途的使用数量,从而保持或增加了它们的价值。

对宝石的需求,则完全是由于它的美观。宝石除用做装饰品外,没有其他用处。其美观的价值,又因为它的稀缺性而增加,也就是说宝石的价值因为开采极其困难且费用巨大而增加。因此,在大多数情况下,工资和利润几乎构成了宝石高价格的全部。地租在宝石价格中只占很小的比例,甚至不占任何份额,只有储藏量最丰富的矿山才提供相当客观的地租。珠宝商塔弗尼埃访问戈尔康达和维沙博耳两地的钻石矿山时得知,当地的矿山只是为国王的利益而开采的,而国王曾下令,只保留生产最大和最美的钻石的矿山,其余所有矿山一律关闭①。其余所有矿山在所有者看来都是不值得开采的。

世界各地贵金属和宝石的价格,都是由世界上藏量最丰富矿

---

① 《约翰·巴浦提斯塔·塔弗尼埃,一位至今健在的法国贵族的六次航海记——从土耳其进入波斯和东印度》(J. P. 译,1678 年)中并没有包括这样的说明。有可能只在塔弗尼埃的备注中发见"在戈尔康达和维沙博耳发现了矿山,国王由于那里的欺诈行为而被迫关闭了他们,因为他们在那里发现了一种石头,外面是绿色的,纯洁而透明的,比任何其他的都要纯,但是到了磨坊却都被磨成了碎片"(第 2 部分,第 138 页)。

mine in it, the rent which a mine of either can afford to its proprietor is in proportion, not to its absolute, but to what may be called its relative fertility, or to its superiority over other mines of the same kind.

<small>The rent of mines of precious metals and precious stones is in proportion to their relative and not to their absolute fertility.</small>　If new mines were discovered as much superior to those of Potosi as they were superior to those of Europe, the value of silver might be so much degraded as to render even the mines of Potosi not worth the working. Before the discovery of the Spanish West Indies, the most fertile mines in Europe may have afforded as great a rent to their proprietor as the richest mines in Peru do at present. Though the quantity of silver was much less, it might have exchanged for an equal quantity of other goods, and the proprietor's share might have enabled him to purchase or command an equal quantity either of labour or of commodities. The value both of the produce and of the rent, the real revenue which they afforded both to the public and to the proprietor, might have been the same.

<small>Abundant supplies would add little to the wealth of the world.</small>　The most abundant mines either of the precious metals or of the precious stones could add little to the wealth of the world. A produce of which the value is principally derived from its scarcity, is necessarily degraded by its abundance. A service of plate, and the other frivolous ornaments of dress and furniture, could be purchased for a smaller quantity of labour, or for a smaller quantity of commodities; and in this would consist the sole advantage which the world could derive from that abundance.

<small>But in estates above ground both produce and rent are regulated by absolute fertility.</small>　It is otherwise in estates above ground. The value both of their produce and of their rent is in proportion to their absolute, and not to their relative fertility. The land which produces a certain quantity of food, cloaths, and lodging, can always feed, cloath, and lodge a certain number of people; and whatever may be the proportion of the landlord, it will always give him a proportionable command of the labour of those people, and of the commodities with which that labour can supply him. The value of the most barren lands is not diminished by the neighbourhood of the most fertile. On the contrary, it is generally increased by it. The great number of people maintained by the fertile lands afford a market to many parts of the produce of the barren, which they could never have found among those whom their own produce could maintain.

藏的价格所决定的,所以贵金属或宝石矿藏所能提供的地租,不是与绝对丰富程度成比例,而是与其相对丰富程度成比例,也即与它比同种类其他矿山的优良程度成比例。如果有优于波托西矿山的新矿山被发现,正像当初波托西矿山优于欧洲矿山一样,那么银价就会大大下跌,甚至连波托西矿山也会失去开采的价值。在西班牙所属西印度群岛被发现以前,欧洲最丰富矿山为其所有者提供的地租,也像今天秘鲁藏量最丰富的矿山为其所有者所提供的地租一样大。当时的银量虽然比现在少得多,但却可以交换与现在等量的其他货物,而所有者的收益也能换得与现在等量的劳动或商品。产品和地租的价值,也即产品和地租给公众和所有者所提供的实际收入,与今天可能也是完全一样的。

<small>贵金属和宝石矿的地租与它们的相对丰富程度成比例,而并不与其绝对丰富程度成比例。</small>

  贵金属或宝石藏量最丰富的矿山,不会增加世界的财富。如果某种产品的价值,主要来自于它们的稀缺性,那么如果产品供给增加其价值必然会随之而下跌。人们使用的金银餐具,以及其他衣服家具的华丽装饰,就能以较少的劳动或商品买入。这就是世界能从金银宝石供应丰富得到的唯一好处。

<small>供应充足并不能增加世界的财富。</small>

  而土地上的产品情况就不同了。土地的产品和地租这两者的价值,不与土地的相对丰富程度成比例,而是与其绝对丰富程度成比例。能生产一定量的衣服、食物和住宅的土地,总能为一定数量的人们提供衣、食、住。不论地主享有的份额是多少,总能使地主有权支配相应数量的劳动,以及这些劳动为他生产的商品。最贫瘠土地的价值不会因靠近最肥沃土地而减少。相反,它的价值常常因此而增加。肥沃的土地所养活的众多的人口,正好给贫瘠土地的许多产品提供了市场,而贫瘠土地的产品,在能够自给自足的那些人中是找不到市场的。

<small>但在土地上,产品和地租是由绝对丰富程度决定的。</small>

Abundance of food raises the value of other produce.   Whatever increases the fertility of land in producing food, increases not only the value of the lands upon which the improvement is bestowed, but contributes likewise to increase that of many other lands, by creating a new demand for their produce. That abundance of food, of which, in consequence of the improvement of land, many people have the disposal beyond what they themselves can consume, is the great cause of the demand both for the precious metals and the precious stones, as well as for every other conveniency and ornament of dress, lodging, houshold furniture, and equipage. Food not only constitutes the principal part of the riches of the world, but it is the abundance of food which gives the principal part of their value to many other sorts of riches. The poor inhabitants of Cuba and St. Domingo, when they were first discovered by the Spaniards, used to wear little bits of gold as ornaments in their hair and other parts of their dress. They seemed to value them as we would do any little pebbles of somewhat more than ordinary beauty, and to consider them a s just worth the picking up, but not worth the refusing to any body who asked them. They gave them to their new guests at the first request, without seeming to think that they had made them any very valuable present. They were astonished to observe the rage of the Spaniards to obtain them; and had no notion that there could anywhere be a country in which many people had the disposal of so great a superfluity of food, so scanty always among themselves, that for a very small quantity of those glittering baubles they would willingly give as much as might maintain a whole family for many years. Could they have been made to understand this, the passion of the Spaniards would not have surprised them.

PART III
Of the Variations in the Proportion between the respective Values of that Sort of Produce which always affords Rent, and of that which sometimes does and sometimes does not afford Rent

The general course of progress is for produce other than food to become dearer.   The increasing abundance of food, in consequence of increasing improvement and cultivation, must necessarily increase the demand for every part of the produce of land which is not food, and which can be applied either to use or to ornament. In the whole progress of improvement, it might therefore be expected, there should be only one variation in the comparative values of those two different sorts of produce. The value of that sort which sometimes does and sometimes does not afford rent, should constantly rise in proportion to that which always affords some rent. As art and

凡是可以提高生产食物的土地肥沃程度的东西,都不仅会提高被改良土地的价值,而且也会提高许多其他土地的价值,因为它为这些土地的产品创造了新的需求。由于土地的改良而使粮食供应充足,使许多人都有了超出自己消费需求的剩余食物,因而对贵金属和宝石也有了需求,这也是对于衣服、住宅、家具和设备以及其他一切便利品和装饰品有需求的原因。食物不仅是世界上财富的主要部分,而且正是食物的丰富使其他各种财富具有了价值。当古巴和圣多明戈刚被西班牙人发现时,那里的穷苦居民经常用小金块作为头饰和服饰。在他们眼里,这些小金块的价值和我们眼中那些比普通石头稍微漂亮的小鹅卵石的价值相同,值得捡回来,但如果有人要时就可以赠送给他。当新来的客人开口索取时,他们会立即赠送,而且并不认为赠送了非常珍贵的礼物。他们对西班牙人那么热切地想获得金块感到惊讶。他们想不到世界上竟有这样的国家,那里的人们拥有大量剩余的粮食,而他们总是缺乏粮食。那里的人为了得到一点会发亮的小玩意儿,竟然愿意支付足够养活一家人好几年的食物。如果他们能够理解其中的缘由,他们就不会对西班牙人的黄金热感到惊讶了。

<small>食物丰富提高了其他产品的价值。</small>

第三节 论总能提供地租的产品和有时能、有时不能提供地租的产品两者价值比例的变化

由于土地的不断改良和耕种的不断扩大,粮食供应日渐丰富,这必然增加了对土地上生产的除了食物以外的具有实用和装饰作用的产品的需求。因此,可以预期在土地改良的过程中,这两种产品的相对价值只有一种变动。有时能、有时不能提供地租的产品的价值会随着总能提供地租的产品价值的增长而相应地

<small>一般的过程使得食物以外的商品价格提高了,</small>

industry advance, the materials of cloathing and lodging, the useful fossils and minerals of the earth, the precious metals and the precious stones should gradually come to be more and more in demand, should gradually exchange for a greater and a greater quantity of food, or in other words, should gradually become dearer and dearer. This accordingly has been the case with most of these things upon most occasions, and would have been the case with all of them upon all occasions, if particular accidents had not upon some occasions increased the supply of some of them in a still greater proportion than the demand.

but there are interruptions, The value of a free-stone quarry, for example, will necessarily increase with the increasing improvement and population of the country round about it; especially if it should be the only one in the neighbourhood. But the value of a silver mine, even though there should not be another within a thousand miles of it, will not necessarily increase with the improvement of the country in which it is situated. The market for the produce of a free-stone quarry can seldom extend more than a few miles round about it, and the demand must generally be in proportion to the improvement and population of that small district. as in the case of silver, when new fertile mines are discovered. But the market for the produce of a silver mine may extend over the whole known world. Unless the world in general, therefore, be advancing in improvement and population, the demand for silver might not be at all increased by the improvement even of a large country in the neighbourhood of the mine. Even though the world in general were improving, yet, if, in the course o f its improvement, new mines should be discovered, much more fertile than any which had been known before, though the demand for silver would necessarily increase, yet the supply might increase in so much a greater proportion, that the real price of that metal might gradually fall; that is, any given quantity, a pound weight of it, for example, might gradually purchase or command a smaller and a smaller quantity of labour, or exchange for a smaller and a smaller quantity of corn, the principal part of the subsistence of the labourer.

The great market for silver is the commercial and civilized part of the world.

Silver would grow dearer in the general progress of improvement, If by the general progress of improvement the demand of this market should increase, while at the same time the supply did not increase in the same proportion, the value of silver would gradually rise in proportion to that of corn. Any given quantity of silver

增长。随着技术和产业的进步,人们对衣服、居住材料、地下的有用化石和矿物以及贵金属和宝石的需求越来越大。它们所能交换的食物也逐渐增多,换句话说,它们变得更加昂贵了,这就是大多数商品通常发生的情况。如果没有特殊事件使其中某些物品的供给增加,大大超过了需求的增加,那么所有的商品都会是这种情况。

比如,一个砂石矿的价值,会随着周围土地的改良以及人口的增加而提高,尤其当这个石矿是附近唯一的石矿时更是如此。然而银矿则不然,即使在周围1000里以内没有第二个银矿,其价值也不见得会随矿山所在国土地的改良而增加。砂石矿产品的市场,一般不超过方圆几里的地方,因而对它的需求,也要和这个区域的土地改良与人口成比例。但是银矿产品的市场,却可以扩大到全世界。所以,除非全世界的土地都改良,人口都增加,否则只有银矿附近某大国的改良,对白银的需求是不会增加的。而且即使全世界都有了改良,但如果在改良的过程中,发现了更加丰富的新矿山,那么即便白银的需求由于改良而增加,白银供给的增加也有可能使得银的真实价格逐渐低落。任何数量的白银,比如说一镑白银,所能支配或购买的劳动量会越来越少。也就是说,一镑白银所能交换的劳动者主要生活资料即谷物的量,可能会越来越少。

白银的巨大市场,存在于世界上商业进步和文明发达的地区。

如果对白银的需求,随着一般的改良而增加,供给却不同比增加,那么白银相对于谷物的价值就会有所提高。也即一定数量的白银能够交换越来越多的谷物,换句话说,谷物的货币价格将

would exchange for a greater and a greater quantity of corn; or, in other words, the average money price of corn would gradually become cheaper and cheaper.

<small>but might grow heaper if some accident increased the supply for many years together:</small> If, on the contrary, the supply by some accident should increase for many years together in a greater proportion than the demand, that metal would gradually become cheaper and cheaper; or, in other words, the average money price of corn would, in spite of all improvements, gradually become dearer and dearer.

<small>or remain stationary if demand and supply increased equally.</small> But if, on the other hand, the supply of the metal should increase nearly in the same proportion as the demand, it would continue to purchase or exchange for nearly the same quantity of corn, and the average money price of corn would, in spite of all improvements, continue very nearly the same.

<small>These three things have happened during the last 400 years.</small> These three seem to exhaust all the possible combinations of events which can happen in the progress of improvement; and during the course of the four centuries preceding the present, if we may judge by what has happened both in France and Great Britain, each of those three different combinations seem to have taken place in the European market, and nearly in the same order too in which I have here set them down.

Digression concerning the Variations in the Value of Silver during the Course of the Four last Centuries

FIRST PERIOD

<small>From 1350 to 1570 silver gradually fell.</small> In 1350, and for some time before, the average price of the quarter of wheat in England seems not to have been estimated lower than four ounces of silver, Tower-weight, equal to about twenty shillings of our present money. From this price it seems to have fallen gradually to two ounces of silver, equal to about ten shillings of our present money, the price at which we find it estimated in the beginning of the sixteenth century, and at which it seems to have continued to be estimated till about 1570. ①

---

① [The evidence for this statement, which does not agree with the figures in the table at the end of the chapter, is given in the next eleven paragraphs.]

逐渐降低。合物的货币价格将越来越便宜。

反之，如果由于某种意外事件，白银供给增加，在连续几年内增加的比例大于需求的增加，那么白银的价格就会逐渐降低。而谷物的货币价格就会随着改良而逐渐增高。

另一方面，如果白银的供给和需求是按照同一比例增加，那么它就能继续购买或交换等量的谷物。所以尽管有了改良，谷物的平均货币价格却不会发生任何变化。

以上三种情况应该包括了在改良过程中所能发生的一切可能的事情。在过去的四个世纪里，如果我们以法国和英国发生的实际情况作为依据，这三种不同的组合在欧洲市场上似乎都发生过，而发生的顺序也大致如此。

但在改良过程中，某种事故发生了，使白银的增加供给，其价格就会低一些；或者当持续的价格求平衡话，价格就保持不变。过去的四个世纪里这三种情况都曾发生过。

关于过去的四个世纪中
白银价值变动的捎带论述

第一期

在1350年以及以前的几年里，英格兰每夸特小麦的平均价格，据估计似乎一直不低于陶衡（tower-weight）4盎司白银，约折合现在的货币20先令。以后，这个价格似乎逐渐降低到2盎司，约等于现在的货币10先令。我们认为，这每夸特10先令的价格，是16世纪初小麦的估计价格，这个价格一直持续到1570年①。

1350—1570年用白银表示的谷物价格逐渐下跌。

---

① 关于这段论述的证据，与本章最后的统计表不一致，将在下面的十一段里给出。

> 国民财富的性质与原理

In 1350 wheat was 402. of silver per quarter, In 1350, being the 25th of Edward Ⅲ, was enacted what is called, The statute of labourers. In the preamble it complains much of the insolence of servants, who endeavoured to raise their wages upon their masters. It therefore ordains, that all servants and labourers should for the future be contented with the same wages and liveries (liveries in those times signified, not only cloaths, but provisions) which they had been accustomed to receive in the 20th year of the king, and the four preceding years; ①that upon this account their livery wheat should no-where be estimated higher than ten-pence a bushel, and that it should always be in the option of the master to deliver them either the wheat or the money. Ten-pence a bushel, therefore, had, in the 25th of Edward Ⅲ, been reckoned a very moderate price of wheat, since it required a particular statute to oblige servants to accept of it in exchange for their usual livery of provisions; and it had been reckoned a reasonable price ten years before that, or in the 16th year of the king, the term to which the statute refers. But in the 16th year of Edward Ⅲ, ten-pence contained about half an ounce of silver, Tower-weight, and was nearly equal to half a crown of our present money. ②Four ounces of silver, Tower-weight, therefore, equal to six shillings and eight-pence of the money of those times, and to near twenty shillings of that of the present, must have been reckoned a moderate price for the quarter of eight bushels.

and was not less than that at the beginning of the century, This statute is surely a better evidence of what was reckoned in those times a moderate price of grain, than the prices of some particular years which have generally been recorded by historians and other writers on account of their extraordinary dearness or cheapness, and from which, therefore, it is difficult to form any judgment concerning what may have been the ordinary price. ③There are, besides, other reasons for believing that in the beginning of the fourteenth century, and for some time before, the common price of wheat was not less than four ounces of silver the quarter, and that of other grain in proportion.

---

① [*I. e.* , four years before the twentieth year.]

② [This and the other reductions of ancient money to the eighteenth century standard are probably founded on the table in Martin Folkes, *Table of English Silver Coins*, 1745, p. 142.]

③ [*E. g.* , Fleetwood's prices in the table at the end of the chapter.]

1350年,即爱德华三世二十五年,通过了所谓的劳动法。在法规的绪论里用了很大篇幅抱怨雇工的蛮横无理,因为他们企图迫使雇主增加工资。因此,该法规规定:所有的雇工以及劳动者,此后应接受爱德华三世二十年及前四年①施行的工资及配给(这些配给在当时不仅包括衣服,也包括食物)水平。由于这个原因,他们所得到的作为配给的小麦,无论在什么地方都不能超过每蒲式耳10便士,而且必须由雇主选择,是交付小麦还是交付货币。在爱德华三世二十五年,每蒲式耳10便士被认为是很适中的小麦价格,因为它要求通过特别的法令来迫使雇工接受,作为一般的配给口粮的价格。这个价格在以前的10年中,也就是法令所指的爱德华三世十六年,是一个合理的价格。但在爱德华三世十六年,10便士约含有陶衡半盎司白银,约等于现在的货币半克朗②。所以,陶衡四盎司白银约等于当时货币6先令8便士,也等于现在的货币20先令,在当时被认为是1夸特也即8蒲式耳小麦的中等价格。

<small>1350年每夸特小麦的平均价格约为陶衡4盎司白银。</small>

关于什么样的价格被当作是当时谷物的中等价格,这项法规肯定比历史学家及其他作者的记载提供了更好的证明,因为他们的记载,强调特别昂贵或特别便宜的价格,所以以此作为判断当时的中等价格的依据是不合适的③。另外,我们还有令人信服的其他理由,14世纪初以及前几年小麦的平均价格,不少于每夸特4盎司白银,而其他各种谷物的价格可以由此推出。

<small>在本世纪初也不低于这个价格。</small>

---

① 即爱德华三世第二十年往前数的4年内。
② 这些以及古代货币的其他减少,达到18世纪的标准,有可能出现在马丁的统计表《英国银铸币统计表》(1745年,第142页)中。
③ 弗利特伍德的价格在本章最后的统计表中列出。

In 1309, Ralph de Born, prior of St. Augustine's, Canterbury, gave a feast upon his installation-day, of which William Thorn has preserved, not only the bill of fare, but the prices of many particulars. In that feast were consumed, 1st, Fifty-three quarters of wheat, which cost nineteen pounds, or seven shillings and two-pence a quarter, equal to about one-and-twenty shillings and six-pence of our present money; 2 dly, Fifty-eight quarters of malt, which cost seventeen pounds ten shillings, or six shillings a quarter, equal to about eighteen shillings of our present money: 3 dly, Twenty quarters of oats, which cost four pounds, or four shillings a quarter, equal to about twelve shillings of our present money. ①The prices of malt and oats seem here to be higher than their ordinary proportion to the price of wheat.

These prices are not recorded on account of their extraordinary dearness or cheapness, but are mentioned accidentally as the prices actually paid for large quantities of grain consumed at a feast which was famous for its magnificence.

_{and for some time before.} In 1262, being the 51st of Henry Ⅲ, was revived an ancient statute called, *The Assize of Bread and Ale*, which, the king says in the preamble, had been made in the times of his progenitors sometime kings of England. it is probably, therefore, as old at least as the time of his grandfather Henry Ⅱ, and may have been as old as the conquest. It regulates the price of bread according as the prices of wheat may happen to be, from one shilling to twenty shillings the quarter of the money of those times. But statutes of this kind are generally presumed to provide with equal care for all deviations from the middle price, for those below it as well as for those above it. Ten shillings, therefore, containing six ounces of silver, Tower-weight, and equal to about thirty shillings of our present money, must,

---

① [The date 1262 is wrong, as 51 Hen. Ⅲ. ran from October 28, 1266, to October 27, 1267. But the editions of the statutes which ascribe the statute to 51 Hen. Ⅲ. appear to have no good authority for doing so; see *Statutes of the Realm*, vol. i. , p. 199, notes. The statute has already been quoted above, p. 28, and is quoted again below, p. 183.]

1309年,坎特布里[1]的圣奥古斯都修道院副院长拉尔夫.波恩在就职时曾举行宴会。威廉·桑恩记录了关于这次筵席的菜单以及许多食物的价格。其记录如下:第一,53夸特小麦,价值19镑,合每夸特6先令2便士,约等于现在的货币21先令2便士;第二,56夸特麦芽,价值17镑10先令,合每夸特6先令,约等于现在的货币18先令;第三,20夸特燕麦,价值4镑,合每夸特4先令,约等于现在的货币12先令。根据这个记载麦芽和燕麦的价格,似乎比它们和小麦的普通比价要高。

这些价格并不是因为它们特别昂贵或特别便宜而记载的,而只是偶然间对一次奢华宴会所消费大量谷物实际价格的真实记载。

1262年,即亨利三世五十一年,恢复了一项古老的法令,即所谓"面包和麦酒法定价格"①的法令。亨利三世在序言里讲到,该项法令乃是他的祖先即英格兰国王所制定的。因此,该法令很可能是亨利二世制订的或者可能是更早期的征服时代制订的。该法令按照当时小麦的价格,即每夸特由一先令至20先令,来规定面包价格。但是我们假定这种法律一般会考虑到对中等价格的偏离,即超过中等价格或低于中等价格的情况,所以在这一假设下,10先令含有陶衡6盎司白银,相当于现在的30先令,在该法以及以前的一些时期。

---

① 262年这个日期有可能是错误的,因为亨利三世五十一年是从1266年10月28日到1267年10月27日。但是来自亨利三世五十一年法令的这个版本好像没有得到很有力的授权来这样做,见《领土法》,这项法令在前面引用过,后面还会引用到。

[1] 坎特伯雷(Canterbury),英格兰东南部一座自治市,位于伦敦东南偏东斯道尔河畔。坎特伯雷大教堂(建于11~16世纪)是英国圣公会的大主教和首席主教的住地。建在由圣奥古斯都在公元600年建立的一个修道院的遗址上。

upon this supposition, have been reckoned the middle price of the quarter of wheat when this statute was first enacted, and must have continued to be so in the 51st of Henry Ⅲ. We cannot therefore be very wrong in supposing that the middle price was not less than one-third of the highest price at which this statute regulates the price of bread, or than six shillings and eight-pence of the money of those times, containing four ounces of silver, Tower-weight.

From these different facts, therefore, we seem to have some reason to conclude, that about the middle of the fourteenth century, and for a considerable time before, the average or ordinary price of the quarter of wheat was not supposed to be less than four ounces of silver, Towerweight.

<small>From that it sank gradually to 2 0z. at the beginning of the sixteenth century and remained at that till 1570.</small> From about the middle of the fourteenth to the beginning of the sixteenth century, what was reckoned the reasonable and moderate, that is the ordinary or average price of wheat, seems to have sunk gradually to about one-half of this price; so as at last to have fallen to about two ounces of silver, Tower-weight, equal to about ten shillings of our present money. It continued to be estimated at this price till about 1570.

In the houshold book of Henry, the fifth earl of Northumberland, drawn up in 1512, there are two different estimations of wheat. In one of them it is computed at six shillings and eight-pence the quarter, in the other at five shillings and eight-pence only. In 1512, six shillings and eight-pence contained only two ounces of silver, Tower-weight, and were equal to about ten shillings of our present money.

From the 25th of Edward Ⅲ, to the beginning of the reign of Elizabeth, during the space of more than two hundred years, six shillings and eight-pence, it appears from several different statutes, had continued to be considered as what is called the moderate and reasonable, that is the ordinary or average price of wheat. The quantity of silver, however, contained in that nominal sum was, during the course of this period, continually diminishing, in consequence of some alterations which were made in the coin. But the increase of the value of silver had, it seems, so far compensated the diminution of the quantity of it contained in the same nominal sum, that the legislature did not think it worth while to attend to this circumstance. ①

Thus in 1436 it was enacted, that wheat might be exported without a licence when the price was so low as six shillings and eight-pence1 And in 1463 it was enacted, that no wheat should be imported

---

① [15 Hen. Ⅵ., c.2.]

令最初制定的时候,一定被认为是每夸特小麦的中等价格,而且,直到亨利三世五十一年都是这样认为的。因此,我们假定,这个中等价格不低于法定的最高面包价格的 1/3,即不低于含有陶衡 4 盎司白银的当时的货币 6 先令 8 便士,应该不会有很大的错误。

因此根据以上事实,我们有充分的理由做出以下结论:即在 14 世纪中期以及以前一个相当长的时期中,每夸特小麦的平均价格或中等价格,大概在陶衡 4 盎司白银以上。

从大约 14 世纪中期至 16 世纪初,被当作是小麦平均的或适中的价格,换句话说,小麦的普通或平均的价格,似乎已经逐渐减少了一半,以至于最后降到大约等于陶衡 2 盎司白银,约折合现在的货币 10 先令。直到 1570 年,仍被估计为这个价格。

1512 年,在诺森伯兰郡第五世伯爵亨利的家务开支记录中,有两种不同的小麦价格的计算方法:一是,每一夸特按照 6 先令 8 便士计算;二是,每一夸特只按 5 先令 8 便士计算。在 1512 年,6 先令 8 便士只含有陶衡 2 盎司白银,约等于现在的货币 10 先令。

从多种不同的法律来看,从爱德华三世二十五年到伊丽莎白在位初期这 200 多年的时间中,6 先令 8 便士似乎一直被认为是小麦的适中的价格或平均的价格,亦即所谓中等的合理价格。然而,在这一时期内,这个名义金额中所包含的银量由于银币的某些变革在不断的减少。不过,银价的增加似乎足以补偿含银量的减少。所以在立法当局看来,名义金额含银量的减少是不足为虑的。

1436 年的法律规定,小麦价格如果降低到每夸特 6 先令 8 便士,就可以随便出口而无需国家的许可①。1463 年的法律规定,如

---

① 亨利六世十五年第 2 号法令。

if the price was not above six shillings and eight-pence the quarter. ① The legislature had imagined, that when the price was so low, there could be no inconveniency in exportation, but that when it rose higher, it became prudent to allow of importation. Six shillings and eight-pence, therefore, containing about the same quantity of silver as thirteen shillings and four-pence of our present money (one third part less than the same nominal sum contained in the time of Edward Ⅲ), had in those times been considered as what is called the moderate and reasonable price of wheat. ②

In 1554, by the 1st and 2d of Philip and Mary; and in 1558, by the 1st of Elizabeth, ③the exportation of wheat was in the same manner prohibited, whenever the price of the quarter should exceed six shillings and eight-pence, which did not then contain two penny worth more silver than the same nominal sum does at present. But it had soon been found that to restrain the exportation of wheat till the price was so very low, was, in reality, to prohibit it altogether. In 1562, therefore, by the 5th of Elizabeth, ④ the exportation of wheat was allowed from certain ports whenever the price of the quarter should not exceed ten shillings, containing nearly the same quantity of silver as the like nominal sum does at present. This price had at this time, therefore, been considered as what is called the moderate and reasonable price of wheat. ⑤ It agrees nearly with the estimation of the Northumberland book in 1512.

The same fall has been observed in France.

That in France the average price of grain was, in the same manner, much lower in the end of the fifteenth and beginning of the sixteenth century, than in the two centuries preceding, has been observed

---

① [3 Ed Iv ,c. 2.]
② [1 and 2 P. and M. , e. 5, §7.]
③ [1 Eliz. , c. 11, §11.]
④ [5 Eliz. c. 5, §17.]
⑤ [Neither his *Recherches sur la valeur des Monnoies et sur les prix des grains avant et après le concile de Francfort*, 1762, nor his *Essai sur les Monnoies, ou réplexions sur le rapport entre l' argent et les denrées*, 1746, contain any clear justification for this reference.]

果小麦的价格不超过每夸特 6 先令 8 便士,就不允许进口①。立法当局认为,当小麦价格非常低的时候,自由出口不会造成什么不方便,但如果麦价升高,则允许自由进口是明智的选择。因此,当时 6 先令 8 便士所含的银相当于现在 13 先令 4 便士的含银量(比爱德华三世时代同一名义金额所含的银量少 1/3),就是当时所谓小麦的中等的、合理的价格。

1554 年,菲利普国王和玛利女王一年和二年的法令②,以及 1558 年伊丽莎白女王第一年的法令③,都有这样的规定,当小麦的价格超过每夸特价格 6 先令 8 便士时,就禁止出口。当时 6 先令 8 便士所包含的银,并不比现在同一名义金额多两便士。但很快就发现,要在小麦价格降到如此低价时才不限制出口,实际上等于永远禁止小麦出口。因此,在 1562 年,即伊丽莎白五年④,又规定在小麦价格不超过每夸特 10 先令时,就可以在指定的港口出口。当时 10 先令和现在同一名义金额的含银量几乎相等。所以,这个价格在当时被认为是中等的、合理的小麦价格,这和亨利伯爵在 1512 年的家务记录中所估计的价格,大致相等。

法国的情形也大致是这样的。杜普雷·得·圣莫尔以及有关谷物政策的论文的作者都这样认为,该国谷物的平均价格,在 15 世纪末和 16 世纪初,比在过去的两个世纪低许多⑤。在同一时

<small>在法国也可以看到同样的下降。</small>

---

① 爱德华四世三年第 2 号法令。
② 菲利普和玛利一年和二年第 5 号法令第 7 条。
③ 伊丽莎白　年第 11 号法令第 11 条。
④ 伊丽莎白五年第 5 号法令第 17 条。
⑤ 圣莫尔于 1762 年和 1746 年出版的两个著作里面都没有为此处的引证提供明显的证据。

both by Mr. Duprède St. Maur, and by the elegant author of the Essay on the police of grain. Its price, during the same period, had probably sunk in the same manner through the greater part of Europe.

It may have been due to the increase of demand for silver or to a diminution of supply.
This rise in the value of silver, in proportion to that of corn, may either have been owing altogether to the increase of the demand for that metal, in consequence of increasing improvement and cultivation, the supply in the mean time continuing the same as before: Or, the demand continuing the same as before, it may have been owing altogether to the gradual diminution of the supply; the greater part of the mines which were then known in the world, being much exhausted, and consequently the expence of working them much increased: Or it may have been owing partly to the one and partly to the other of those two circumstances. In the end of the fifteenth and beginning of the sixteenth centuries, the greater part of Europe was approaching towards a more settled form of government than it had enjoyed for several ages before. The increase of security would naturally increase industry and improvement ; and the demand for the precious metals, as well as for every other luxury and ornament, would naturally increase with the increase of riches. A greater annual produce would require a greater quantity of coin to circulate it; and a greater number of rich people would require a greater quantity of plate and other ornaments of silver. It is natural to suppose too, that the greater part of the mines which then supplied the European market with silver, might be a good deal exhausted, and have become more expensive in the working. They had been wrought many of them from the time of the Romans.

Most writers, however, have supposed that the value of silver continually fell.
It has been the opinion, however, of the greater part of those who have written upon the prices of commodities in ancient times, that, from the Conquest, perhaps from the invasion of Julius Cæsar, till the discovery of the mines of America, the value of silver was continually diminishing. This opinion they seem to have been led into, partly by the observations which they had occasion to make upon the prices both of corn and of some other parts of the rude produce of land; and partly by the popular notion, that as the quantity of silver naturally increases in every country with the increase of wealth, so its value diminishes as its quantity increases.

They have been misled in their observations on the price of corn, (I) by confusing con version prices with market prices;
In their observations upon the prices of corn, three different circumstances seem frequently to have misled them.

First, In ancient times almost all rents were paid in kind; in a certain quantity of corn, cattle, poultry, &c. It sometimes happened, however, that the landlord would stipulate, that he should be at liberty to demand of the tenant, either the annual payment in kind, or a certain sum of money instead of it. The price at which the payment in kind was in this manner exchanged for a certain

期,谷物价格在欧洲大部分国家也许同样下降。

白银价值相对于谷物价值的提高,也许完全是因为随着土地改良及耕种的进步,供给保持不变而需求增加;也可能完全是因为,需求保持不变而供给逐渐减少。当时世界上已知的银矿,大部分都已开采得接近枯竭,因而继续开采的费用大大增加;或者也可能是上述两种情况共同作用的结果。在15世纪末和16世纪初,欧洲大多数国家的政局比过去几个世纪更加稳定。安全稳定性的增强,自然促进了工业的发展,而对于贵金属以及其他各种装饰品和奢侈品的需求,也随财富的增加而增加。年产出的增加,需要有更多的铸币来使其流通。富人数量增多,对银制器皿及其他银制装饰品的需求酒会增加。而且当时供给欧洲市场白银的大部分银矿,都接近枯竭,因而开采费用变大,这是可以推测的,因为有许多银矿是从古罗马时代起就开采的。

> 可能是由于银的需求增加或供给减少。

古代大部分论述商品价格的作者都认为,从诺尔曼征服时代起,或者从朱利阿·恺撒侵略时代起,直到发现美洲银矿的时候止,银价是在不断下降的。他们之所以会有这种看法,一方面是由于他们对谷物及其他土地原生产物价格所作的偶然的观察,另一方面则是由于一种流行的说法,即任何国家的白银,会自然地随财富的增加而增加,其价值则自然地随数量的增加而下降。

> 大作家们会认为白银价格持续下跌。然而多数者认为白银价格持续下跌。

在他们对谷物价格进行观察时,以下三种情况很容易使他们走入歧途:

第一,在古代几乎所有的地租都是用实物支付,即以一定数量的谷物、家禽、牲畜等来支付的。不过,地主有时候也会规定他可随意地要求佃户用实物支付年租,也可以用等于实物的一定

> 他们对谷物价格的观察受到误导;(1)换算价格与市场价格被混淆;

sum of money, is in Scotland called the conversion price. As the option is always in the landlord to take either the substance or the price, it is necessary for the safety of the tenant, that the conversion price should rather be below than above the average market price. In many places, accordingly, it is not much above one-half of this price. Through the greater part of Scotland this custom still continues with regard to poultry, and in some places with regard to cattle. It might probably have continued to take place too with regard to corn, had not the institution of the public fiars put an end to it. These are annual valuations, according to the judgment of an assize, of the average price of all the different sorts of grain, and of all the different qualities of each, according to the actual market price in every different county. This institution rendered it sufficiently safe for the tenant, and much more convenient for the landlord, to convert, as they call it, the corn rent, rather at what should happen to be the price of the fiars of each year, ① than at any certain fixed price. But the writers who have collected the prices of corn in ancient times, seem frequently to have mistaken what is called in Scotland the conversion price for the actual market price. Fleetwood acknowledges, upon one occasion, that he had made this mistake. As he wrote his book, however, for a particular purpose, he does not think proper to make this acknowledgment till after transcribing this conversion price fifteen times. The price is eight shillings the quarter of wheat. This sum in 1423, the year at which he begins with it, contained the same quantity of silver as sixteen shillings of our present money. But in 1562, the year at which he ends with it, it contained no more than the same nominal sum does at present.

(2) by the slovenly transcription of ancient statutes of assize;

Secondly, They have been misled by the slovenly manner in

① [*Chronicon Preciosum*, 1707, pp. 121, 122. Fleetwood does not ' acknowledge ' any ' mistake, ' but says that though the price was not the market price it might have been ' well agreed upon '. His particular purpose ' was to prove that in order to qualify for a fellowship a man might conscientiously swear his income to be much less than it was.]

数额的货币支付。在苏格兰,像这样用来代替实物的一定量的货币价格,被称为换算价格。因为地主总是掌握着收取实物还是收取货币的权力,所以为了保护佃户的安全,其换算价格必须订得低于平均的市场价格,而不是相反。因此在许多地方,这一换算价格,只比平均市场价格的一半略高。直到今天,在苏格兰大部分地区,在家禽方面还保持着这种习惯,在有些地方,对牲畜也是这样。如果不是法定谷价制度的实施废除了换算,恐怕至今在谷物方面还会沿用这种换算办法。法定谷价,就是根据谷价法定委员会的意见,每年按照各县区的实际市场价格,对不同种类、不同品质的谷物的平均价格所评定的一个价格。根据这一制度,在换算谷物地租时,都是按照当年的法定价格而不是依据其他任何定价方法;这样一来,佃户的利益得到保障,而对地主也很方便。但是一些搜集古代谷物价格的作者们,往往把苏格兰的换算价格误当作实际的市场价格。弗利特伍德就曾经承认自己犯过一次这样的错误。但是,他是为了特殊的写书的目的才使用这种换算价格,直到用了 15 次以后①,他才敢承认自己的错误。那时小麦的换算价格是每夸特 8 先令。1423 年是他从事研究的第一年,这一年 8 先令的含银量与现在的 16 先令所含银量相同,但在他所研究的最后一年即 1562 年,8 先令所含的银量,则与现在同一名义金额货币的含银量相同。

第二,有些抄写人在抄写关于法定价格的法规时潦草粗 (2) 由于古代价格的法律抄写潦草;

---

① 《宝贵的纪念考证》(1707 年,第 121、122 页),弗利特伍德不承认犯了错误,而是说这个价格虽不是市场价格,但却是被普遍接受的价格。他的特别目的是在于证明一个人为了得到一种会员资格,会愿意心安理得地发誓自己的收入比真实的少得多。

which some ancient statutes of assize had been sometimes transcribed by lazy copiers; and sometimes perhaps actually composed by the legislature.

The ancient statutes of assize seem to have begun always with determining what ought to be the price of bread and ale when the price of wheat and barley were at the lowest, and to have proceeded gradually to determine what it ought to be, according as the prices of those two sorts of grain should gradually rise above this lowest price. But the transcribers of those statutes seem frequently to have thought it sufficient, to copy the regulation as far as the three or four first and lowest prices; saving in this manner their own labour, and judging, I suppose, that this was enough to show what proportion ought to be observed in all higher prices.

Thus in the assize of bread and ale, of the 51st of Henry III, the price of bread was regulated according to the different prices of wheat, from one shilling to twenty shillings the quarter, of the money of those times. But in the manuscripts from which all the different editions of the statutes, preceding that of Mr. Ruffhead, were printed, the copiers had never transcribed this regulation beyond the price of twelve shillings. Several writers, therefore, being misled by this faulty transcription, very naturally concluded that the middle price, or six shillings the quarter, equal to about eighteen shillings of our present money, was the ordinary or average price of wheat at that time.

or by misunderstandings of those statutes; In the statute of Tumbrel and Pillory, enacted nearly about the same time, the price of ale is regulated according to every sixpence rise in the price of barley, from two shillings to four shillings the quarter. That four shillings, however, was not considered as the highest price to which barley might frequently rise in those times, and that these prices were only given as an example of the proportion which ought to be observed in all other prices, whether higher or lower, we may infer from the last words of the statute; "et sic deinceps "crescetur vel diminuetur per sex denarios. "The expression is very slovenly, but the meaning is plain enough; "That the price of ale is" in this manner to be increased or diminished according to every "sixpence rise or fall in the price of barley." In the composition of this statute the legislature itself seems to have been as negligent as the copiers were in the transcription of the other.

心,有时立法当局在制定法规时也不够认真严肃,这些都会对这些作者们产生误导。

古代关于法定价格的法令,似乎总是首先这样规定,在小麦和大麦价格最低时,面包和麦酒的价格应该是多少,然后,在这两种谷物超过这最低价格时,面包和麦酒的价格应该是多少。然而那些法规的抄写人往往以为,抄写前面三四个最低价格就够了,我觉得他们想省点力气,因为他们认为,这已足以说明价格较高时应按什么比例来计算。

例如,在亨利三世五十一年关于面包、麦酒法定价格的法令中,面包的价格就是根据小麦的价格确定的,小麦的价格在当时是每夸特 1 先令到 20 先令。然而在拉弗赫先生出版法令汇编以前,其他所有法律汇编所根据的抄本,其抄写人都抄到 12 先令的价格为止。因此,受这些不完整抄本所误导的一些作者,就很自然地认为,当时小麦的一般价格或平均价格就是每夸特 6 先令,也就是大约等于现在的 18 先令。

又比如,大约在同一时期制定的《刑车法》和《颈手枷法》中规定,麦酒的价格按大麦的价格每夸特是 2 先令到 4 先令,每上涨 6 便士就调整一次。不过,在当时这 4 先令的价格,并没有被当做是大麦能够经常达到的最高价格,而只是作为例子,来说明当价格较高或较低时应按照什么样的比例来计算增减。这一点从该法令的最后一句话中可以看出来:"et sic deinceps ' crescetur vel diminuetur per sex denarios '"。这句话表达虽不够精确,但意思却很明显,就是说:"麦酒的价格,应该根据大麦的价格每增减 6 便士,而随之增减。"立法当局以及抄写在制定和抄写这法令时,似乎像都是同样地粗心潦草。

<small>或由于对法律的错误理解;</small>

国民财富的性质与原理

In an ancient manuscript of the Regiam Majestatem, an old Scotch law book, there is a statute of assize, in which the price of bread is regulated according to all the different prices of wheat, from ten-pence to three shillings the Scotch boll, equal to about half an English quarter. Three shillings Scotch, at the time when this assize is supposed to have been enacted, were equal to about nine shillings sterling of our present money. Mr. Ruddiman seems to conclude from this, that three shillings was the highest price to which wheat ever rose in those times, and that ten-pence, a shilling, or at most two shillings, were the ordinary prices. Upon consulting the manuscript, however, it appears evidently, that all these prices are only set down as examples of the proportion which ought to be observed between the respective prices of wheat and bread. The last words of the statute are, "reliqua "judicabis secundum præscripta habendo respectum ad pretium bladi." "You shall judge of the remaining cases according to what is above"written having a respect to the price of corn."

and (3) by attributing too much importance to excessively low prices.

Thirdly, They seem to have been misled too by the very low price at which wheat was sometimes sold in very ancient times; and to have imagined, that as its lowest price was then much lower than in later times, its ordinary price must likewise have been much lower. They might have found, however, that in those ancient times, its highest price was fully as much above, as its lowest price was below any thing that had ever been known in later times. Thus in 1270, Fleetwood gives us two prices of the quarter of wheat. The one is four pounds sixteen shillings of the money of those times, equal to fourteen pounds eight shillings of that of the present; the other is six pounds eight shillings, equal to nineteen pounds four shillings of our present money. No price can be found in the end of the fifteenth, or beginning of the sixteenth century, which approaches to the extravagance of these. The price of corn, though at all times liable to variation, varies most in those turbulent and disorderly societies, in which the interruption of all commerce and communication hinders the plenty of one part of the country from relieving the scarcity of

在苏格兰的一部古代法律《苏格兰古代法》(Regiam Majestatem)的古老抄本中,记载着有关法定价格的规定,其中面包的价格是根据小麦价格的变动调整的。这些价格从每苏格兰博耳[1] 10 便士到 3 先令不等。可以推测在这法令制定的时候,苏格兰的 3 便士约合现在英币 9 先令。拉迪曼先生似乎由此得出,3 先令是当时小麦的最高价格,10 便士、1 先令,或最多 2 先令,则是中等的价格。但是查阅抄本就很明白了,那些价格只是作为例子来说明小麦和面包价所应该有的比例。这法令最后有一句话:"reliqua judicabis secundum Praescripta? scripta habendo respectum ad Pretium bladi."即"在其他情况下应该按照以上所提到的谷物价格来进行推算"。

第三,这些作者有时也会被古代偶尔出现小麦的极低价格所误导,他们推测,既然当时的小麦最低价格,比后来的小麦最低价格低得多,那么其普通价格,一定也比后来的低许多。不过他们也许又发现,古代小麦的最高价格,也比后来的小麦最高价格高得多,如同最低价格比后来的最低价格低得多一样。例如在 1270 年,弗利特伍德谈到每夸特小麦的两种价格:一种是当时的货币 4 镑 16 先令,折合现在的货币 14 镑 8 先令;另一种是当时货币 6 镑 8 先令,折合现在的货币 19 镑 4 先令。在 15 世纪末或 16 世纪初,像这样过高的价格是不会见到的。虽然,在各个时期谷物的价格都会有所变动,但在动荡不安的社会里价格变动得更为剧烈。因为在这样的社会,所有的商业和交通被中断,国内富裕的

──────────

〔1〕 博耳(boll),英格兰和英格兰北部的容量单位;苏格兰的重量单位。

another. In the disorderly state of England under the Plantagenets, who governed it from about the middle of the twelfth, till towards the end of the fifteenth century, one district might be in plenty, while another at no great distance, by having its crop destroyed either by some accident of the seasons, or by the incursion of some neighbouring baron, might be suffering all the horrors of a famine; and yet if the lands of some hostile lord were interposed between them, the one might not be able to give the least assistance to the other. Under the vigorous administration of the Tudors, who governed England during the latter part of the fifteenth, and through the whole of the sixteenth century, no baron was powerful enough to dare to disturb the public security.

<small>The figures at the end of the chapter confirm this account.</small> The reader will find at the end of this chapter all the prices of wheat which have been collected by Fleetwood from 1202 to 1597, both inclusive, reduced to the money of the present times, and digested according to the order of time, into seven divisions of twelve years each. At the end of each division too, he will find the average price of the twelve years of which it consists. In that long period of time, Fleetwood has been able to collect the prices of no more than eighty years, so that four years are wanting to make out the last twelve years. I have added, therefore, from the accounts of Eton College, the prices of 1598, 1599, 1600, and 1601. It is the only addition which I have made. The reader will see, that from the beginning of the thirteenth, till after the middle of the sixteenth century, the average price of each twelve years grows gradually lower and lower; and that towards the end of the sixteenth century it begins to rise again. The prices, indeed, which Fleetwood has been able to collect, seem to have been those chiefly which were remarkable for extraordinary dearness or cheapness; and I do not pretend that any very certain conclusion can be drawn from them. So far, however, as they prove any thing at all, they confirm

地区无法救济贫穷的地区。从 12 世纪中期到 15 世纪末,英国处在普兰塔日尼王室统治之下,其时政局紊乱,一个地区可能很富饶,而另一个相距不很远的地区,就可能由于季节性的灾害或邻近贵族的入侵,庄稼被毁坏而陷于灾荒;如果入侵的贵族的领地介于贫富两地区中间,富者就不能对穷者提供援助。然而,在都铎王朝[1]强力统治下的 15 世纪后半叶和 16 世纪,就没有一个贵族强大得敢于武力破坏社会安全。

读者在本章末尾将会看到弗利特伍德所搜集的 1202—1597 年(包括这二年在内)的小麦价格,这些价格被换算为现在的货币,并按照年代顺序分为七阶段,每一阶段包含 12 年。每一阶段的末尾,列出了该阶段 12 年的平均价格。弗利特伍德在这样漫长的时期内只搜集到了 80 年的价格,在最后一个阶段还差 4 个年份的数据。因此我根据伊顿公学[2]的记载,补充了 1598 年、1599 年、1600 年及 1601 年的价格。只有这 4 年的数字是我所增补的。从这些数字读者可以看到,每 12 年的小麦平均价格,从 13 世纪初一直到 16 世纪中期逐渐下降,到 16 世纪末期以后又逐渐上升。弗利特伍德所搜集的价格,似乎主要是侧重于过高或过低的价格,所以我不敢确定,从他所搜集的这些价格能得出很正确的结论。但是如果这些价格,的确能证明什么的话,那么它们证

本章末尾的数字证实了这一观点。

---

〔1〕 都铎王朝(Tudor),英格兰统治王朝(1485~1603 年),包括亨利七世及其后代亨利八世、爱德华六世、玛丽一世和伊丽莎白一世。

〔2〕 伊顿(Eton),英国中部偏西南一个城镇,临近泰晤士河与温莎相对,此城镇内的伊顿学院,是英格兰最大和最有名望的公立寄宿学校,1440 年由亨利四世创建。伊顿公学(Eton College),培养英国上层政界人物的一所学校。

the account which I have been endeavouring to give. Fleetwood himself, however, seems, with most other writers, to have believed, that during all this period the value of silver, in consequence of its increasing abundance, was continually diminishing. The prices of corn which he himself has collected, certainly do not agree with this opinion.① They agree perfectly with that of Mr. Dupr de St. Maur, and with that which I have been endeavouring to explain. Bishop Fleetwood and Mr. Duprè de St. Maur are the two authors who seem to have collected, with the greatest diligence and fidelity, the prices of things in ancient times. It is somewhat curious that, though their opinions are so very different, their facts, so far as they relate to the price of corn at least, should coincide so very exactly.

<small>Sometimes the value of silver has been measured by the price of cattle, poultry, etc. But the low price of these things shows their cheapness, not the dearness of silver.</small> It is not, however, so much from the low price of corn, as from that of some other parts of the rude produce of land, that the most judicious writers have inferred the great value of silver in those very ancient times. ② Corn, it has been said, being a sort of manufacture, was, in those rude ages, much dearer in proportion than the greater part of other commodities; it is meant, I suppose, than the greater part of unmanufactured commodities; such as cattle, poultry, game of all kinds, &c. That in those times of poverty and barbarism these were proportionably much cheaper than corn, is undoubtedly true. But this cheapness was not the effect of the high value of silver, but of the low value of those commodities. It was not because silver would in such times purchase or represent a greater quantity of labour, but because such commodities would purchase or represent a much smaller quantity than in times of more opulence and improvement. Silver must certainly be cheaper in Spanish America than in Europe; in the country where it is produced, than in the country to which it is brought, at the expence of a long carriage both by land and by sea, of a freight and an insurance. One-and-twenty pence halfpenny sterling, however, we are told by Ulloa, was, not many years ago, at Buenos Ayres, the price of an ox chosen from a herd of three or four hundred. Sixteen shillings sterling, we are told by Mr. Byron, was the price of a good horse in the capital of Chili. In a country naturally fertile,

---

① [This appears to be merely an inference from the fact that he does not take notice of fluctuations.]

② [Narrative of the Hon. John Byron, containing an account of the Great Distresses suffered by himself and his companions on the Coast of Patagonia from 1740 to 1746, 1768, pp. 212, 220.]

明的也就是我一直在力图说明的了。弗利特伍德本人像大多数其他作者一样,似乎都相信银价在此期间①,由于产量的日益增多而不断降低。但他所搜集的谷物价格,却不支持这种观点,而是支持杜普雷·得·圣莫尔的意见,也是我所努力说明的那种观点。弗利特伍德和圣莫尔这两位作者,似乎都一直在勤勉踏实地搜集古代的各种物价。但令人感到惊讶的是,尽管他们两人的意见是那么不相同,而他们两人所搜集的事实,至少关于谷物价格的部分,是完全一致的。

然而,一些很有见地的作者在推断古代银价的昂贵时,不是根据谷物的低廉价格,而是根据其他许多土地产品的低廉价格。据说谷物作为一种制造品,在原始未开化时代,比其他大部分商品贵得多。我想,所谓的大部分商品,是指家禽、牲畜和猎物等的非制造品。在那贫困和野蛮时代,这些物品当然会比谷物便宜得多。但是这个便宜,不是由于银价过高而是由于这些商品本身价值低。不是因为白银在那个时代比富裕时代能购买或者代表更多的劳动量,而是因为这些商品在那个时代能够购买或者可以代表非常少的劳动量。在西班牙,美洲白银必然比在欧洲价格低,也就是说白银在生产国肯定要比进口国便宜,因为要花费长途水陆运输的运费和保险费。但是乌洛阿却告诉我们,不久以前在布宜诺斯艾利斯,仅花费21便士半就可以从400头牛中挑一头。拜伦先生告诉我们,在智利首都,一匹好马的价格仅为16先令②。

有时用牲畜、家禽等的价格来表示白银的价格,但这些物品能廉价只能说明它们自身价值低,而不能说明白银价昂。

---

① 这似乎只是从他并没有关注波动这一事实得出的推断。
② 《尊敬的约翰·拜伦的故事,包含1740~1746年他和他同伴们在南美洲巴塔哥尼亚海岸遭受巨大灾难的叙述》,1768年,第212页、220页。

but of which the far greater part is altogether uncultivated, cattle, poultry, game of all kinds, &c. as they can be acquired with a very small. quantity of labour, so they will purchase or command but a very small quantity. The low money price for which they may be sold, is no proof that the real value of silver is there very high, but that the real value of those commodities is very low.

<small>for labour is the real measure.</small> Labour, it must always be remembered, and not any particular commodity or set of commodities, is the real measure of the value both of silver and of all other commodities.

<small>Cattle, poultry, etc., are produced by very different quantities of labour at different times,</small> But in countries almost waste, or but thinly inhabited, cattle, poultry, game of all kinds, &c. as they are the spontaneous productions of nature, so she frequently produces them in much greater quantities than the consumption of the inhabitants requires. In such a state of things the supply commonly exceeds the demand. In different states of society, in different stages of improvement, therefore, such commodities will represent, or be equivalent to, very different quantities of labour.

<small>whereas corn scarcely varies at all,</small> In every state of society, in every stage of improvement, corn is the production of human industry. But the average produce of every sort of industry is always suited, more or less exactly, to the average consumption; the average supply to the average demand. In every different stage of improvement, besides, the raising of equal quantities of corn in the same soil and climate, will, at an average, require nearly equal quantities of labour; or what comes to the same thing, the price of nearly equal quantities; the continual increase of the productive powers of labour in an improving state of cultivation being more or less counterbalanced by the continually increasing price of cattle, the principal instruments of agriculture. Upon all these accounts, therefore, we may rest assured, that equal quantities of corn will, in every state of society, in every stage of improvement, more nearly represent, or be equivalent to, equal quantities of labour, than equal quantities of any other part of the rude produce of land. Corn, accordingly, it has already been observed, is, in all the different stages of wealth and improvement, a more accurate measure of value than any other commodity or set of commodities. In all those different

<small>and also regulates the money price of labour.</small> stages, therefore, we can judge better of the real value of silver, by comparing it with corn, than by comparing it with any other commodity, or set of commodities.

Corn, besides, or whatever else is the common and favourite

在一个土壤肥沃而大部分土地又没有开发的国家,家禽、牲畜和猎物都可以用很少的劳动量就可以获得,因此它们所能购买或支配的劳动量也很少。这些商品在那里只能以极便宜的货币价格出售,只能证明这些商品在那里的真实价值很低而并不能证明那里白银的真实价值很高。

我们应当牢记,衡量白银或其他一切商品价值的真正尺度,不是任何一种商品或任何一类商品,而是劳动。

劳动是衡量商品价值的真实尺度。

在土地几乎荒芜或人口稀少的国家,人自然所提供的家禽、牲畜和各种猎物,往往大大多于居民所能够消费的。在这种状态下,供给通常是超过需求。所以,在不同的社会状态和不同的改良阶段,这些商品所代表或可以交换的劳动量相差很大。

家禽、牲畜等,在不同时代所需要的劳动量不同。

但是无论在什么社会状态下以及什么样的改良阶段,谷物都是人类劳动的产物。但各种劳动的平均产量,一般说来总是和其平均消费量相适应,就是说,供需总是基本平衡的。而且,无论在什么改良阶段,在相同的土壤和气候条件下,生产同一数量的谷物需要花费的劳动量大体是相等的,或者说,其价值是几乎相等的(两者是一回事)。在耕种得到改良的情况下,劳动生产力的不断增加,或多或少要被牲畜(主要的农业工具)价格的不断增加所抵消。由以上原因可知:一定量的谷物在任何社会状态和任何改良阶段中,比等量的其他土地产品,能更准确地代表或交换等量劳动。所以,在改良的不同阶段中,谷物比其他任何一个或一种商品更适合做价值尺度。因此,在上述不同阶段,我们通过比较白银和谷物来正确判定银的真实价值比把白银同其他任何一个或一种商品相比更合适。

谷物代表的劳动量很少有变动,而且决定劳动的货币价格。

再者,谷物或其他任何普通人民喜爱的植物性食物,在每一

vegetable food of the people, constitutes, in every civilized country, the principal part of the subsistence of the labourer. In consequence of the extension of agriculture, the land of every country produces a much greater quantity of vegetable than of animal food, and the labourer every-where lives chiefly upon the wholesome food that is cheapest and most abundant. Butcher's-meat, except in the most thriving countries, or where labour is most highly rewarded, makes but an insignificant part of his subsistence; poultry makes a still smaller part of it, and game no part of it. In France, and even in Scotland, where labour is somewhat better rewarded than in France, the labouring poor seldom eat butcher's-meat, except upon holidays, and other extraordinary occasions. The money price of labour, therefore, depends much more upon the average money price of corn, the subsistence of the labourer, than upon that of butcher's-meat, or of any other part of the rude produce of land. The real value of gold and silver, therefore, the real quantity of labour which they can purchase or command, depends much more upon the quantity of corn which they can purchase or command, than upon that of butcher's-meat, or any other part of the rude produce of land.

<small>The authors were also misled by the notion that silver falls in value as its quantity increases.</small> Such slight observations, however, upon the prices either of corn or of other commodities, would not probably have misled so many intelligent authors, had they not been influenced, at the same time, by the popular notion, that as the quantity of silver naturally increases in every country with the increase of wealth, so its value diminishes as its quantity increases. This notion, however, seems to be altogether groundless.

<small>Increase of quantity arising from greater abundance of the mines is connected with diminution of value.</small> The quantity of the precious metals may increase in any country from two different causes: either, first, from the increased abundance of the mines which supply it; or, secondly, from the increased wealth of the people, from the increased produce of their annual labour. The first of these causes is no doubt necessarily connected with the diminution of the value of the precious metals; but the second is not.

When more abundant mines are discovered, a greater quantity of the precious metals is brought to market, and the quantity of the necessaries and conveniencies of life for which they must be exchanged being the same as before, equal quantities of the metals must be exchanged for smaller quantities of commodities. So far, therefore, as the increase of the quantity of the precious metals in any country arises from the increased abundance of the mines, it is necessarily connected

个文明国家里都是劳动者的主要生活资料。由于农业的发展,各国土地所生产的植物性食物比动物性食物多得多,各国的劳动者都是以这种最便宜、最丰富且健康卫生的食物为主要生活资料。除了最繁荣的国家,或劳动报酬极高的地方,家畜肉在劳动者生活资料中只占极小的比例,家禽的比例更小,猎物则没有。在法国,甚至在劳动报酬比法国略高的苏格兰,贫穷的劳动者,除了在节日或其他特殊场合,是很少吃肉的。因此,劳动的货币价格,更多地取决于谷物即劳动者主要生活资料的平均货币价格,在很小程度上取决于家畜肉或其他土地产品的平均货币价格。所以,金银的真实价值,或者说金银所能购买或所能支配的真实劳动量,主要取决于金银所能购买的谷物量,只是在很小程度上受金银所能支配的家畜肉量或任何其他土地产品量的影响。

然而,关于谷物和其他商品价格的上述不仔细的观察,如果他们不是同时受到以下流行观念的影响,也许未必会让那么多聪明的作者受到误导,即由于各国的银的数量随着财富的增加而自然增加,而银的价值则随白银的数量的增加而减少。显然这种观念是毫无根据的。

在任何一个国家贵金属数量增加的原因有两个:第一,由于生产贵金属的矿山的产量的增加;第二,由于人民财富即每年劳动产量的增加。第一个原因必然会引起贵金属价值的减少,但第二个原因则不能。

一旦更丰富矿山的被发现,就会有更大数量的贵金属进入市场,而这些贵金属所要交换的生活必需品和便利品,在数量上如果和从前一样,那么同等数量的贵金属就只能交换的比从前更少的商品量。所以,如果任何国家贵金属量的增加是由于矿山丰富

国民财富的性质与原理

with some diminution of their value.

<small>but increase of quantity resulting from the increased wealth of a country is not.</small>
When, on the contrary, the wealth of any country increases, when the annual produce of its labour becomes gradually greater and greater, a greater quantity of coin becomes necessary in order to circulate a greater quantity of commodities: and the people, as they can afford it, as they have more commodities to give for it, will naturally purchase a greater and a greater quantity of plate. The quantity of their coin will increase from necessity; the quantity of their plate from vanity and ostentation, or from the same reason that the quantity of fine statues, pictures, and of every other luxury and curiosity, is likely to increase among them. But as statuaries and painters are not likely to be worse rewarded in times of wealth and prosperity, than in times of poverty and depression, so gold and silver are not likely to be worse paid for.

<small>Gold and silver are dearer in a rich country.</small>
The price of gold and silver, when the accidental discovery of more abundant mines does not keep it down, as it naturally rises with the wealth of every country, so, whatever be the state of the mines, it is at all times naturally higher in a rich than in a poor country. Gold and silver, like all other commodities, naturally seek the market where the best price is given for them, and the best price is commonly given for every thing in the country which can best afford it. Labour, it must be remembered, is the ultimate price which is paid for every thing, and in countries where labour is equally well rewarded, the money price of labour will be in proportion to that of the subsistence of the labourer. But gold and silver will naturally exchange for a greater quantity of subsistence in a rich than in a poor country, in a country which abounds with subsistence, than in one which is but indifferently supplied with it. If the two countries are at a great distance, the difference may be very great; because though the metals naturally fly from the worse to the better market, yet it may be difficult to transport them in such quantities as to bring their price nearly to a level in both. If the countries are near, the difference will be smaller, and may sometimes be scarce perceptible; because in this case the transportation will be easy. China is a much richer country than any part of Europe, and the difference between the price of subsistence in China and in Europe is very great. Rice in China is much cheaper than

程度的增加,那就必然会降低贵金属的价值。

　　相反,当一国财富增加时,或者当该国劳动的年产量逐渐增多时,就需要有更多的通货来使这更多的量商品的流通起来。而人民,只要他们支付得起,而且也拥有更多的商品来交换,自然会购买越来越多的金银器皿。商品流通的需求使得他们的通货量增加,追求虚荣和浮华而增加了他们的金银器皿量,或者由于同样的原因,精致的雕像、绘画及其他各种奢侈品和珍奇品也可能增加。但是,因为雕刻家和画家在富足和繁荣时期所得到的报酬,不可能比贫穷萧条时期低,所以金银也不可能价格更低。

当一国财富增长的时候则贵金属的数量自然会增加但是金银增长情况不然。

　　如果更丰富矿山的偶然发现,并没有使金银价格下落,反而由于金银的价格会随着各国财富的增加而提高,那么,不论矿山是否丰富,金银在富国的价格总是会高于其在穷国的价格。金银像其他一切商品一样,自然的要寻找开出最好价格的市场,通常能对金银出得起最好价格的国家就是对每一种商品都出得起最好价格的国家。必须记住,劳动是对于一切货物所支付的最终价格。如果在一个国家里劳动都能得到同样良好回报,那么劳动的货币价格与劳动者生活资料的货币价格成比例。然而,金银在富国自然比在穷国能交换更多的生活资料,换句话说,金银在生活资料丰富的国家比在生活资料贫乏的国家所换得的生活资料多。这两个国家如果相隔很远,其差异就会很大,因为虽然金银会自然地从差的市场流入好的市场,但很难运送如此大量的金银以使两个国家金银的价格接近同一个水平。如果两个国家离得很近,那么这个差别就可能由于运输方便而较小,有时几乎看不出来。中国比欧洲任何一个国家都富足得多,中国和欧洲生活资料的价格悬殊大。中国大米的价格比欧洲各地的小麦价格都要便宜。

金银在更富的国家贵一些,

^{as may be shown by comparing China with Europe and Scotland with England as to the price of subsistence} wheat is any-where in Europe. England is a much richer country than Scotland; but the difference between the money-price of corn in those two countries is much smaller, and is but just perceptible. In proportion to the quantity or measure, Scotch corn generally appears to be a good deal cheaper than English; but in proportion to its quality, it is certainly somewhat dearer. Scotland receives almost every year very large supplies from England, and every commodity must commonly be somewhat dearer in the country to which it is brought than in that from which it comes. English corn, therefore, must be dearer in Scotland than in England, and yet in proportion to its quality, or to the quantity and goodness of the flour or meal which can be made from it, it cannot commonly be sold higher there than the Scotch corn which comes to market in competition with it.

The difference between the money price of labour in China and in Europe, is still greater than that between the money price of subsistence; because the real recompence of labour is higher in Europe than in China, the greater part of Europe being in an improving state, while China seems to be standing still. The money price of labour is lower in Scotland than in England, because the real recompence of labour is much lower; Scotland, though advancing to greater wealth, advancing much more slowly than England. The frequency of emigration from Scotland, and the rarity of it from England, sufficiently prove that the demand for labour is very different in the two countries.

2 The proportion between the real recompence of labour in different ^{Gold and silver are cheapest among the poorest nations.} countries, it must be remembered, is naturally regulated, not by their actual wealth or poverty, but by their advancing, stationary, or declining condition.

^{The fact that corn is dearer in towns is due to its dearness there, not to the cheapness of silver,} Gold and silver, as they are naturally of the greatest value among the richest, so they are naturally of the least value among the poorest nations. Among savages, the poorest of all nations, they are of scarce any value.

In great towns corn is always dearer than in remote parts of the country. This, however, is the effect, not of the real cheapness of silver, but of the real dearness of corn. It does not cost less labour to bring silver to the great town than to the remote parts of the country; hut it costs a great deal more to bring corn.

英格兰也比苏格兰富足得多,但这两个国家谷物的货币价格的差异则很小,只不过刚好能看得出来。就数量来说,苏格兰产的谷物的价格比英格兰产的便宜得多,然而就质量来说,其价格却比英格兰产的要略贵些。苏格兰几乎每年都从英格兰进口大量谷物。不论什么物品,进口国的价格一般总是比出口国高些。因此,英格兰的谷物在苏格兰销售的价格自然比在英格兰高。可是,就品质而言即谷物所能制成的面粉或饭食的数量及品质而言说,英格兰谷物一般不能比与它竞争的苏格兰谷物在市场上卖得更贵。

中国与欧洲在生活资料的货币价格上有很大的差异,而在劳动的货币价格上则有更大的差异。这是因为欧洲大部分地区都处在改良的状态,而中国似乎停滞不前,所以在欧洲,劳动的真实报酬高于中国。苏格兰劳动的货币价格要低于英格兰劳动的货币价格,因为苏格兰虽然也在变得越来越富裕,但是比英格兰慢得多,所以其劳动的真实报酬也低得多。苏格兰人民频繁地迁移到国外,而英格兰人民却很少迁移,这足以证明两国的劳动需求的差别之大。必须记住,不同国家劳动的真实报酬,不是由各国实际的贫富程度决定,而是由各国所处的进步、停滞或退步等状态决定。

金银在最富裕的地区自然会有最大的价值,而在最贫穷的国家只有最小价值。在最穷的野蛮民族当中,金银是根本没有价值的。

在大城市,谷物总是在比偏远地区昂贵。但这并不是白银实际价格便宜的结果,而是谷物实际昂贵的结果。把银运往大城市并不比运往偏远地方所耗费的劳动量少,而把谷物运往大城市却要花费多得多的劳动。

<small>and this is true also in Holland, Genoa, etc.</small>   In some very rich and commercial countries, such as Holland and the territory of Genoa, corn is dear for the same reason that it is dear in great towns. They do not produce enough to maintain their inhabitants. They are rich in the industry and skill of their artificers and manufacturers; in every sort of machinery which can facilitate and abridge labour; in shipping, and in all the other instruments and means of carriage and commerce: but they are poor in corn, which, as it must be brought to them from distant countries, must, by an addition to its price, pay for the carriage from those countries. It does not cost less labour to bring silver to Amsterdam than to Dantzick; but it costs a great deal more to bring corn. The real cost of silver must be nearly the same in both places; but that of corn must be very different. Diminish the real opulence either of Holland or of the territory of Genoa, while the number of their inhabitants remains the same: diminish their power of supplying themselves from distant countries; and the price of corn, instead of sinking with that diminution in the quantity of their silver, which must necessarily accompany this declension either as its cause or as its effect, will rise to the price of a famine. When we are in want of necessaries we must part with all superfluities, of which the value, as it rises in times of opulence and prosperity, so it sinks in times of poverty and distress. It is otherwise with necessaries. Their real price, the quantity of labour which they can purchase or command, rises in times of poverty and distress, and sinks in times of opulence and prosperity, which are always times of great abundance; for they could not otherwise be times of opulence and prosperity. Corn

在某些很富有的商业国,如荷兰及热那亚[1]地区,谷物昂贵的原因与同其在大城市昂贵的原因是一样的。这些国家自己不能生产足够的谷物来维持当地居民的生活。他们之所以富有,是源自于技工和制造者的勤勉与技术、各种方便省力的机器,源自于船舶运输,也源自于其他一切运输工具和他们的商业。然而,由于他们自己生产的谷物很少,所需要的谷物必须从遥远的国家运来,所以除谷物价格以外,还必须支付从这些国家运来的费用。把白银运到阿姆斯特丹并不比运到丹泽克所需要的劳动量少,但把谷物运到阿姆斯特丹需要的劳动量则多得多。在这两个地区,白银的真实成本肯定是几乎相等的,但这两地谷物的真实成本却差别很大。如果减少荷兰或热那亚地区的真实富裕程度,而保持他们的居民人数不变,再降低他们从遥远国家进口谷物满足自己需求的能力,那么不论是作为衰退的原因还是衰退的结果,这种衰退必然会伴随着白银数量的减少。但谷物的价格不但不会随着白银数量减少而下降,反而还会提高,达到饥荒时期的价格。当我们的生活必需品缺乏时,我们必将会舍弃所有的非必需品。非必需品的价值,在富足和繁荣的时期会上升,而在贫穷萧条的时期则会下降。必需品的情况则正好相反,他们的真实价格,即他们所能购买或支配的劳动量,在贫穷和萧条的时期会上升,而在富足繁荣的时期下降。富足繁荣时期也总是谷物非常充足的时期,否则就不能被称作是富足繁荣时期。在这样的时期谷物是

> 在荷兰和热那亚等地区也是这样的。

---

〔1〕 热那亚(Genoa),意大利西北的一座城市,濒临利古里亚海的一个港湾热那亚湾。作为一个古老的聚居地,热那亚在罗马人统治下繁盛起来,并在十字军东征期间聚敛了大量财富。今天,它是意大利的主要港口和重要的商业、工业中心。

is a necessary, silver is only a superfluity.

<small>So no increase of silver due to the increase of wealth could have reduced its value.</small> Whatever, therefore, may have been the increase in the quantity of the precious metals, which, during the period between the middle of the fourteenth and that of the sixteenth century, arose from the increase of wealth and improvement, it could have no tendency to diminish their value either in Great Britain, or in any other part of Europe. If those who have collected the prices of things in ancient times, therefore, had, during this period, no reason to infer the diminution of the value of silver, from any observations which they had made upon the prices either of corn or of other commodities, they had still less reason to infer it from any supposed increase of wealth and improvement.

SECOND PERIOD

<small>No doubt exists as to the second period,</small> But how various soever may have been the opinions of the learned concerning the progress of the value of silver during this first period, they are unanimous concerning it during the second.

<small>silver sank, and a quartet of corn came to be worth 6 oz. or 8 oz. of silver.</small> From about 1570 to about 1640, during a period of about seventy years, the variation in the proportion between the value of silver and that of corn, held a quite opposite course. Silver sunk in its real value, or would exchange for a smaller quantity of labour than before; and corn rose in its nominal price, and instead of being commonly sold for about two ounces of silver the quarter, or about ten shillings of our present money, came to be sold for six and eight ounces of silver the quarter, or about thirty and forty shillings of our present money.

<small>This was owing to the discovery of the abundant American mines.</small> The discovery of the abundant mines of America, seems to have been the sole cause of this diminution in the value of silver in proportion to that of corn. It is accounted for accordingly in the same manner by every body; and there never has been any dispute either about the fact, or about the cause of it. The greater part of Europe was, during this period, advancing in industry and improvement, and the demand for silver must consequently have been increasing. But the increase of the supply had, it seems, so far exceeded that of the demand, that the value of that metal sunk considerably. The discovery of the mines of America, it is to be observed, does not seem to have

必需品,而白银只是不必要的东西。

因此,在14世纪中期到16世纪中期的这一时期,贵金属数量的增长是来自于财富的增加和改良,但不管贵金属数量的增长达到何种程度,贵金属的价值在不列颠或欧洲其他任何国家,都不可能出现降低的趋势。所以,如果搜集古代物价的人们没有理由根据对谷物或其他物品价格的观察,来推断在此期间里白银的价值降低,他们也就更没有理由根据假定的财富的增长和改良来推断白银价格的下降了。

> 由财富增加带来的白银增加所不会降低银的价值。

第二期

不管学者们对于第一期白银价值的变动持有多么不同的意见,他们对于第二期白银价值的变动意见却完全一致。

从1570年左右到1640年左右,在这大约70年的时期里,白银和谷物价值之比的变动方向是完全相反的。白银的真实价值下降了,或者说它所能交换的劳动量少于从前;谷物的名义价格上升了,其售价由从前的每夸特大约2盎司白银,约等于现在的10先令,降低到每夸特6盎司或8盎司白银,约等于现在的货币30先令或40先令。

> 关于第二期不存在疑问,银的价值下降,每夸特谷物价值大约由白银2盎司到6到8盎司。

美洲发现丰富的矿山,似乎是这一时期白银价值相对于谷物价值降低的唯一原因。每一个人都这样解释,关于白银的比价下降这一事实以及造成这种下降的原因,从来没有发生过任何争论。在这一时期,欧洲的大部分地区实现了产业进步和土地改良,因而对白银的需求必然会大大增加。但是,供给的增加,似乎远远超过了需求的增加,所以银价因此而降低。但是应当注意,

> 这是由于美洲矿山丰富的发现。

had any very sensible effect upon the prices of things in England till after 1570; though even the mines of Potosi had been discovered more than twenty years before. ①

<small>Wheat rose at Windsor market.</small> From 1595 to 1620, both inclusive, the average price of the quarter of nine bushels of the best wheat at Windsor market, appears from the accounts of Eton College, to have been 2*l*. 1*s*. 6*d*. $\frac{9}{13}$. From which sum, neglecting the fraction, and deducting a ninth, or 4*s*. 7*d*. $\frac{1}{3}$, the price of the quarter of eight bushels comes out to have been 1*l*. 16*s*. 10*d*. $\frac{2}{3}$. And from this sum, neglecting likewise the fraction, and deducting a ninth, or 4*s*. 1*d*. $\frac{1}{6}$, for the difference between the price of the best wheat and that of the middle wheat, ② the price of the middle wheat comes out to have been about 1*l*. 12*s*. 8*d*. $\frac{3}{9}$, or about six ounces and one-third of an ounce of silver.

From 1621 to 1636, both inclusive, the average price of the same measure of the best wheat at the same market, appears, from the same accounts, to have been 2*l*. 10*s*. ; from which making the like deductions as in the foregoing case, the average price of the quarter of eight bushels of middle wheat comes out to have been 1*l*. 19*s*. 6*d*. or about seven ounces and two-thirds of an ounce of silver.

THIRD PERIOD

<small>The effect of the discovery of the American mines was complete about 1636.</small> BETWEEN 1630 and 1640, or about 1636, the effect of the

① [In 1545. Ed. I.]

② [The deduction of this ninth is recommended by Charles Smith, *Three Tracts on the Corn Trade and Corn Laws*, 2nd ed. , 1766, p. 104, because, ' it hath been found that the value of all the wheat fit for bread, if mixed together, would be eight-ninths of the value of the best wheat. ']

美洲银矿的发现,似乎没有明显的影响英格兰的物价,直到1570年以后为止。尽管波托西银矿在二十多年前就被发现了①,也没有影响英格兰的物价。

从1595年到1620年包括1595年和1620这两年,根据伊顿公学的记载,温莎市场上上等小麦每夸特或9蒲式耳的平均价格为2镑1先令6$\frac{9}{13}$便士,根据这金额,不计算零头,再减去1/9,即减去4先令7$\frac{1}{3}$便士,得到每夸特或8蒲式耳的价格为1镑16先令10$\frac{2}{3}$便士。根据这个金额再减去零头,再减去1/9,或4先令1$\frac{1}{9}$便士,即上等小麦与中等小麦这二者价格的差额,得到中等小麦的价格②,大约是1镑12先令8$\frac{3}{9}$便士,约合白银6$\frac{1}{3}$盎司。〔在温莎市场上小麦的价格上涨。〕

从1621年到1636年(同样包含这两个年头),根据同一记载,在同一市场上该数量上等小麦的平均价格,约为2镑10先令。根据这个金额按上述计算方法,得到中等小麦的平均价格为每夸特或8蒲式耳1镑19先令6便士,约合白银7$\frac{1}{3}$盎司。

第三期

在1630年到1640年之间,或大约在1636年,美洲矿山发现〔银矿发现影响大,在1636年终止了。美洲银矿的影响,约〕

---

① 1545年被发现的。
② 查理·史密斯提出要减掉这1/9,参见《关于谷物贸易和谷物法的三个论文》,第二版,1766年,第104页,"人们发现所有适合做面包的小麦的价值如果合在一起的话,将是最好小麦的九分之八"。

discovery of the mines of America in reducing the value of silver, appears to have been completed, and the value of that metal seems never to have sunk lower in proportion to that of corn than it was about that time. It seems to have risen somewhat in the course of the present century, and it had probably begun to do so even some time before the end of the last.

<small>From 1637 to 1700 there was a very slight rise of wheat at Windsor,</small>　From 1637 to 1700, both inclusive, being the sixty-four last years of the last century, the average price of the quarter of nine bushels of the best wheat at Windsor market, appears, from the same accounts, to have been 2*l*. 11*s*. 0*d*. $\frac{1}{3}$; which is only 1*s*. 0*d*. $\frac{1}{3}$ dearer than it had been during the sixteen years before. But in the course of these sixty-four years there happened two events which must have produced a much greater scarcity of corn than what the course of the seasons would otherwise have occasioned, and which, therefore, without supposing any further reduction in the value of silver, will much more than account for this very small enhancement of price.

<small>due to the civil war,</small>　The first of these events was the civil war, which, by discouraging tillage and interrupting commerce, must have raised the price of corn much above what the course of the seasons would otherwise have occasioned. It must have had this effect more or less at all the different markets in the kingdom, but particularly at those in the neighbourhood of London, which require to be supplied from the greatest distance. In 1648, accordingly, the price of the best wheat at Windsor market, appears, from the same accounts, to have been 4*l*. 5*s*. and in 1649 to have been 4*l*. the quarter of nine bushels. The excess of those two years above 2*l*. 10*s*. (the average price of the sixteen years preceding 1637) is 3*l*. 5*s*. ; which divided among the sixty-four last years of the last century, will alone very nearly account for that small enhancement of price which seems to have taken place in them. These, however, though the highest, are by no means the only high prices which seem to have been occasioned by the civil wars.

<small>the bounty on the exportation of corn,</small>　The second event was the bounty upon the exportation of corn, granted in 1688. ①The bounty, it has been thought by many people,

---

① [By 1 W. & M. , c. 12.]

对银价降低的影响,就已经终止了。白银价值相对于谷物价值的降低似乎从来没有低到这种程度。在本世纪,白银的价值似乎有所上升,或许在上世纪终了之前上升趋势就已经开始了。

从 1637 年到 1700 年(含这两个年头)的时期里,即上个世纪的最后 64 年,根据同一记载,温莎市场上上等小麦的平均价格为每 9 蒲式耳一夸特大约 2 镑 11 先令 $\frac{1}{3}$ 便士。这平均价格,比 16 年前的平均价格贵 1 先令 $\frac{1}{3}$ 便十。但在这 64 年中,发生了两个事件,造成了当时谷物的稀缺远远超过收成情况所能造成的程度。即使不对白银价值的进一步下跌做出假定,仅这两个事件就足以说明谷物价格的少量上升。_{1637—1700 年小麦在温莎有少量的上升,}

第一个事件是内乱。它阻碍了耕种,扰乱了商业。使得谷物价格的上涨大大超过了由于收成状况所造成的程度。它不同程度的影响到了不列颠的所有市场,尤其是伦敦附近的市场,因为他们所需要的谷物必须从偏远的地方输入。因此,根据同样的记载,在温莎市场上,最好小麦的价格在 1648 年为 9 蒲式耳一夸特约值 4 镑 5 先令,第二年为 4 镑。这两年谷物的价格,比 2 镑 10 先令(1637 年以前 16 年的平均价格)高出 3 镑 5 先令。如果把这个金额在上个世纪的最后 64 年中分摊,就足够说明为什么谷价在这些年中会略有上升。这两年的价格,虽然属于最高价格,但却似乎并非内乱引起的、唯一的最高价格。_{由于内战,}

第二件事是 1688 年颁发的谷物出口补贴制度①。在多数人_{谷物出口奖励,}

---

① 威廉一世和玛利第 12 号法令。

by encouraging tillage, may, in a long course of years, have occasioned a. greater abundance, and consequently a greater cheapness of corn in the home-market, than what would otherwise have taken place there. How far the bounty could produce this effect at any time, I shall examine hereafter; I shall only observe at present, that between 1688 and 1700, it had not time to produce any such effect. During this short period its only effect must have been, by encouraging the exportation of the surplus produce of every year, and thereby hindering the abundance of one year from compensating the scarcity of another, to raise the price in the home-market. The scarcity which prevailed in England from 1693 to 1699, both inclusive, though no doubt principally owing to the badness of the seasons, and, therefore, extending through a considerable part of Europe, must have been somewhat enhanced by the bounty. In 1699, accordingly, the further exportation of corn was prohibited for nine months. ①

<small>and the clipping and wearing of the coin.</small> There was a third event which occurred in the course of the same period, and which, though it could not occasion any scarcity of corn, nor, perhaps, any augmentation in the real quantity of silver which was usually paid for it, must necessarily have occasioned some augmentation in the nominal sum. This event was the great debasement of the silver coin, by clipping and wearing. This evil had begun in the reign of Charles Ⅱ. and had gone on continually increasing till 1695; at which time, as we may learn from Mr. Lowndes, the current silver coin was, at an average, near five-and-twenty per cent. below its standard value. ②But the nominal sum which constitutes the market-price of every commodity is necessarily regulated, not so much by the quantity of silver, which, according to the standard, ought to be contained in it, as by that which, it is found by experience, actually is contained in it. This nominal sum, therefore, is necessarily higher when the coin is much debased by clipping and wearing, than when near to its standard value.

In the course of the present century, the silver coin has not at any time been more below its standard weight than it is at present.

---

① [The Act 10 Will. Ⅲ. , c. 3,] prohibits exportation for one year from loth February, 1699.

② [Lowndes says on p. 107 of his *Report Containing an Essay for the Amendment of the Silver Coins*, 1695, But in the text above, the popular estimate, as indicated by the price of silver bullion, is accepted, as in the next paragraph.]

看来,这种补贴可以鼓励耕种,在长时期内增加谷物的产量,使其超出往年的产量从而降低国内市场上的谷物价格。补贴究竟能在多大程度上,使得谷物增加产量降低价格,我将留待以后考察,现在所要说的,只是 1688 年到 1700 年间,它还没有产生任何这样的结果。在这个短期中,补贴的唯一效果是,由于每年鼓励剩余产品的出口,使得丰收年份的收获不够弥补匮乏年份谷物的短缺,反而抬高了国内市场上的谷价。从 1693 年到 1699 年间,英格兰普遍存在的谷物短缺虽然主要是由于当时的自然条件恶劣,因而扩展到欧洲的大部分地区,但是补贴的发放确实加剧了谷物的短缺。所以,在 1699 年有九个月的时间禁止谷物出口①。_{谷物出口奖励,}

在同一时期还有第三件事发生,这件事虽不会造成谷物短缺,也不会使对谷物实际支付所需要的白银增多,但却引起了谷物名义价格较大增长。这个事件就是银币受到的切削和磨损,大大降低了银币的价值。这种恶劣行为从查理二世时期就开始出现,一直到 1695 年不断地加剧。我们从朗兹那里得知:当时通用银币的价值比它的标准价值平均降低了接近 25%②。但是,构成所有商品市场价格的名义金额,必定不是由标准银币所应含有的银量决定,而是由银币根据经验判断所实际包含的银量决定的。因此,当银币受到的切削和磨损时,这个名义金额必然比其在接近标准价值时要高一些。_{银币受到的切削和磨损,}

在本世纪,银币从来没有像现在这样严重的低于其标准重

---

① 威廉三世十年,第 3 号法令,该法令从 1699 年 2 月 10 日开始禁止谷物出口一年。

② 《含有一篇关于银币改造的论文的报告》,朗兹,1695 年,第 107 页。在前面文章中关于银币价格的估计被接受了,在后面的段落也是如此。

<small>which was then much greater than in the present century.</small> But though very much defaced, its value has been kept up by that of the gold coin for which it is exchanged. For though before the late recoinage, the gold coin was a good deal defaced too, it was less so than the silver. In 1695, on the contrary, the value of the silver coin was not kept up by the gold coin; a guinea then commonly exchanging for thirty shillings of the worn and clipt silver. ①Before the late recoinage of the gold, the price of silver bullion was seldom higher than five shillings and seven pence an ounce, which is but five-pence above <small>Moreover the bounty has been long enough in existence to produce any possible effect in lowering the price of corn.</small> the mint price. But in 1695, the common price of silver bullion was six shillings and five-pence an ounce,②which is fifteen-pence above the mint price. Even before the late re-coinage of the gold, therefore, the coin, gold and silver together, when compared with silver. bullion, was not supposed to be more than eight per cent. below its standard value. In 1695, on the contrary, it had been supposed to be near five-and-twenty per cent. below that value. But in the beginning of the present century, that is, immediately after the great re-coinage in King William's time, the greater part of the current silver coin.

must have been still nearer to its standard weight than it is at present. In the course of the present century too there has been no great public calamity, such as the civil war, which could either discourage tillage, or interrupt the interior commerce of the country. And though the bounty which has taken place through the greater part of this century, must always raise the price of corn somewhat higher than it otherwise would be in the actual state of tillage;③ yet as, in the course of this century, the bounty has had full time to produce all the good effects commonly imputed to it, to encourage tillage, and thereby to increase the quantity of corn in the home market, it may, upon the principles of a system which I shall explain and examine hereafter, be supposed to have done something to lower the price of that commodity the one way, as well as to raise it the other. It is by many people supposed to have done more. In the sixty-four first years of the present century accordingly, the average price of the quarter of nine bushels of the

---

① [Lowndes, Essay, p. 88.]

② Lowndes's Essay on the Silver Coin, p. 68.

③ [The meaning is 'given a certain area and intensity of cultivation, the bounty will raise the price of corn'.]

量。但是尽管银币受到很大的磨损,其价值却由于能够兑换金币而得到了维持。因为虽然最近金币在重新铸造以前,也受到了不少磨损,然而终究没有银币磨损得那么厉害。相反的,在 1695 年,银币的价值没有因兑换金币而维持;当时,金币 1 几尼通常可换 30 先令被切削和磨损的银币①。在最近的金币改铸以前,银块的价格每盎司很少能超过 5 先令 7 便士,只比造币厂的价格高 5 便士。但 1695 年,银块的通常价格,是每盎司 6 先令 5 便士,比造币厂的价格高出了 15 便士②。所以,就是在最近金币改铸以前,金银铸币和银块比较,也假定其低于标准价值不会超过 8%。反之,在 1695 年,却假定其低于标准价值接近 25%。但是,在本世纪初,即在威廉国王进行大规模重铸之后,大部分通用的银币一定比今天的银币更接近其标准重量。本世纪中,也没有发生类似内乱那样阻碍耕种扰乱商业的天灾人祸。虽然本世纪一直采用的谷物出口补贴制度,必然会使谷物的价格高于在当时实际耕种情况条件下所维持的价格,③但因为这种补贴在本世纪已经有充分时间来产生它本来所应产生的所有好结果,即鼓励耕种从而增加国内市场上的谷物供给。所以,在我后面将要解释和考察的某一体系的原理基础上,可以假定,它已经产生了某些影响,即一方面可能提高商品的价格,同时在另一方面也与可能降低商品价格。许多人还假定它在降低物价方面起了更大的作用。所以根据伊顿公学的记载,在本世纪最初的 64 年间,温莎市场上上等小

---

① 朗兹:《论银币(增补版)》,第 88 页。
② 朗兹:《论银币》,第 68 页。
③ 这句话的意思是"如果给予一定面积的土地和施以一定强度的耕种,那么津贴就会提高谷物的价格"。

best wheat at Windsor market, appears, by the accounts of Eton College, to have been 2*l*. 0*s*. 6*d*. $\frac{19}{32}$,⁸ which is about ten shillings and sixpence, or more than five-and-twenty per cent. cheaper than it had been during the sixty-four last years of the last century; and about nine shillings and sixpence cheaper than it had been during the sixteen years preceding 1636, when the discovery of the abundant mines of America may be supposed to have produced its full effect; and about one shilling cheaper than it had been in the twenty-six years preceding 1620, before that discovery can well be supposed to have produced its full effect. According to this account, the average price of middle wheat, during these sixty-four first years of the present century, comes out to have been about thirty-two shillings the quarter of eight bushels.

<small>Silver has risen somewhat since the beginning of the century, and the rise began before; as is shown by Mr. King's calculations.</small>

The value of silver, therefore, seems to have risen somewhat in proportion to that of corn during the course of the present century, and it had probably begun to do so even some time before the end of the last.

In 1687, the price of the quarter of nine bushels of the best wheat at Windsor market was 1*l*. 5*s*. 2*d*. the lowest price at which it had ever been from 1595.

In 1688, Mr. Gregory King, a man famous for his knowledge in matters of this kind, estimated the average price of wheat in years of moderate plenty to be to the grower 3*s*. 6*d*. the bushel, or eight-and-twenty shillings the quarter. ①The grower's price I understand to be the same with what is sometimes called the contract price, or the price at which a farmer contracts for a certain number of years to deliver a certain quantity of corn to a dealer. As a contract of this kind saves the farmer the expence and trouble of marketing, the contract price is generally lower than what is supposed to be the average market price. Mr. King had judged eight-and-twenty shillings the quarter to be at that time the ordinary contract price in years of moderate plenty. Before the scarcity occasioned by the late extraordinary course of bad seasons, it was, I have been assured, the ordinary contract price in all common years.

---

① [*Natural and Political Observations and Conclusions upon the State and Condition of England*, by Gregory King,]

麦的平均价格为九蒲式耳一夸特约 2 磅 6 $\frac{19}{32}$ 便士。这个价格比上世纪最后 64 年间的平均价格,低大约 10 先令 8 便士,超过 25%;比 1636 年以前的 16 年间的平均价格,低大约 9 先令 6 便士,那时候美洲丰富矿山早已发现并充分发挥了影响;比 1620 年以前 26 年间的平均价格,低大约 1 先令,那时候美洲矿山已发现但是尚未充分发挥作用。根据以上记载,在本世纪初的 64 年中,中等小麦的平均价格是八蒲式耳一夸特约为 32 先令。

由此可知,在本世纪中,相对于谷物价格,白银的价格似乎稍有上升,但或许在上世纪末以前的时候就已开始有上升趋势了。

1687 年在温莎市场上,上等小麦的价格是九蒲式耳一夸特约为 1 磅 5 先令 2 便士。这个价格是 1595 年以来的最低价格。

1688 年,格雷戈里·金,一位因在这些事情方面知识丰富而闻名的学者,估计道,对于生产者来说小麦的平均价格,在丰收的年份为每蒲式耳 3 先令 6 便士,即每夸特 28 先令①。我理解,所谓的生产者价格有时被称作合同价格,就是农场主与商人签订合同,承诺在一定年限内供给商人一定数量谷物时所约定的价格。因为这种合同,使农场主节约了在市场上讨价还价的费用和麻烦,所以合同价格通常低于一般认为的平均市场价格。金先生认为,当时丰收年份的普通合同价格为每夸特 28 先令。据我所知,这个价格,在最近异常的恶劣天气造成的谷物缺乏以前,的确是所有一般年份的普通合同价格。

在本世纪初银价略有上升,但这上升似乎更早时候就已开始,如戈里·金先生的计算所说明的那样,

---

① 格雷戈里·金:《关于英格兰的现状的自然的和政治的观察与结论》。

In 1688 was granted the parliamentary bounty upon the exportation of corn. The country gentlemen, who then composed a still greater proportion of the legislature than they do at present, had felt that the money price of corn was falling. The bounty was an expedient to raise it artificially to the high price at which it had frequently been sold in the times of Charles I. and II. It was to take place, therefore, till wheat was so high as forty-eight shillings the quarter; that is twenty shillings, or $\frac{5}{7}$ths dearer than Mr. King had in that very year estimated the grower's price to be in times of moderate plenty. If his calculations deserve any part of the reputation which they have obtained very universally, eight-and-forty shillings the quarter was a price which, without some such expedient as the bounty, could not at that time be expected, except in years of extraordinary scarcity. But the government of King William was not then fully settled. It was in no condition to refuse any thing to the country gentlemen, from whom it was at that very time soliciting the first establishment of the annual land-tax.

The value of silver, therefore, in proportion to that of corn, had probably risen somewhat before the end of the last century; and it seems to have continued to do so during the course of the greater part of the present; though the necessary operation of the bounty must have hindered that rise from being so sensible as it otherwise would have been in the actual state of tillage.

Apart from its effect in extending tillage, the bounty raises the price of corn, both in times of plenty and of scarcity.

In plentiful years the bounty, by occasioning an extraordinary exportation, necessarily raises the price of corn above what it otherwise would be in those years. To encourage tillage, by keeping up the price of corn even in the most plentiful years, was the avowed end of the institution.

In years of great scarcity, indeed, the bounty has generally been suspended. It must, however, have had some effect even upon the prices of many of those years. By the extraordinary exportation which it occasions in years of plenty, it must frequently hinder the plenty of one year from compensating the scarcity of another.

Both in years of plenty and in years of scarcity, therefore, the bounty raises the price of corn above what it naturally would be in the actual state of tillage. If, during the sixty-four first years of the present century, therefore, the average price has been lower than during

第一篇 第十一章

1688年,颁发了议会津贴来鼓励谷物的出口。当时乡绅在立法机关所占的席位比现在多。他们觉得谷物的货币价格在不断下降。津贴人为地将谷物价格抬高到查理一世以及查理二世时代的水平,但也只是权宜之计,所以,在谷价涨到每夸特48先令以前要继续执行。这个价格比格雷戈里.金先生在同年推算的一般年份的生产者价格大约高出20先令,即5/7。假使金先生的计算,的确与他当时所博得的普遍赞誉名实相符,那么除了特别歉收的年份,每夸特48先令的价格,如果不借助于津贴等人为的手段是绝不可能实现的。不过,当时威廉国王政府还没有完全巩固,在制定年度土地税法方面对乡绅有所求,因而无法拒绝乡绅的任何要求。

由此可见,白银价格相对于谷物价格的上升,在上世纪末以前就已经开始了。到了本世纪大部分时间里,上升趋势仍在继续,只是由于津贴的必然作用,上升不能根据实际耕种的情况出现显著的效果。

在丰收的年份,由于津贴极大的促进谷物出口,必然会使谷物的价格大大高于其在这些年份本来应有的水平。但是津贴制度公开的目的,本来就是在最丰收的年份也要设法维持谷物的高价以鼓励耕种。

除了扩大耕种以外,津贴在丰收的年份和歉收的年份都提高了谷价。

的确,在谷物歉收严重的年份,津贴一般会暂停发放。但是,即使在这许多歉收的年份里,这津贴一定也对谷物的价格产生了某些影响。因为在丰收的年份谷物由于受到津贴的鼓励而大量出口,必然会阻碍了以丰收年份的产量来弥补歉收年份的不足。

因此,不论是在丰收年份还是歉收年份,津贴都会使谷价升高,超过其在实际耕种条件下所应有的价格。因此,如果本世纪初64年中谷物的平均价格低于上世纪末64年中的谷物平均价格,那么要是

the sixty-four last years of the last century, it must, in the same state of tillage, have been much more so, had it not been for this operation of the bounty.

<small>It is said to have extended tillage (and so to have reduced the price), but the rise of silver has not been peculiar to England.</small>   But without the bounty, it may be said, the state of tillage would not have been the same. What may have been the effects of this institution upon the agriculture of the country, I shall endeavour to explain hereafter, when I come to treat particularly of bounties. I shall only observe at present, that this rise in the value of silver, in proportion to that of corn, has not been peculiar to England. It has been observed to have taken place in France during the same period, and nearly in the same proportion too, by three very faithful, diligent, and laborious collectors of the prices of corn, Mr. Duprède St. Maur, Mr. Messance, and the author of the Essay on the police of grain. But in France, till 1764, the exportation of grain was by law prohibited; and it is somewhat difficult to suppose, that nearly the same diminution of price which took place in one country, notwithstanding this prohibition, should in another be owing to the extraordinary encouragement given to exportation.

<small>The alteration should be regarded as a rise of silver rather than a fall of corn.</small>   It would be more proper, perhaps, to consider this variation in the average money price of corn as the effect rather of some gradual rise in the real value of silver in the European market, than of any fall in the real average value of corn. Corn, it has already been observed, is at distant periods of time a more accurate measure of value than either silver, or perhaps any other commodity. When, after the discovery of the abundant mines of America, corn rose to three and four times its former money price, this change was universally ascribed, not to any rise in the real value of corn, but to a fall in the real value of silver. If during the sixty-four first years of the present century, therefore, the average money price of corn has fallen somewhat below what it had been during the greater part of the last century, we should in the same manner impute this change, not to any fall in the real value of corn, but to some rise in the real value of silver in the European market.

<small>The recent high price of corn is merely the effect of unfavourable seasons.</small>   The high price of corn during these ten or twelve years past, indeed, has occasioned a suspicion that the real value of silver still continues to fall in the European market. This high price of corn, however, seems evidently to have been the effect of the extraordinary unfavourableness of the seasons, and ought therefore to be regarded, not as a permanent, but as a transitory and occasional event. The seasons for these ten or twelve years past have been unfavourable through the greater part of Europe; and the disorders of Poland have very much increased the scarcity in all those countries, which, in dear years, used to be supplied from that market. So long a course of

没有津贴制度的存在,在同样的耕种状态下,谷物价格一定会更低。

但是有人可能会说,如果没有津贴,耕种状态或许就会不一样。津贴制度对一个国家的农业究竟有什么样的影响,我将在后面专门讨论津贴的时候做出说明。在这里,我只想说明白银价格相对于谷物价格的上涨,并不是英格兰特有的现象。杜普雷·德·圣莫尔先生、麦桑斯先生和另外一位有关谷物政策论文的作者,这三位是忠实、勤奋而辛苦的谷物价格搜集者,他们曾经观察到在同一时期的法国也发生过几乎同一比例的银价上涨。但法国在1764年以前,曾经是禁止谷物出口的。我们很难想象,在一个禁止谷物出口的国家出现的类似的价格下降现象,在另一个国家却是由于奖励谷物出口造成的。

把谷物平均货币价格上的这种变动,当作是欧洲市场上白银的真实价值逐渐上涨的结果,而不是谷物真实价值下降的结果,或许会更合适。前面已经讲过,谷物在相当长时期内是比白银或任何其他商品更正确的价值尺度。美洲那些丰富的矿山被发现后,谷物的货币价格比从前上涨了三倍乃至四倍。当时这种变动的原因,一般人都认为是白银的真实价格下降而不是谷物真实价值的提高。所以,如果本世纪最初64年间的谷物平均价格低于上世纪大部分年度的谷物平均价格,我们同样应该认为,这变动的原因是银的真实价值上升而不是谷物真实价值的下降。

在过去10年甚至12年间谷物价格的高昂,引起了一种怀疑,即欧洲市场上白银的真实价值是否还会继续下降。但这种高昂的谷价,似乎明显是异常恶劣的气候造成的,是偶然而并非持久的原因。在最近10年甚至12年间,欧洲大部分地区都遭受了恶劣的气候。而波兰发生的动乱,又大大加剧了那些在谷物昂贵年

bad seasons, though not a very common event, is by no means a singular one; and whoever has enquired much into the history of the prices of corn in former times, will be at no loss to recollect several other examples of the same kind. Ten years of extraordinary scarcity, besides, are not more wonderful than ten years of extraordinary plenty. The low price of corn from 1741 to 1750, both inclusive, may very well be set in opposition to its high price during these last eight or ten years. From 1741 to 1750, the average price of the quarter of nine bushels of the best wheat at Windsor market, it appears from the accounts of Eton College, was only 1l. 13s. 9d. $\frac{4}{5}$, which is nearly 6s. 3d. below the average price of the sixty-four first years of the present century. ① The average price of the quarter of eight bushels of middle wheat, comes out, according to this account, to have been, during these ten years, only 1l. 6s. 8d. ②

The bounty kept up the price between 1741 and 1750.

Between 1741 and 1750, however, the bounty must have hindered the price of corn from falling so low in the home market as it naturally would have done. During these ten years the quantity of all sorts of grain exported, it appears from the custom-house books, amounted to no less than eight millions twenty-nine thousand one hundred and fifty-six quarters one bushel. The bounty paid for this amounted to 1,514,962 l. 17s. 4d. $\frac{1}{2}$.

In 1749 accordingly, Mr. Pelham, at that time prime minister, observed to the House of Commons, that for the three years③ preceding,

---

① [See the table at the end of the chapter.]

② [This figure is obtained, as recommended by Charles Smith (*Tracts on the Corn Trade*, 1766, p. 104), by deducting one-ninth for the greater size of the Windsor measure and oneninth from the remainder for the difference between best and middling wheat.]

③ ['Years' is apparently a mistake for 'months'. 'There is such a superabundance of corn that incredible quantities have been lately exported. I should be afraid to mention what quantities have been exported if it did not appear upon our custom-house books; but from them it appears that lately there was in three months' time above £220,000 paid for bounties upon corn exported. ' — *Parliamentary History* (Hansard), vol. xiv. , p. 589.]

份从他那里进口谷物的国家谷物短缺的程度。像这样长期的恶劣气候,虽然不是很平常的事件,但也绝不是什么特别罕见的事件。那些研究古代谷物价格的人,都很容易举出许多类似的实例来。此外,异常歉收的 10 年并不比异常丰收的 10 年更为稀奇少见。从 1741 年到 1750 年(包括这两个年头)低廉的谷价,与最近 8 年或 10 年间高昂的谷价正好是鲜明的对比。根据伊顿公学的记录,1741 年到 1750 年间,温莎市场上上等小麦每九蒲式耳一夸特的平均价格约为 1 镑 13 先令 9$\frac{4}{5}$便士。这比本世纪最初 64 年间的平均价格,大约低了 6 先令 3 便士①。由此可知,在这 10 年间,中等小麦八蒲式耳每夸特的平均价格仅约为 1 镑 6 先令 8 便士②。

但是,1741 年与 1750 年间,津贴一定阻止了谷物价格的下降,使它免于降到国内市场在自然条件下应有的水平。据海关统计,这十年间各种谷物所出口的数量,共计 8029156 夸特一蒲式耳。为此而支付的津贴累计为 1514962 镑 17 先令 4$\frac{1}{2}$便士。1749 年,首相佩勒姆[1]对下议院说,过去的三年中③,为鼓励

津贴维持了 1741 年—1750 年间的谷价。

---

① 参见本章末尾的统计表。
② 根据查理·史密斯的计算,这个数字是这样得到的:先从温莎市场的九蒲式耳一夸特减去九分之一,再从余下的减去最好小麦与最差小麦差额的九分之一。
③ 三年显然错误,应为三月。"谷物产量如此丰富,最近有令人难以置信的大量谷物被出口,如果不是海关统计上有记载,我都几乎不敢提及,但是从上面可以看出,在三个月中有 220000 镑被作为津贴付出。"《议会史》(汉萨得),第 14 卷,589 页。

[1] 佩勒姆(Henry Pelham),执政时期从 1743 年 8 月 27 日至 1754 年 3 月 7 日。

a very extraordinary sum had been paid as bounty for the exportation of corn. He had good reason to make this observation, and in the following year he might have had still better. In that single year the bounty paid amounted to no less than 324, 176*l*. 10*s*. 6*d*. ①It is unnecessary to observe how much this forced exportation must have raised the price of corn above what it otherwise would have been in the home market.

<small>The sudden change at 1750 was due to accidental variation of the seasons.</small>   At the end of the accounts annexed to this chapter the reader will find the particular account of those ten years separated from the rest. He will find there too the particular account of the preceding ten years, of which the average is likewise below, though not so much below, the general average of the sixty-four first years of the century. The year 1740, however, was a year of extraordinary scarcity. These twenty years preceding 1750, may very well be set in opposition to the twenty preceding 1770. As the former were a good deal below the general average of the century, notwithstanding the intervention of one or two dear years; so the latter have been a good deal above it, notwithstanding the intervention of one or two cheap ones, of 1759, for example. If the former have not been as much below the general average, as the latter have been above it, we ought probably to impute it to the bounty. The change has evidently been too sudden to be ascribed to any change in the value of silver, which is always slow and gradual. The suddenness of the effect can be accounted for only by a cause which can operate suddenly, the accidental variation of the seasons.

<small>The rise in the price of labour has been due to increase of demand for labour, not to a diminution in the value of silver.</small>   The money price of labour in Great Britain has, indeed, risen during the course of the present century. This, however, seems to be the effect, not so much of any diminution in the value of silver in the European market, as of an increase in the demand for labour in Great Britain, arising from the great, and almost universal prosperity of the country. In France, a country not altogether so prosperous, the money price of labour has, since the middle of the last century, been observed to sink gradually with the average money price of corn. Both in the last century and in the present, the day-wages of common labour are there said to have been pretty uniformly about the twentieth part of the average price of the septier of wheat, a measure which contains a

---

① See *Tracts on the Corn Trade*; Tract 3d.

谷物出口支付了巨大金额的津贴。他这样说是有很正当理由的，第二年这样说的理由更充分。因为仅这一年，付出的津贴就达到324176镑16先令6便士①。只是没有必要说明这种强制的出口，使国内市场上的谷价在多大程度上超过没有津贴时所应有的价格。

在本章所附的统计表的最后，读者可以看到，这10年的统计同其他各年的统计分开的。还可以可看到单独列出的这之前10年的统计数据。这10年的平均数，虽然低于本世纪最初64年的总平均数，但只低于此平均数很少。1740年是特别歉收的年份。1750年以前的那20年正好可以和1770年以前的那20年形成对比。前者虽然间或有一两年谷价昂贵的年份，但显然大大低于本世纪的总平均数；后者虽然间或有一两年谷价低廉的年份（例如1759年），但显然大大高于总平均数。如果前者低于总平均数的程度不像后者超过总平均数的程度那么大，则其原因应该是由于津贴制度。而且银价变动总是很缓慢的，显然不能很好的解释这突然的恶化。突发的效果，只能用突然的原因来说明，也就是气候的意外变化。

[旁注：1750年的突然变化是由于偶然的气候变化。]

在本世纪中，大不列颠的劳动的货币价格确实提高了。但这种提高，并不是由于欧洲市场上白银价值的降低，而是由于大不列颠普遍的繁荣导致了对劳动需求的增加。法国，一个并不十分繁荣的国家，自从上个世纪中期以来，其劳动的货币价格不断随谷物的平均货币价格逐渐降低。在上世纪和本世纪，法国普通工人每天的工资，据说始终不变地等于一塞蒂〔1〕小麦平均价格的1/20，

[旁注：劳动价格的上升是由于劳动需求增加，而不是由于白银价值的降低。]

---

① 参见《关于谷物贸易的论文集》，第三篇。

〔1〕 塞蒂（Septier），古代法国156公升的谷量，即法国古代谷物计量单位，约合现在的151公升。

little more than four Winchester bushels. In Great Britain the real recompence of labour, it has already been shown, the real quantities of the necessaries and conveniencies of life which are given to the labourer, has increased considerably during the course of the present century. The rise in its money price seems to have been the effect, not of any diminution of the value of silver in the general market of Europe, but of a rise in the real price of labour in the particular market of Great Britain, owing to the peculiarly happy circumstances of the country.

<small>The decrease in the rent and profit of mines of gold and silver</small>   For some time after the first discovery of America, silver would continue to sell at its former, or not much below its former price. The profits of mining would for some time be very great, and much above their natural rate. Those who imported that metal into Europe, however, would soon find that the whole annual importation could not be disposed of at this high price. Silver would gradually exchange for a smaller and a smaller quantity of goods. Its price would sink gradually lower and lower till it fell to its natural price; or to what was just sufficient to pay, according to their natural rates, the wages of the labour, the profits of the stock, and the rent of the land, which must be paid in order to bring it from the mine to the market. In the greater part of the silver mines of Peru, the tax of the king of Spain, amounting to a tenth of the gross produce, eats up, it has already been observed, the whole rent of the land. This tax was originally a half; it soon afterwards fell to a third, then to a fifth, and at last to a tenth, at which rate it still continues. In the greater part of the silver mines of Peru, this, it seems, is all that remains, after replacing the stock of the undertaker of the work, together with its ordinary profits; and it seems to be universally acknowledged that these profits, which were once very high, are now as low as they can well be, consistently with carrying on the works.

The tax of the king of Spain was reduced to a fifth part of the registered silver in 1504, one-and-forty years before 1545, the date of the discovery of the mines of Potosi. In the course of ninety years, or before 1636, these mines, the most fertile in all America, had time sufficient to produce their full effect, or to reduce the value of silver in the European market as low as it could well fall, while it continued to pay this tax to the king of Spain. Ninety years is time sufficient to reduce any commodity, of which there is no monopoly, to its natural price, or to the lowest price at which, while it pays a particular tax, it can continue to be sold for any considerable time together.

一塞蒂约比 4 温切斯特蒲式耳略多。前面已经提到过,大不列颠劳动的实际报酬,也就是支付给劳动者的生活必需品和便利品的实际数量,在本世纪中已经增加不少。劳动货币价格的上升,似乎不是由于欧洲一般市场上白银价值的下降,而是由于大不列颠特别优良的环境使得这个市场上劳动的真实价格上升。

在第一次发现美洲之后的一段时间里,白银仍然按照原来的价格或者比原来的低不太多的价格出售。所以有一阵采矿业的利润很大,远远超过了自然水平。但是不久那些将白银进口到欧洲的人就发现,这些进口的白银不可能全部都以高价卖出。白银所能交换的货物数量逐渐越来越少,这样白银的价格也不断降低,直到降到自然价格的水平,即降到只能按照自然率支付将其从矿山送往市场所必须花费的劳动工资、资本利润和土地地租。前面已经说过,秘鲁的大部分银矿都必须支付西班牙国王总产量 1/10 的赋税,这样就吞掉了全部地租。起初这种赋税为总产量的一半,随后又降为 1/3,接着又降到 1/5,最后降到 1/10,这个比率一直维持到现在。在秘鲁的大部分银矿里,似乎在补偿了开矿者资本及其平均利润后所剩下的也就是这个 1/10 了。因此开采者的利润一度非常高,现今低到大家公认的只能使其维持继续开采的程度了。

金银矿地租和利润的下降。

1504 年(这一年也是 1545 年发现波托西银矿前的 41 年),西班牙国王的赋税降为登记银的 1/5。1545 年后的 90 年里,即 1636 年以前,这些美洲最丰富的矿山在继续向西班牙国王交纳赋税的情况下有足够时间充分发挥它们的影响,使整个欧洲市场的银价,降到无法再低的程度。90 年的时间,足以使任何非垄断的商品降低到其自然价格,也就是说降低到在它继续缴纳某种赋税的情况下仍能长时间继续出售的最低价格。

| 国民财富的性质与原理

^{has been stayed by the gradual enlargement of the market,} The price of silver in the European market might perhaps have fallen still lower, and it might have become necessary either to reduce the tax upon it, not only to one tenth, as in 1736, but to one twentieth, in the same manner as that upon gold, or to give up working the greater part of the American mines which are now wrought. The gradual increase of the demand for silver, or the gradual enlargement of the market for the produce of the silver mines of America, is probably the cause which has prevented this from happening, and which has not only kept up the value of silver in the European market, but has perhaps even raised it somewhat higher than it was about the middle of the last century.

Since the first discovery of America, the market for the produce of its silver mines has been growing gradually more and more extensive.

(1) in Europe, First, The market of Europe has become gradually more and more extensive. Since the discovery of America, the greater part of Europe has been much improved. England, Holland, France, and Germany; even Sweden, Denmark, and Russia, have all advanced considerably both in agriculture and in manufactures. Italy seems not to have gone backwards. The fall of Italy preceded the conquest of Peru. Since that time it seems rather to have recovered a little. Spain and Portugal, indeed, are supposed to have gone backwards. Portugal, however, is but a very small part of Europe, and the declension of Spain is not, perhaps, so great as is commonly imagined. In the beginning of the sixteenth century, Spain was a very poor country, even in comparison with France, which has been so much improved since that time. It was the well-known remark of the Emperor Charles V. who had travelled so frequently through both countries, that every thing abounded in France, but that every thing was wanting in Spain. The increasing produce of the agriculture and manufactures of Europe must necessarily have required a gradual increase in the quantity of silver coin to circulate it; and the increasing number of wealthy individuals must have required the like increase in the quantity of their plate and other ornaments of silver.

(2) in America itself, Secondly, America is itself a new market for the produce of its own silver mines; and as its advances in agriculture, industry, and population, are much more rapid than those of the most thriving countries in Europe, its demand must increase much more rapidly. The English colonies are altogether a new market, which partly for coin and partly for plate, requires a continually augmenting supply of silver through a great continent where there never was any demand before.

欧洲市场上的白银的价格,原本有可能会降得更低,这样就使得税率,不仅可能降到像 1736 年的 1/10 那样的税率,而且还可能降到像对黄金的 1/20 那样的税率。甚至使得现在还在继续开采的大部分美洲矿山关闭停产。但之所以这些情况没有出现,或许是因为对白银需求的逐渐增长,美洲银矿产品市场的逐渐扩大,不仅维持住了欧洲市场上的白银的价格,甚至还将其价格抬高到略微高于上世纪中叶的价格。

<small>白银价格的下降被市场的逐渐扩大所阻止。</small>

自首次发现美洲以来,美洲银矿产品市场一直在逐渐扩大。

第一,欧洲市场逐渐变得越来越大。自从发现美洲之后,欧洲大部分地区都有很大的发展。英格兰、荷兰、法兰西和德意志,甚至瑞典、丹麦、俄罗斯在农业和制造业方面都有了相当大的进步。意大利似乎也没有退步。意大利的没落是在征服秘鲁之前,自那以后就似乎渐有起色。西班牙和葡萄牙的确被认为退步了。但葡萄牙只占欧洲的很小一部分,而西班牙的或许也并没有衰退到普遍想象的那个程度。在 16 世纪初叶,与法国相比西班牙也是一个非常贫穷的国家。自那时起法国就已经有很大改进。因此,经常游历这个两国的查理五世,曾说过这样一句有名的话:法国是什么都有,而在西班牙是什么都没有。既然欧洲农业和制造业的产量增大了,也就必然要增加流通所需的银币数量。既然富人人数增加了,也就必须要增加银制器皿和其他银饰品的数量。<small>(1)在欧洲,</small>

第二,美洲本身是其银矿产品的新市场,并且由于农业、工业和人口方面都比欧洲最繁荣的国家还要发展得快得多,所以美洲本身对于白银的需求增长也必然快得多。英国领属殖民地完全是一个新市场,那里以前一向对白银没有需求。部分因为铸币需要,部分因为打制器皿需要,那里才要求不断增加对白银的供应。<small>(2)在美洲本身,</small>

The greater part too of the Spanish and Portuguese colonies are altogether new markets. New Granada, the Yucatan, Paraguay, and the Brazils were, before discovered by the Europeans, inhabited by savage nations, who had neither arts nor agriculture. A considerable degree of both has now been introduced into all of them. Even Mexico and Peru, though they cannot be considered as altogether new markets, are certainly much more extensive ones than they ever were before. After all the wonderful tales which have been published concerning the splendid state of those countries in ancient times, whoever reads, with any degree of sober judgment, the history of their first discovery and conquest, will evidently discern that, in arts, agriculture, and commerce, their inhabitants were much more ignorant than the Tartars of the Ukraine are at present. Even the Peruvians, the more civilized nation of the two, though they made use of gold and silver as ornaments, had no coined money of any kind. Their whole commerce was carried on by barter, and there was accordingly scarce any division of labour among them. Those who cultivated the ground were obliged to build their own houses, to make their own houshold furniture, their own clothes, shoes, and instruments of agriculture. The few artificers among them are said to have been all maintained by the sovereign, the nobles, and the priests, and were probably their servants or slaves. All the ancient arts of Mexico and Peru have never furnished one single manufacture to Europe. ① The Spanish armies, though they scarce ever exceeded five hundred men, and frequently did not amount to half that number, found almost every-where great difficulty in procuring subsistence. The famines which they are said to have occasioned almost wherever they went, in countries too which at the same time are represented as very populous and wellcultivated,

---

① [Below, vol. ii. , p. 70. Raynal, *Histoire philosophique*, Amsterdamed. 1773, tom. iii. , pp. 113, 116, takes the same view of the Peruvians.]

大部分西班牙和葡萄牙领属殖民地也完全是新市场。新格拉纳达[1]、尤卡坦、巴拉圭、巴西等地的居民,在被欧洲人发现以前,属于没有工艺和农业的野蛮民族。可是现在,他们都有了相当程度的工艺和农业。甚至墨西哥和秘鲁两国,虽然不能完全被视为新市场,但也是比过去扩大了的市场。不管记述这两国辉煌历史的神奇故事如何描绘,那些读它们的发现史及征服史的人,只要具有清醒的判断能力,就会看出,当时那里的居民在工艺、农业和商业上比如今乌克兰的鞑靼人还要无知。即使是两国中比较进步的秘鲁人,虽然也知道利用金银作为装饰品,却不知道铸金银为货币。他们的商业完全是物物交换,因而不存在劳动分工。耕种土地的人,同时不得不自行建造房屋,自行打造家具,自行缝制衣物、鞋子,自行制作农具等。他们中间虽然有少数工匠,但是据说这些人都是由国王、贵族和僧侣供养的,可能就是他们的仆人或奴隶。墨西哥和秘鲁的所有古代工艺,从来没有向欧洲供应过任何制造品①。西班牙在这里的军队,虽然不超过 500 人,甚至往往不到 250 人,却觉得几乎到处都难以获得食物。据说,这些军队所到之处,即使是人口稠密、耕种发达的地方,也常常发生饥荒。这充分说明,这些有关人口稠密、耕种发达的故事,在很大程度上是虚

---

① 后面,第三篇。雷纳尔:《历史哲学》,阿姆斯特丹,1773 年,第 3 部,第 113、116 页,秘鲁人也这样认为。
[1] 新格拉纳达(New Granada),西班牙在南美北部的一个殖民地,包括现在的哥伦比亚、厄瓜多尔、巴拿巴和委内瑞拉。从 16 世纪 30 年代到 1819 年属西班牙管制。

sufficiently demonstrate that the story of this populousness and high cultivation is in a great measure fabulous. The Spanish colonies are under a government in many respects less favourable to agriculture, improvement and population, than that of the English colonies. ①They seem, however, to be advancing in all these much more rapidly than any country in Europe. In a fertile soil and happy climate, the great abundance and cheapness of land, a circumstance common to all new colonies, is, it seems, so great an advantage as to compensate many defects in civil government. Frezier, who visited Peru in 1713, represents Lima as containing between twenty-five and twenty-eight thousand inhabitants. ②Ulloa, who resided in the same country between 1740 and 1746, represents it as containing more than fifty thousand. ③The difference in their accounts of the populousness of several other principal towns in Chili and Peru is nearly the same; ④and as there seems to be no reason to doubt of the good information of either, it marks an increase which is scarce inferior to that of the English colonies. America, therefore, is a new market for the produce of its own silver mines, of which the demand must increase much more rapidly than that of the most thriving country in Europe.

(3) in the East Indies, Thirdly, The East Indies is another market for the produce of the silver mines of America, and a market which, from the time of the first discovery of those mines, has been continually taking off a greater and a greater quantity of silver. Since that time, the direct trade between America and the East Indies, which is carried on by means of the Acapulco ships, ⑤ has been continually augmenting, and the indirect intercourse by the way of Europe has been augmenting in a still greater proportion. During the sixteenth century, the Portuguese were the only European nation who carried on any regular trade to the East Indies. In the last years of that century the Dutch began to encroach upon this monopoly, and in a few years expelled them from their

---

① [Below, vol. ii. , *passim.*]

② [*Voyage to the South Sea*, p. 218,]

③ [*Voyage historique*, tom. i. , p. 443, 445:]

④ [E. g. , Santiago and Callao, Frezier, *Voyage*, pp. 102, 202]

⑤ [Originally one ship, and, after 1720, two ships, were allowed to sail between Acapulco in Mexico and the Philippines. For the regulations applied to the trade see Uztariz, *Theory and Practice of Commerce and Maritime Affairs*, trans. by John Kippax, 1751, vol i. , pp. 206-208.]

构的。西班牙领属殖民地的政府统治,在许多方面比不上英国领属殖民地那样有利于农业发展、技术改进和人口增长①。但是,西班牙领属殖民地在所有这几个方面,却比欧洲任何国家都进步得快。因为这些殖民地具有一切新殖民地所共有的优点,即土壤肥沃、气候宜人、土地广大而低廉。这些大的优点足以补偿其政治上的许多缺点。佛雷泽曾于1713年访问过秘鲁。他说,利马市人口在25000人至28000人之间②。但是,1740年到1746年间曾在秘鲁居住的乌洛阿却说利马市人口超过了50000人③。关于智利和秘鲁的其他几个主要城市的人口数,他们两个的说法同样有差异④。他们两人报告的正确性无可置疑。只能说那里人口的增加并不逊于英国领属殖民地。因此,美洲是其本地银矿产品的新市场。它对于白银的需求必然比欧洲最繁荣国家的需求增长更快。

第三,东印度是美洲银矿产品的另一个市场,并且自从最初发现这些矿山以来,该市场所吸收的白银越来越多。从那时起,通过阿卡普尔科船舶⑤而进行的美洲和东印度之间的直接贸易一直不断扩大,而经由欧洲的间接交易则增加得更多。在16世纪期间,欧洲民族中只有葡萄牙人与东印度进行正规贸易。但16

(3)在东印度,

---

① 后面,第二篇,多处可见。
② 《南海航行记》,第218页。
③ 《航海史》,第1部,第443、445页。
④ 例如圣地亚哥和卡亚俄。佛雷泽《航海史》,第102、202页。
⑤ 最初是一只船,1720年以后是两只船,被允许在墨西哥的阿卡普尔科和菲律宾之间航行。这种规定用于贸易的事情,参见乌兹塔利兹:《商业和战争的理论与实践》,约翰·基帕克斯译,1751年版,第一篇,第206~208页。

principal settlements in India. During the greater part of the last century those two nations divided the most considerable part of the East India trade between them; the trade of the Dutch continually augmenting in a still greater proportion than that of the Portuguese declined. The English and French carried on some trade with India in the last century, but it has been greatly augmented in the course of the present. The East India trade of the Swedes and Danes began in the course of the present century. Even the Muscovites now trade regularly with China by a sort of caravans which go over land through Siberia and Tartary to Pekin. The East India trade of all these nations, if we except that of the French, which the last war had well nigh annihilated, has been almost continually augmenting. The increasing consumption of East India goods in Europe is, it seems, so great, as to afford a gradual increase of employment to them all. Tea, for example, was a drug very little used in Europe before the middle of the last century. At present the value of the tea annually imported by the English East India Company, for the use of their own countrymen, amounts to more than a million and a half a year; and even this is not enough; a great deal more being constantly smuggled into the country from the ports of Holland, from Gottenburg in Sweden, and from the coast of France too, as long as the French East India Company was in prosperity. The consumption of the porcelain of China, of the spiceries of the Moluccas, of the piece goods of Bengal, and of innumerable other articles, has increased very nearly in a like proportion. The tonnage accordingly of all the European shipping employed in the East India trade, at any one time during the last century, was not, perhaps, much greater than that of the English East India Company before the late reduction of their shipping. ①

---

① ['In order to prevent the great consumption of timber fit for the construction of large ships of war, the East India Company were prohibited from building, or allowing to be built for their service, any new ships, till the shipping in their employment should be reduced under 45, 000 tons, or employing any ships built after 18th March, 1772. But they are at liberty to build any vessel whatever in India or the colonies, or to charter any vessel built in India or the colonies, 12 Geo. III., c. 54. '-Macpherson, *Annals of Commerce*, 1805, A. D. 1772, vol. iii., pp. 521, 522.]

世纪末期,荷兰人开始起来竞争,而且不到几年,就把葡萄牙人逐出了他们在印度的主要居留地。在上世纪的大部分时间里,这两个国家瓜分了大部分的东印度贸易。葡萄牙人的贸易日见衰退,而荷兰人的贸易却以比这衰退更快的速度不断增长。英国人和法国人在上世纪与印度进行过一些贸易,而本世纪他们之间的贸易已经大为增长。瑞典人和丹麦人与东印度的贸易开始于本世纪。甚至俄罗斯人,最近也组织所谓商队,经由西伯利亚和鞑靼,到达北京,与中国进行正规贸易。总之,除了法国对东印度的贸易因为最近的战争而被毁灭了以外,其他各国对东印度的贸易几乎都在继续扩大。欧洲对东印度货物的消费量的日益增多,看来好像使得东印度各行各业逐渐发展。例如,16世纪中叶以前,茶叶还是欧洲很少使用的一种药品。然而现在,英国东印度公司每年为本国国民当作饮料而进口的茶叶,价值就达150万镑。但是,即使这样也不能满足需要,又要经由荷兰各港口、瑞典的哥登堡以及在法国东印度公司繁荣时期经由法国海岸,不断秘密大量进口。此外,对于中国的瓷器、马六甲群岛的香料、孟加拉的布匹,以及其他无数货物,欧洲的消费量也都以几乎同样的比例增加。所以,就用在东印度贸易上的船舶来讲,上世纪任何时候全欧洲所用的船舶吨位,比最近航运缩减以前的英国东印度公司一家所用的船舶吨位,恐怕多不了多少①。

————————

① 为了建造大型战船,阻止对原木的大量消费,东印度公司被禁止建造楼房、服务设施以及新船,直到他们利用的船只减少到45000吨,或者利用1772年3月18日以后建造的船只。但他们能在印度或殖民地自由打造或者包租任何器皿。参见马克菲尔森:《商业年鉴》,1805年版,公元1772年,第3卷,第521、522页。

国民财富的性质与原理

<small>where the value of gold and silver was, and still is, higher than in Europe.</small>   But in the East Indies, particularly in China and Indostan, the value of the precious metals, when the Europeans first began to trade to those countries, was much higher than in Europe; and it still continues to be so. In rice countries, which generally yield two, sometimes three crops in the year, each of them more plentiful than any common crop of corn, the abundance of food must be much greater than in any corn country of equal extent. Such countries are accordingly much more populous. In them too the rich, having a greater super-abundance of food to dispose of beyond what they themselves can consume, have the means of purchasing a much greater quantity of the labour of other people. The retinue of a grandee in China or Indostan accordingly is, by all accounts, much more numerous and splendid than that of the richest subjects in Europe. The same super-abundance of food, of which they have the disposal, enables them to give a greater quantity of it for all those singular and rare productions which nature furnishes but in very small quantities; such as the precious metals and the precious stones, the great objects of the competition of the rich. Though the mines, therefore, which supplied the Indian market had been as abundant as those which supplied the European, such commodities would naturally exchange for a greater quantity of food in India than in Europe. But the mines which supplied the Indian market with the precious metals seem to have been a good deal less abundant, and those which supplied it with the precious stones a good deal more so, than the mines which supplied the European. The precious metals, therefore, would naturally exchange in India for somewhat a greater quantity of the precious stones, and for a much greater quantity of food than in Europe. The money price of diamonds, the greatest of all superfluities, would be somewhat lower, and that of food, the first of all necessaries, a great deal lower in the one country than in the other. But the real price of labour, the real quantity of the necessaries of life which is given to the labourer, it has already been observed, is lower both in China and Indostan, the two great markets of India, than it is through the greater part of Europe. The wages of the labourer will there purchase a smaller quantity of food; and as the money price of food is much lower in India than in Europe, the money price of labour is there lower upon a double account; upon account both of the small quantity of food which it will purchase, and of the low price of that food. But in countries of e-qual art and industry, the money price of the greater part of manufactures will be in proportion to the money price of labour; and in

但在东印度,尤其是在中国与印度斯坦,当欧洲人首次与他们进行贸易时,贵金属的价值都要比在欧洲高得多,而且至今仍然是这样。生产稻米的国家通常每年能收获两三次,而每次收获的产量又比小麦的一般收成更多,其粮食的富足程度必然大大超过任何相同面积的生产小麦的国家。因此,这些国家的人口更为众多。此外,这些国家的富人,拥有自己消费不了的大量剩余粮食可以自由处置,于是有条件购买更多数量的他人劳动。因此,根据所有记载,中国和印度斯坦的达官显贵比欧洲最富裕的人,都拥有更多的仆役和更大的气派。而且,他们的大量剩余粮食也使得他们能够支付较大数量的粮食来交换那些产量极少的珍奇物品,比如富人们竞相争购的贵金属和宝石。所以,尽管供应印度市场的矿山和供应欧洲市场的矿山一样丰饶,其产物在印度所能交换到的粮食也必然更多。可是,以贵金属供应印度市场的矿山比以贵金属供应欧洲市场的矿山贫瘠得多,而以宝石供应印度市场的矿山却比以宝石供应欧洲市场的矿山丰饶得多。因此,贵金属在印度自然要比在欧洲能交换到稍多的宝石,并能交换到更多的粮食。印度与欧洲相比,像钻石那样的非必需品的货币价格要略微低一些,而像粮食这样的最重要必需品的货币价格要低得多。但是前面说过,在中国和印度斯坦这两个大市场,劳动的实际价格,即劳动者得到的生活必需品的实际量,却比欧洲大部分地区要低。因此那里的劳动者的工资只能购买到较少量的粮食。同时由于粮食价格在印度要比在欧洲低得多,所以,劳动的货币价格在印度要比在欧洲低得更多,因为一方面它所能购买到的粮食量少,一方面粮食的价格又便宜。但在技术和勤勉程度相同的国家,大部分制造品的货币价格与其劳动的货币价格成比例。中

无论过去和现在,金银的价值在印度都比在欧洲高。

manufacturing art and industry, China and Indostan, though inferior, seem not to be much inferior to any part of Europe. The money price of the greater part of manufactures, therefore, will naturally be much lower in those great empires than it is any-where in Europe. Through the greater part of Europe too the expence of land-carriage increases very much both the real and nominal price of most manufactures. It costs more labour, and therefore more money, to bring first the materials, and afterwards the complete manufacture to market. In China and Indostan the extent and variety of inland navigations save the greater part of this labour, and consequently of this money, and thereby reduce still lower both the real and the nominal price of the greater part of their manufactures. Upon all these accounts, the precious metals are a commodity which it always has been, and still continues to be, extremely advantageous to carry from Europe to India. There is scarce any commodity which brings a better price there; or which, in proportion to the quantity of labour and commodities which it costs in Europe, will purchase or command a greater quantity of labour and commodities in India. It is more advantageous too to carry silver thither than gold; because in China, and the greater part of the other markets of India, the proportion between fine silver and fine gold is but as ten, or at most as twelve, to one; whereas in Europe it is as fourteen or fifteen to one. In China, and the greater part of the other markets of India, ten, or at most twelve, ounces of silver will purchase an ounce of gold. in Europe it requires from fourteen to fifteen ounces. In the cargoes, therefore, of the greater part of European ships which sail to India, silver has generally been one of the most valuable articles. ①It is the most valuable article in the

---

① [Newton, in his *Representation to the Lords of the Treasury*, 1717 (reprinted in the *Universal Merchant*, quoted on the next page), says that in China and Japan the ratio is 9 or 10 to 1 and in India 12 to 1, and this carries away the silver from all Europe. Magens, in a note to this passage (*Universal Merchant*, p. 90), says that down to 1732 such quantities of silver went to China to fetch back gold that the price of gold in China rose and it became no longer profitable to send silver there.]

国和印度斯坦制造业上的技术和勤勉程度,虽然比不上欧洲各地,但也差不了多少。它们大部分制造品的货币价格自然要比欧洲任何地方低得多。还有,欧洲大部分地区多由陆路输送货物,由于在把原料和制造品运往市场的过程中需要耗费更多的劳动,也由此需要花费更多的货币,大部分制造品的实际价格和名义价格就因而大大提高。在中国和印度斯坦,则由于内地航运方便,所需运费较少,其大部分制造品的实际价格和名义价格就更加降低。由于这些原因,贵金属由欧洲运往印度,过去和现在都一直极为有利可图。与贵金属相比,没有什么商品能够在印度卖得好价。也就是说,在欧洲制造的价值一定的劳动量和商品量的商品,在印度都不能比贵金属交换到更多数量的劳动和商品。贵金属中,将白银运往印度比将黄金运往印度有利,因为在中国及其他大部分印度市场上,纯银与纯金的比率,通常是 10:1,最多是 12:1,而在欧洲市场上则为 14:1 或 15:1。购买 1 盎司黄金,在中国及其他大部分印度市场上需要 10 盎司或最多 12 盎司白银,而在欧洲市场上则需要 14 盎司到 15 盎司白银。因此,白银通常是大部分从欧洲开往印度的船只上最有价值的运输品之一①,也是从阿卡普尔科开往马尼拉〔1〕

---

① 牛顿在其《领主财富的陈述》(1717 年版,重印于〈环球商人〉,下一页要引用)中说,中国和日本的这个比率为9:1 或 10:1,印度的这个比率为12:1。这从欧洲输出了白银。马根斯在对这种航行做的一篇笔记(〈环球商人〉第 90 页)中说,直到 1732 年,这些运往中国以换来黄金的白银都在增加,使得往中国输出白银不再有利可图。

〔1〕 马尼拉(Manilla 又作 Manila),菲律宾的首都和最大城市,位于吕宋岛和南中国海的马尼拉湾的西南部。1571 年建城,一直由西班牙控制。1898 年在美西战争中被美国军队夺占。

Acapulco ships which sail to Manilla. The silver of the new continent seems in this manner to be one of the principal commodities by which the commerce between the two extremities of the old one is carried on, and it is by means of it, in a great measure, that those distant parts of the world are connected with one another.

<small>The supply of silver must provide for waste as well as increase of plate and coin.</small>   In order to supply so very widely extended a market, the quantity of silver annually brought from the mines must not only be sufficient to support that continual increase both of coin and of plate which is required in all thriving countries; but to repair that continual waste and consumption of silver which takes place in all countries where that metal is used.

<small>Waste is considerable.</small>   The continual consumption of the precious metals in coin by wearing, and in plate both by wearing and cleaning, is very sensible; and in commodities of which the use is so very widely extended, would alone require a very great annual supply. The consumption of those metals in some particular manufactures, though it may not perhaps be greater upon the whole than this gradual consumption, is, however, much more sensible, as it is much more rapid. In the manufactures of Birmingham alone, the quantity of gold and silver annually employed in gilding and plating, and thereby disqualified from ever afterwards appearing in the shape of those metals, is said to amount to more than fifty thousand pounds sterling. We may from thence form some notion how great must be the annual consumption in all the different parts of the world, either in manufactures of the same kind with those of Birmingham, or in laces, embroideries, gold and silver stuffs, the gilding of books, furniture, &c. A considerable quantity too must be annually lost in transporting those metals from one place to another both by sea and by land. In the greater part of the governments of Asia, besides, the almost universal custom of concealing treasures in the bowels of the earth, of which the knowledge frequently dies with the person who makes the concealment, must occasion the loss of a still greater quantity.

<small>Six millions of gold and silver are imported at Cadiz and Lisbon,</small>   The quantity of gold and silver imported at both Cadiz and Lisbon

的船只上最有价值的运输品。新大陆的白银似乎就因此而成为旧大陆两端通商的主要商品之一。世界各处相距遥远的地区在很大程度上也正是通过这种方式而得以联结起来。

为了供应如此广大的市场,每年由矿山运出的白银数量,不但要足以满足所有繁荣国家因铸造货币和打制器皿而不断增加的需求,还必须足以弥补一切使用白银的国家银币、银器皿的不断磨损。_{白银的供应必须考虑铸币和器皿制造以及铸币器皿磨损的需求增加。银的磨损毁损很可观。}

由于磨损和洗擦,贵金属用作铸币和器皿的消耗很大。单就这些使用范围非常广泛的各种商品的不断消耗来说,每年就必须供应极大数量的贵金属。某些特殊制造业中所消耗的贵金属,虽然整个来说可能不会多于这种逐渐消耗,但由于消耗得更快而特别显著。据说,单是伯明翰[1]的制造品,每年为镀金和包金而使用的金银量就超过英币5万镑,而且这些金银被这样使用后就再也不能恢复原状。我们据此可以想到,在与伯明翰的制造品相类似的制造品上,或者在镶边、彩饰、金银器、书边镀金及家具等方面,世界各地每年所消耗的金银一定数量巨大。而且金银每年经由海上和陆地从一处运往另一处,在途中的损失也一定有相当数量。另外,亚洲各国几乎都有掘地藏宝的习俗,而埋藏的地方往往在埋藏者死后再也无人知道,这必然增加金银的损失量。

根据极其可靠的记载,经由卡迪兹及里斯本[2]进口的金银量 _{经由卡迪兹及里斯本每年进口600万镑的金银,}

---

〔1〕 伯明翰(Birmingham),英国中部伦敦西北一城市,为主要工业中心和交通中心。

〔2〕 里斯本(Lisbon),葡萄牙首都和最大的城市。位于太加斯河湾区域的西部。它是一个古老的伊比利亚人定居点,曾被腓尼基人和迦太基人占有。公元前205年被罗马人占领,并于公元714年被摩尔人征服,1147年葡萄牙人重新征服该城。在16世纪向非洲和印度的殖民扩张的全盛时期最为繁荣,在1755年一场人地震中被夷为平地。

(including not only what comes under register, but what may be supposed to be smuggled) amounts, according to the best accounts, to about six millions sterling a year.

<small>as shown by Magens,</small> According to Mr. Meggens① the annual importation of the precious metals into Spain, at an average of six years; viz. from 1748 to 1753, both inclusive;② and into Portugal, at an average of seven years; viz. from 1747 to 1753, both inclusive; amounted in silver to 1,101,107 pounds weight; and in gold to 49,940 pounds weight. The silver, at sixty-two shillings the pound Troy, amounts to 3,413,431l. 10s.③ sterling. The gold, at forty-four guineas and a half the pound Troy, amounts to 2,333,446l. 14s. sterling. Both together amount to 5,746,878l. 4s. sterling. The account of what was imported under register, he assures us is exact. He gives us the detail of the particular places from which the gold and silver were brought, and of the particular quantity of each metal, which, according to the register, each of them afforded. He makes an allowance too for the quantity of each metal which he supposes may have been smuggled. The great experience of this judicious merchant renders his opinion of considerable weight.

<small>Raynal,</small> According to the eloquent and, sometimes, well-informed Author of the Philosophical and Political History of the Establishment of the Europeans in the two Indies, the annual importation of registered gold and silver into Spain, at an average of eleven years; viz. from 1754 to 1764, both inclusive; amounted to 13,984,185$\frac{3}{4}$ piastres of ten reals. On account of what may have been smuggled, however, the whole annual importation, he supposes, may have amounted to

---

① [Postscript to the Universal Merchant, p. 15 and 16. This Postscript was not printed till 1756, three years after the publication of the book, which has never had a second edition.]

② [The two periods are really five years, April, 1748, to April, 1753, and six years, January, 1747, to January, 1753, but the averages are correct, being taken from Magens.]

③ [The 10s. here should be 14s. , and two lines lower down the 14s. should be 10s.]

（包括正式登记的和可能走私的），每年约值 600 万镑。

　　据马根斯先生说①，1748 年到 1753 年这 6 年期间西班牙每年进口的平均量，和 1747 年到 1753 年这 7 年期间葡萄牙每年进口的平均量②，共计白银 1101107 镑，黄金 49940 镑。白银每金衡镑值 62 先令，共值 3413431 镑 10 先令③。黄金每金衡镑值 44 几尼半，共值 2333446 镑 14 先令。两项合计共值 5746878 镑 4 先令。他认为这些登记的进口数字是正确的。他根据登记簿详细地介绍了出口金银的各个地点以及从每一地点进口的金银量。他也对他认为可能是走私进口的金银量做出了估计。这位商人经验丰富，卓有见识，他的意见也因此具有相当的分量。

　　《欧洲人在东西印度建立殖民地的哲学史和政治史》一书的作者能言善辩而且消息灵通。据他说，自 1754 年到 1764 年的 11 年间，每年正式登记的进口西班牙的金银量，以 10 雷阿尔银币为 1 比索计算，平均达到 13984185 $\frac{3}{4}$ 比索。要是再加上走私进口量，每年总进口量可能达到 1700 万比索。如果以 1 比索为 4 先令

---

　　① 《环球商人后记》第 15、16 页。该书出版后 3 年（即 1756 年）才印了后记，没有第二版。

　　② 据马根斯说，两个时期实际上分别为五年（1748 年 4 月至 1753 年 4 月）和六年（1747 年 1 月至 1753 年 1 月），但平均数是正确的。

　　③ 这里 10 先令应为 14 先令，下面一行的 14 先令应为 10 先令。

seventeen millions of piastres; which, at 4s. 6d. the piastre, is equal to 3, 825, 000l. sterling. He gives the detail too of the particular places from which the gold and silver were brought, and of the particular quantities of each metal which, according to the register, each of them afforded. ①He informs us too, that if we were to judge of the quantity of gold annually imported from the Brazils into Lisbon by the amount of the tax paid to the king of Portugal, which it seems is one-fifth of the standard metal, we might value it at eighteen millions of cruzadoes, or forty-five millions of French livres, equal to about two millions sterling. On account of what may have been smuggled, however, we may safely, he says, add to this sum an eighth more, or 250, 000l. sterling, so that the whole will amount to 2, 250, 000l. sterling. ②According to this account, therefore, the whole annual importation of the precious metals into both Spain and Portugal, amounts to about 6, 075, 000l. sterling.

<small>and other authors.</small> Several other very well authenticated, though manuscript, accounts, I have been assured, agree, in making this whole annual importation amount at an average to about six millions sterling; sometimes a little more, sometimes a little less.

<small>This is not the whole of the annual supply, but by far the greater part</small> The annual importation of the precious metals into Cadiz and Lisbon, indeed, is not equal to the whole annual produce of the mines of America. Some part is sent annually by the Acapulco ships to Manilla; some part is employed in the contraband trade which the Spanish colonies carry on with those of other European nations; and some part, no doubt, remains in the country. The mines of America, besides, are by no means the only gold and silver mines in the world. They are, however, by far the most abundant. The produce of all the other mines which are known, is insignificant, it is acknowledged, in comparison with theirs; and the far greater part of their produce, it is likewise acknowledged, is annually imported into Cadiz and Lisbon. But the consumption of Birmingham alone, at the rate of fifty thousand pounds a year, is equal to the

---

① [Raynal, *Histoire philosophique et politique des établissemens et du commerce des Européens dans les deux Indes*, Amsterdam ed. , 1773, tom. iii. , p. 310.]

② [Raynal, *Histoire philosophique*, Amsterdam ed. , 1773, tom. iii. , p. 385.]

6便士换算,每年总进口量相当于英币382.5万镑。他曾详细列举了各个金银出口地以及各地每一种金属的登记出口量。① 据他报告,每年由巴西进口到里斯本的金量,如果按葡萄牙国王所征收的税额判断(税率似乎为标准金属的20%),可以估计为葡币1800万克鲁查多[1],即法币4500万里弗,约合英币200万镑。他说,我们有把握以公开进口部分的1/8来计算走私进口部分,这样又可以加上25万镑,因此总量为225万镑②。依据这种计算,西班牙和葡萄牙两国每年进口的贵金属总量就达到607.5万镑。

我确信其他几种记述也是非常可靠的,尽管它们只是抄本以及其他作者所言。它们都认为每年平均进口总量在600万镑左右,有时多一些,有时少一些。

每年进口到卡迪兹和里斯本的贵金属量,并不等于美洲矿山的全年产量。全年产量中,一部分每年由阿卡普尔科船只运往马尼拉,一部分用于西班牙殖民地和其他欧洲国家殖民地之间的走私交易,还有一部分毫无疑问是留在了出产地。此外,美洲矿山虽然不是世界上仅有的金银矿山,但它们是世界上最丰饶的矿山。人们公认,就产量来说,我们所知道的所有其他矿山和美洲矿山相比都微不足道。人们也公认,每年美洲矿山产量的大部分都运进了卡迪兹和里斯本两地。但是,单是伯明翰一地的消耗量

---

① 雷纳尔:《欧洲人在东西印度建立殖民地的哲学史和政治史》,1773年阿姆斯特丹出版,第3部,第310页。

② 雷纳尔:《欧洲人在东西印度建立殖民地的哲学史和政治史》,1773年阿姆斯特丹出版,第3部,第385页。

[1] 兑鲁查多(Cruzado),古时葡萄牙金币单位。

hundred-and-twentieth part of this annual importation at the rate of six millions a year. The whole annual consumption of gold and silver, therefore, in all the different countries of the world where those metals are used, may perhaps be nearly equal to the whole annual produce. The remainder may be no more than sufficient to supply the increasing demand of all thriving countries. It may even have fallen so far short of this demand as somewhat to raise the price of those metals in the European market.

<small>Brass and iron increase, but we do not expect them to fall in value. Why then gold and silver?</small> The quantity of brass and iron annually brought from the mine to the market is out of all proportion greater than that of gold and silver. We do not, however, upon this account, imagine that those coarse metals are likely to multiply beyond the demand, or to become gradually cheaper and cheaper. Why should we imagine that the precious metals are likely to do so ? The coarse metals, indeed, though harder, are put to much harder uses, and, as they are of less value, less care is employed in their preservation. The precious metals, however, are not necessarily immortal any more than they, but are liable too to be lost, wasted, and consumed in a great variety of ways.

<small>In consequence of their durability the metals, especially gold and silver, vary little in value from year to year.</small> The price of all metals, though liable to slow and gradual variations, varies less from year to year than that of almost any other part of the rude produce of land; and the price of the precious metals is even less liable to sudden variations than that of the coarse ones. The durableness of metals is the foundation of this extraordinary steadiness of price. The corn which was brought to market last year, will be all or almost all consumed long before the end of this year. But some part of the iron which was brought from the mine two or three hundred years ago, may be still in use, and perhaps some part of the gold which was brought from it two or three thousand years ago. The different masses of corn which in different years must supply the consumption of the world, will always be nearly in proportion to the respective produce of those different years. But the proportion between the different masses of iron which may be in use in two different years, will be very little affected by any accidental difference in the produce of the iron mines of those two years; and the proportion between the masses of gold will be still less affected by any such difference in the produce of the gold mines. Though the produce of the greater part of metallic mines, therefore, varies, perhaps, still more from year to year than that of the greater part of corn-fields, those variations have not the same effect upon the price of the one species of commodities, as upon that of the other.

每年就有5万镑,相当于每年600万镑进口量的1/120。这样看来,世界各地每年的金银消耗总量也许近似于其每年的产出总量。供大于求的多出部分可能仅足以供应所有繁荣国家不断增加的需求。甚至可能还远远不能满足这种需求,从而使欧洲市场上这些金属的价格略有上升。

就每年由矿山供应市场的数量来看,铜和铁的数量远远多于黄金和白银的数量。但我们绝不能因此就以为,这些低廉金属会大大超过需求,或者价格会越来越低。那么,我们为什么会这样认识贵金属呢?诚然,低廉金属比较坚固,常用于比较容易磨损的用途,而且因为价值较低,人们保存起来也不是多么留心。但是,贵金属并不一定比低廉金属保存得更长久。贵金属也常以各种方式丢失、磨损和消耗。

所有金属的价格,虽然都有缓慢的和逐渐的变动,但与土地其他原生产物相比,其逐年的变动程度较小。而贵金属与低廉金属相比,其价格突然变动的可能性更小。金属的耐久性是其价格不易变动的原因。去年上市的谷物在今年年终就将全部或几乎全部被消费掉。但是,两三百年前由矿山开采的铁可能有一部分现在还在使用,两三千年前由矿山开采的黄金可能也是这样。世界上各年度各种谷物的消费量与其生产量通常保持一定的比例。但是,两个不同年度所使用的铁的数量间的比例,很少受到这两个年度铁矿产量偶然差异的影响,而所使用的黄金的数量间的比例更不会受到金矿产量变动的影响。所以,就逐年的产量来看,虽然大部分金属矿山比大部分谷地也许有更大的变动,但产量变动对这两种不同生产物价格的影响不一样。

Variations in the Proportion betweene the respective Values of Gold and Silver

After the discovery of the American mines silver fell in proportion to gold.
Before the discovery of the mines of America, the value of fine gold to fine silver was regulated in the different mints of Europe, between the proportions of one to ten and one to twelve; that is, an ounce of fine gold was supposed to be worth from ten to twelve ounces of fine silver. About the middle of the last century it came to be regulated, between the proportions of one to fourteen and one to fifteen; that is, an ounce of fine gold came to be supposed worth between fourteen and fifteen ounces of fine silver. Gold rose in its nominal value, or in the quantity of silver which was given for it. Both metals sunk in their real value, or in the quantity of labour which they could purchase; but silver sunk more than gold. Though both the gold and silver mines of America exceeded in fertility all those which had ever been known before, the fertility of the silver mines had, it seems, been proportionably still greater than that of the gold ones.

It is higher in the East
The great quantities of silver carried annually from Europe to India, have, in some of the English settlements, gradually reduced the value of that metal in proportion to gold. In the mint of Calcutta, an ounce of fine gold is supposed to be worth fifteen ounces of fine silver, in the same manner as in Europe. It is in the mint perhaps rated too high for the value which it bears in the market of Bengal. In China, the proportion of gold to silver still continues as one to ten, or one to twelve. In Japan, it is said to be as one to eight. ①

Magens seems to think the proportion of value should be the same as the proportion of quantity.
The proportion between the quantities of gold and silver annually imported into Europe, according to Mr. Meggens's account, is as one to twenty-two nearly; ②that is, for one ounce of gold there are imported a little more than twenty-two ounces of silver. The great quantity of silver sent annually to the East Indies, reduces, he supposes, the quantities of those metals which remain in Europe to the proportion of one to fourteen or fifteen, the proportion of their values. The proportion between their values, he seems to think, ③must necessarily be the same as that between

---

① [Cantillon gives one to ten for China and one to eight for Japan, *Essai*, p. 365.]

② [Above, pp. 208, 209. The exact figure given by Magens, *Farther Explanations*, p. 16, is 1 to 22 $\frac{1}{10}$.]

③ [*Ibid.*, p. 17.]

黄金和白银之间价值比例的变动

在美洲矿山发现以前，欧洲各造币厂规定纯金对纯银的价值比例为1∶10至1∶12，也就是说，1盎司纯金被认定为值10盎司至12盎司纯银。大约在上世纪中叶，这个比例调整为1∶14至1∶15，即1盎司纯金被认定为值14盎司至15盎司纯银。这样，黄金的名义价值上升了，换句话说，黄金所能交换到的白银数量增加了。两种金属的实际价值，即它们所能购买到的劳动量，虽然均有下降，但白银比黄金降得更低。虽然美洲金矿和银矿的丰饶程度超过了以前发现的所有矿山，但银矿的丰饶程度似乎比金矿更大。

美洲矿山发现以后，白银与黄金相比价值下降。

每年从欧洲运往印度的白银数量很大，致使某些英国殖民地的白银相对于黄金的价格逐渐下降。与欧洲一样，加尔各答的造币厂认定1盎司纯金值15盎司纯银。但这种定价和黄金在孟加拉市场上的价值相比似乎显得太高。黄金与白银的价值比例，在中国仍旧是1∶10或1∶12，在日本据说是1∶8①。

白银的价值在东方较高。

根据马根斯先生的记载，每年进口到欧洲的黄金和白银数量之间的比例接近1∶22②，也就是说，进口1盎司黄金就要进口22盎司多点白银。他认为，白银进口到欧洲后又有一部分运往东印度，使得留在欧洲的黄金和白银数量之间的比例降到1∶14或1∶15，大约与它们的价值比例相同。他似乎认为③，这两种金属的价

马根斯认为价值比例应该与数量比例一致。

---

① 在《论一般商业的性质》中第365页，肯提伦认为在中国为1∶10，在日本为1∶8。
② 马根斯书《进一步的说明》第16页所载的准确数字为1∶22.1。
③ 同上书，第17页。

their quantities, and would therefore be as one to twenty-two, were it not for this greater exportation of silver.

<small>but this is absurd.</small>
But the ordinary proportion between the respective values of two commodities is not necessarily the same as that between the quantities of them which are commonly in the market. The price of an ox, reckoned at ten guineas, is about threescore times the price of a lamb, reckoned at 3s. 6d. It would be absurd, however, to infer from thence, that there are commonly in the market threescore lambs for one ox: and it would be just as absurd to infer, because an ounce of gold will commonly purchase from fourteen to fifteen ounces of silver, that there are commonly in the market only fourteen or fifteen ounces of silver for one ounce of gold.

<small>The whole of a cheap commodity is commonly worth more than the whole of a dear one, and this is the case with silver and gold.</small>
The quantity of silver commonly in the market, it is probable, is much greater in proportion to that of gold, than the value of a certain quantity of gold is to that of an equal quantity of silver. The whole quantity of a cheap commodity brought to market, is commonly not only greater, but of greater value, than the whole quantity of a dear one. The whole quantity of bread annually brought to market, is not only greater, but of greater value than the whole quantity of butcher's-meat; the whole quantity of butcher's-meat, than the whole quantity of poultry; and the whole quantity of poultry, than the whole quantity of wild fowl. There are so many more purchasers for the cheap than for the dear commodity, that, not only a greater quantity of it, but a greater value, can commonly be disposed of. The whole quantity, therefore, of the cheap commodity must commonly be greater in proportion to the whole quantity of the dear one, than the value of a certain quantity of the dear one, is to the value of an equal quantity of the cheap one. When we compare the precious metals with one another, silver is a cheap, and gold a dear commodity. We ought naturally to expect, therefore, that there should always be in the market, not only a greater quantity, but a greater value of silver than of gold. Let any man, who has a little of both, compare his own silver with his gold plate, and he will probably find, that, not only the quantity, but the value of the former greatly exceeds that of the latter. Many people, besides, have a good deal of silver who have no gold plate, which, even with those who have it, is generally confined to watch-cases, snuff-boxes, and such like trinkets, of which the whole amount is seldom of great value. In the British coin, indeed, the value of the gold preponderates greatly, but it is not so in that of all countries.

值比例必然与它们的数量比例一致。所以,如果白银没有出口那么多,则它们的价值比例应该是1:22。

但是,两种商品通常的价值比例,并不必须与其在市场上通常的数量比例保持一致。一头牛的价格为10几尼,一头羊的价格为3先令6便士,前者约为后者的60倍。如果由此得出结论说,通常市场上有1头牛就有60头羊,那是荒谬的。如果在市场上以1盎司黄金一般可购买到14到15盎司白银,就由此得出结论说,通常市场上有1盎司黄金就有14到15盎司白银,也同样荒唐可笑。

> 但这是荒谬的。

通常市场上白银与黄金的数量比例,可能比相同数量的黄金与白银的价值比例大得多。在市场上,廉价商品与高价商品相比,不仅总量通常更大,而且总价值也往往更大。每年送入市场的商品来说,面包的总量和总价值都分别依次大于鲜肉、家禽、野禽的总量和总价值。廉价商品的顾客通常比高价商品的顾客更多,以致廉价商品能在市场上售出更多的数量和更大的价值。所以,廉价商品对高价商品的总量比例,通常大于相同数量高价商品对廉价商品的价值比例。就贵金属来说,白银是廉价商品,黄金是高价商品。因此,我们自然而然地可以预期,通常市场上白银的总量和总价值都比黄金大。任何多少拥有一些金银器物的人,只要把自己的银器和金器比较一下,就会发现,银器在数量和价值上都大大超过金器。此外,还有许多人拥有不少银器,却没有金器。即使有一些,也往往只限于表壳、鼻烟盒等诸如此类的小玩意儿,总共也值不了多少钱。诚然,就英国铸币来说,所有金币的价值大于所有银币的价值。但并非其他国家的情况也是这样。在有些国家,其铸币中所有银币的价值差不多与所有金币的

> 所有廉价商品比所有高价商品通常的价值更大,这就是白银和黄金的情况。

In the coin of some countries the value of the two metals is nearly equal. In the Scotch coin, before the union with England, the gold preponderated very little, though it did somewhat,①as it appears by the accounts of the mint. In the coin of many countries the silver preponderates. In France, the largest sums are commonly paid in that metal, and it is there difficult to get more gold than what is necessary to carry about in your pocket. The superior value, however, of the silver plate above that of the gold, which takes place in all countries, will much more than compensate the preponderancy of the gold coin above the silver, which takes place only in some countries.

<small>Gold is nearer its lowest possible price than silver.</small> Though, in one sense of the word, silver always has been, and probably always will be, much cheaper than gold; yet in another sense, gold may, perhaps, in the present state of the Spanish market, be said to be somewhat cheaper than silver. A commodity may be said to be dear or cheap, not only according to the absolute greatness or smallness of its usual price, but according as that price is more or less above the lowest for which it is possible to bring it to market for any considerable time together. This lowest price is that which barely replaces, with a moderate profit, the stock which must be employed in bringing the commodity thither. It is the price which affords nothing to the landlord, of which rent makes not any component part, but which resolves itself altogether into wages and profit. But, in the present state of the Spanish market, gold is certainly somewhat nearer to this lowest price than silver. The tax of the King of Spain upon gold is only onetwentieth part of the standard metal, or five per cent. ; whereas his tax upon silver amounts to one-tenth part of it, or to ten per cent. In these taxes too, it has already been observed, consists the whole rent of the greater part of the gold and silver mines of Spanish America; and that upon gold is still worse paid than that upon silver. The profits of the undertakers of gold mines too, as they more rarely make a fortune, must, in general, be still more moderate than those of the undertakers of silver mines. The price of Spanish gold, therefore, as it affords both less rent and less profit, must, in the Spanish market, be somewhat nearer to the lowest price for which it is possible to bring it thither, than the price of Spanish silver. When all expences

---

① [See Ruddiman's Preface to Anderson's Diplomata, &c. Scotiæ. *Selectus diplomatum et numismatum thesaurus* (quoted above, p. 184), pp. 84, 85; and in the translation, pp. 175, 176.]

价值相等。据造币厂统计,苏格兰在与英格兰合并以前,金币虽然略多于银币,但相差不多①。而其他许多国家的铸币中,占多数的不是金币而是银币。在法国,巨额支付通常都用银币,很难搞到超过随身携带的必要的金币。不过,所有国家的银器价值总是大于其金器价值,这种优势足以补偿某些国家银币对于金币的劣势而有余。

从某种意义上说,白银在过去一直比黄金低廉得多,而且将来恐怕也是这样。但在另一种意义上,目前西班牙市场上的情况,或许可以说黄金比白银略为低廉。说一种商品是昂贵或低廉,不仅可以根据其通常价格的绝对大小,同时也可以根据其价格超过其长期供应市场所可能的最低价格的程度。所谓最低价格,是指仅足以补偿商品投入市场所必需的资本及其适当利润的价格。这种价格,对地主不能提供任何报酬,只可分解为工资和利润而不含地租。在目前的西班牙市场上,黄金肯定比白银多少更接近于这种最低价格。西班牙国王对黄金的课税仅为标准金的1/20,即5%,而对白银的课税则为标准银的1/10,即10%。前面说过,这种赋税包括美洲的西班牙属地大部分金银矿山的全部地租,而且在黄金方面的赋税收入状况还比不上白银方面。经营金矿而发大财的人更少,可见金矿的利润肯定低于银矿的利润。这样,在西班牙市场上,因为黄金的价格只提供较少的地租和利润,所以黄金一定比白银多少更接近于这种最低价格。当把一切费用都计算在内的时候,在西班牙市场上,全部黄金似乎不能像

> 黄金比白银更接近于它可能的最低价格。

---

① 参见鲁迪曼为安德森的《苏格兰古代文书》所写的序言,第84、85页,英译本第175、176页。

are computed, the whole quantity of the one metal, it would seem, cannot, in the Spanish market, be disposed of so advantageously as the whole quantity of the other. The tax, indeed, of the King of Portugal upon the gold of the Brazils, is the same with the ancient tax of the King of Spain upon the silver of Mexico and Peru; or one-fifth part of the standard metal. It may, therefore, be uncertain whether to the general market of Europe the whole mass of American gold comes at a price nearer to the lowest for which it is possible to bring it thither, than the whole mass of American silver.

<small>Diamonds are nearer still.</small>

The price of diamonds and other precious stones may, perhaps, be still nearer to the lowest price at which it is possible to bring them to market, than even the price of gold.

<small>It may be necessary to reduce it still further the tax on silver in Spanish America.</small>

Though it is not very probable, that any part of a tax which is not only imposed upon one of the most proper subjects of taxation, a mere luxury and superfluity, but which affords so very important a revenue, as the tax upon silver, will ever be given up as long as it is possible to pay it; yet the same impossibility of paying it, which in 1736 made it necessary to reduce it from one-fifth to one-tenth, may in time make it necessary to reduce it still further; in the same manner as it made it necessary to reduce the tax upon gold to one-twentieth. That the silver mines of Spanish America, like all other mines, become gradually more expensive in the working, on account of the greater depths at which it is necessary to carry on the works, and of the greater expence of drawing out the water and of supplying them with fresh air at those depths, is acknowledged by every body who has enquired into the state of those mines.

<small>The greater cost of raising silver must lead to an increase of its price, or a reduction of the tax upon it, or both.</small>

These causes, which are equivalent to a growing scarcity of silver (for a commodity may be said to grow scarcer when it becomes more difficult and expensive to collect a certain quantity of it), must, in time, produce one or other of the three following events. The increase of the expence must either, first, be compensated altogether by a proportionable increase in the price of the metal; or, secondly, it must be compensated altogether by a proportionable diminution of the tax upon silver; or, thirdly, it must be compensated partly by the one, and partly by the other of those two expedients. This third event is very possible. As gold rose in its price in proportion to silver, notwithstanding a great diminution of the tax upon gold; so silver might rise in its price in pro. portion to labour and commodities, notwithstanding an equal diminution of the tax upon silver.

Such successive reductionsof the tax, however, though they may not prevent altogether, must certainly retard, more or less, the rise of the value of silver in the European market. In consequence of such reductions, many mines may be wrought which could not be wrought before,

全部白银那样有利地销售出去。诚然,葡萄牙国王对巴西黄金的课税,与以往西班牙国王对墨西哥和秘鲁的白银的课税一样,同为标准金属的1/5。因此,就供应欧洲一般市场来说,美洲的全部黄金是否比其全部白银更接近于可能的最低价格,还不能肯定。

钻石及其他宝石的价格,也许比黄金的价格更接近于可能的最低价格。〔钻石更接近于最低价格。〕

白银不仅是一种奢侈品,是最合适的课税对象之一,而且对白银的课税也是国王的重要收入来源。所以,只要还有征收可能,这种课税就难于放弃。但是,征税困难已于1736年使对白银的课税由1/5降到1/10,也许有一天,同样的原因将使其不得不再次降低,就像对黄金的课税不得不降到1/20那样。与其他矿山一样,美洲西班牙属地的银矿,由于采掘更为深入,由于排出深处的积水以及供应深处以新鲜空气等费用越来越高,开采费用也逐渐增高。这是每一个曾经调查过这些矿山状况的人都承认的。〔可能有必要对美洲西班牙属地的白银进一步降低课税。〕

这些原因,等于增加白银的稀缺性(因为,如果获得某种商品的困难和费用增加,就可以说它越来越稀缺了),必然会产生以下三种结果之一。第一,费用的增加必须通过金属价格成比例提高而取得全部补偿;第二,必须通过对白银的课税成比例减少而取得全部补偿;第三,必须部分地通过提价,部分地通过减税而取得全部补偿。第三种结果是最可能发生的。就像尽管对黄金的课税大减而和白银相比的黄金价格仍然上升一样,尽管对白银的课税同样减少,但和劳动及其他商品相比,白银价格仍然可能上升。〔白银的生产成本增大,必致价格上升或银税降低,或者两同时发生。〕

可是,不断减少对白银的课税,虽然不能完全阻止欧洲市场上白银价值的上升,但肯定总会多少推迟其上升。由于对白银的课税减少,以前因不堪重税而无法开采的矿山,现在可以开采了。

The reduction of the tax in the past makes silver at least 10 per cent. lower than it would otherwise have been. because they could not afford to pay the old tax; and the quantity of silver annually brought to market must always be somewhat greater, and, therefore, the value of any given quantity somewhat less, than it otherwise would have been. In consequence of the reduction in 1736, the value of silver in the European market, though it may not at this day be lower than before that reduction, is, probably, at least ten per cent. lower than it would have been, had the Court of Spain continued to exact the old tax.

Silver has probably risen somewhat in the present century. That, notwithstanding this reduction, the value of silver has, during the course of the present century, begun to rise somewhat in the European market, the facts and arguments which have been alleged above, dispose me to believe, or more properly to suspect and conjecture; for the best opinion which I can form upon this subject scarce, perhaps, deserves the name of belief. The rise, indeed, supposing there has been any, has hitherto been so very small, that after all that has been said, it may, perhaps, appear to many people uncertain, not only whether this event has actually taken place; but whether the contrary may not have taken place, or whether the value of silver may not still continue to fall in the European market.

The annual consumption must at length equal the annual importation, It must be observed, however, that whatever may be the supposed annual importation of gold and silver, there must be a certain period, at which the annual consumption of those metals will be equal to that annual importation. Their consumption must increase as their mass increases, or rather in a much greater proportion. As their mass increases, their value diminishes. They are more used, and less cared for, and their consumption consequently increases in a greater proportion than their mass. After a certain period, therefore, the annual consumption of those metals must, in this manner, become equal to their annual importation, provided that importation is not continually increasing; which, in the present times, is not supposed to be the case.

and will then accommodate itself to changes in the importation. If, when the annual consumption has become equal to the annual importation, the annual importation should gradually diminish, the annual consumption may, for some time, exceed the annual importation. The mass of those metals may gradually and insensibly diminish, and their value gradually and insensibly rise, till the annual importation becoming again stationary, the annual consumption will gradually and insensibly accommodate itself to what that annual importation can maintain.

这样,每年投入市场的白银数量必然要有所增加,而一定数量白银的价值也必然要有所降低。1736年西班牙国王减少对白银的课税,使得欧洲市场上的白银价值,虽然比以往没有实际降低,但与白银的课税没有减少时比较,可能至少要低10%。

<small>以往的课税使白银价比不时减低至少10%。</small>

上述事实和讨论使我相信,或者更恰当地说,使我揣测,尽管有了减税,白银价值却在本世纪的欧洲市场上有所上升。之所以说揣测,是因为我就这个问题所能形成的最好意见也许都不能算作信念。的确,假定白银价值上升了一些,其上升程度到目前为止也必然很有限。所以,尽管上面说了很多,也许仍然还有许多人不能肯定,究竟白银价值是否真正上升过,是否发生过相反的现象,即白银价值在欧洲市场上是否仍旧在下降。

<small>白银价值在本世纪也许略有上升。</small>

不过,必须注意以下的讨论。不管假定每年黄金和白银的进口量是多少,必定有一个时期,其年消费量等于其年进口量。黄金和白银的消费量必然随着它们数量的增加而增加,有时消费量增加的比例还要更大一些。黄金和白银的价值必然因它们数量的增加而减少。人们对黄金和白银使用得越多,就越不那么爱惜,因此它们的消费量比其数量增加得更多。所以,经过一定时期后,在进口量不继续增加的条件下,这些金属的每年消费量,必然与其每年进口量趋于一致。可是,目前的进口量仍然在继续增加。

<small>每年的消费量必然终等于每年的进口量。</small>

在黄金和白银每年消费量等于其每年进口量时,如果每年进口量逐渐减少,则可能有一段时间每年消费量会超过每年进口量。于是,这些金属的数量可能逐渐不知不觉地减少,而价值逐渐不知不觉地上升,一直到每年进口量不增不减时为止。这时候,每年消费量将逐渐不知不觉地适应每年进口量所能维持的数额。

<small>然后消量与进口量的变化自行适应。</small>

Grounds of the Suspicion that the Value of Silver still continues to decrease

<small>Gold and silver are supposed to be still falling because they are increasing in quantity and some sorts of rude produce are rising.</small>   The increase of the wealth of Europe, and the popular notion that, as the quantity of the precious metals naturally increases with the increase of wealth, so their value diminishes as their quantity increases, may, perhaps, dispose many people to believe that their value still continues to fall in the European market; and the still gradually increasing price of many parts of the rude produce of land may confirm them still further in this opinion.

<small>It has already been shown that the increase of the metals need not diminish their value;</small>   That that increase in the quantity of the precious metals, which arises in any country from the increase of wealth, has no tendency to diminish their value, I have endeavoured to show already, Gold and silver naturally resort to a rich country, for the same reason that all sorts of luxuries and curiosities resort to it; not because they are cheaper there than in poorer countries, but because they are dearer, or because a better price is given for them. It is the superiority of price which attracts them, and as soon as that superiority ceases, they necessarily cease to go thither.

<small>and the rise of cattle, etc., is due to a rise in their real price, not to a fall of silver.</small>   If you except corn and such other vegetables as are raised altogether by human industry, that all other sorts of rude produce, cattle, poultry, game of all kinds, the useful fossils and minerals of the earth, &c. naturally grow dearer as the society advances in wealth and improvement, I have endeavoured to show already. Though such commodities, therefore, come to exchange for a greater quantity of silver than before, it will not from thence follow that silver has become really cheaper, or will purchase less labour than before, but that such commodities have become really dearer, or will purchase more labour than before. It is not their nominal price only, but their real price which rises in the progress of improvement. The rise of their nominal price is the effect, not of any degradation of the value of silver, but of the rise in their real price.

怀疑白银价值仍在继续下降的根据

欧洲财富的增加,以及认为由于贵金属的数量随财富增加而自然增加、其价值也随其数量增加而自然减少的流行的观念,可能使许多人相信,欧洲市场上黄金和白银的价值仍在继续下降。而许多土地原生产物的价格还在逐渐上升的事实,更使他们坚持这种看法。_{因为某些原生产物数量的增加,而认为金和银的价值仍在下降。}

我已经努力表明,一个国家财富的增加而使贵金属的数量增加,并没有降低其价值的倾向。所有的奢侈品和珍奇品都流向富裕的国家,同样的原因,金银也自然流向富裕的国家。这不是因为这些物品在富国比在穷国低廉,而是因为它们在富国比在贫国昂贵,或者说在富国能卖得更好的价钱。价格的优越性吸引了这些物品。一旦价格的优越性消失,这些物品就不会进入那里的市场。_{已经说明,金属数量增加一定不会降低其价值;}

我已经努力表明,如果除去谷物及其他全靠人类劳动种植的植物,那么,所有的原生产物,如牲畜、家禽、各种猎物以及地下有用的化石和矿物等,都随社会的财富增长和技术改进而自然变得越来越贵。所以,尽管这些商品能比以前交换到更多白银,仍不能由此断定白银真正变得便宜了,或者说白银能购买的劳动量比以前少了。只能由此断定的是,这些商品真正变得昂贵了,或者说它们能购买的劳动量比以前多了。随着社会的进步,这些商品的名义价格和实际价格都上升了。名义价格的上升,不是白银价值下降的结果,而是这些商品自身实际价格上升的结果。_{牲畜等价格的上升,不是白银价值的下降,而是由它们实际价格上升。}

Different Effects of the Progress of Improvement upon three different Sorts of rude Produce

<small>The real price of three sorts of rude produce rises in the progress of improvement:</small>　These different sorts of rude produce may be divided into three classes. The first comprehends those which it is scarce in the power of human industry to multiply at all. The second, those which it can multiply in proportion to the demand. The third, those in which the efficacy of industry is either limited or uncertain. In the progress of wealth and improvement, the real price of the first may rise to any degree of extravagance, and seems not to be limited by any certain boundary. That of the second, though it may rise greatly, has, however, a certain boundary beyond which it cannot well pass for any considerable time together. That of the third, though its natural tendency is to rise in the progress of improvement, yet in the same degree of improvement it may sometimes happen even to fall, sometimes to continue the same, and sometimes to rise more or less, according as different accidents render the efforts of human industry, in multiplying this sort of rude produce, more or less successful.

First Sort

<small>(1) The sort which cannot be multiplied by human industry, such as game.</small>　The first sort of rude produce of which the price rises in the progress of improvement, is that which it is scarce in the power of human industry to multiply at all. It consists in those things which nature produces only in certain quantities, and which being of a very perishable nature, it is impossible to accumulate together the produce of many different seasons. Such are the greater part of rare and singular birds and fishes, many different sorts of game, almost all wild-fowl, all birds of passage in particular, as well as many other things. When wealth and the luxury which accompanies it increase, the demand for these is likely to increase with them, and no effort of human industry may be able to increase the supply much beyond what it was before this increase of the demand. The quantity of such commodities, therefore, remaining the same, or nearly the same, while the competition to purchase them is continually increasing, their price may rise to any degree of extravagance, and seems not to be limited by any certain boundary. If woodcocks should become

社会进步对三种原生产物的不同影响

原生产物可以分为三类。第一类是人类劳动的力量根本无法使之增加的产物;第二类是人类劳动的力量可以使之随着需求的增加而增加的产物;第三类是人类劳动的力量可以使之增加但效果有限或不确定的产物。第一类产物的实际价格可随财富增长和技术改进而上升到非常昂贵的程度,似乎不受任何限制。第二类产物的实际价格,虽然有时可以大大上升,但有一定的限度,不可能长期超越这个限度。第三类产物的实际价格,虽然随着社会进步而有自然上升的趋势,但在相同进步程度下,有时甚至下降,有时保持不变,有时或多或少地有所上升,使人类增加这类产物的劳动努力取得成功的偶然性增大。

> 原生产物三类价格在社会进步过程中均上升:

第一类

随着社会进步而价格提高的第一类原生产物,是人类劳动的力量根本无法使之增加的产物。它们既不能使产量超过自然生产的限量,又非常容易腐烂,所以不可能把各季节生产的这类产物全部贮积起来。大部分稀有特异的鸟类和鱼类,许多种猎物,几乎所有的野禽,尤其是各种候鸟,以及许多其他东西,都属于这类产物。随着财富的增加以及随之而发生的奢侈的增进,对这类产物的需求很可能会增加,但人类的努力却不可能使其供给大量增加。因此,这些商品的数量保持不变或基本不变,其价格就会随着购买者竞争的加剧而无限制地上升。例如,山鹬即使成为时

> (1)人类劳动使不能增加的原生产物,如猎物。

so fashionable as to sell for twenty guineas a-piece, no effort of human industry could increase the number of those brought to market, much beyond what it is at present. The high price paid by the Romans, in the time of their greatest grandeur, for rare birds and fishes, may in this manner easily be accounted for. These prices were not the effects of the low value of silver in those times, but of the high value of such rarities and curiosities as human industry could not multiply at pleasure. The real value of silver was higher at Rome, for some time before and after the fall of the republic, than it is through the greater part of Europe at present. Three sestertii, equal to about sixpence sterling, was the price which the republic paid for the modius or peck of the tithe wheat of Sicily. This price, however, was probably below the average market price, the obligation to deliver their wheat at this rate being considered as a tax upon the Sicilian farmers. When the Romans, therefore, had occasion to order more corn than the tithe of wheat amounted to, they were bound by capitulation to pay for the surplus at the rate of four sestertii, or eight-pence sterling, the peek; and this had probably been reckoned the moderate and reasonable, that is, the ordinary or average contract price of those times; it is equal to about one-and-twenty shillings the quarter. Eight-and-twenty shillings the quarter was, before the late years of scarcity, the ordinary contract price of English wheat, which in quality is inferior to the Sicilian, and generally sells for a lower price in the European market. The value of silver, therefore, in those ancient times, must have been to its value in the present, as three to four inversely; that is, three ounces of silver would then have purchased the same quantity of labour and commodities which four ounces will do at present. When we read in Pliny, therefore, that Seius[1] bought a white nightingale, as a present for the empress Agrippina, at the price of six thousand sestertii, equal to about fifty pounds of our present money; and that Asinius Celer[2] purchased a surmullet at the price of eight thousand sestertii, equal to about sixty-six pounds thirteen shillings and fourpence of our present money; the extravagance of those prices, how much soever it may surprise us, is apt, notwithstanding, to appear to us about one-third less than it really was. Their real price, the quantity of labour and

---

[1] Lib. x. c. 29.
[2] Lib. ix. c. 17.

尚品,一只可卖到二十几尼,人类也不能由于勤劳而使上市的山鹬数目增加到大大超过现在的情况。这正可用来解释,罗马人在鼎盛时期为何对珍贵的鱼类和鸟类支付高价。这种高价,的确不是因为当时白银价值低落,而是人类不能随意增加的这些珍品本身价值上升的结果。在罗马共和国没落前后一段时间,白银的实际价值比目前欧洲大部分地区都高。罗马共和国支付西西里所缴纳什一税的小麦的价格,每1莫迪斯或1配克付价3塞斯特斯,约合英币6便士。但是,这价格可能要低于平均市场价格,因为西西里农场主认为按这价格交售他们的小麦是在尽纳税义务。所以,当罗马人需要从西西里进口什一税以外的谷物时,他们就必须按照契约对于超出量每配克付给4塞斯特斯,约合英币8便士。这在当时被视为适度而合理的价格,也就是一般或平均的契约价格,换算起来,每夸特约合21先令。英国小麦,品质上比西西里小麦差,在欧洲市场上的售价也通常比西西里小麦低。但在最近歉收年份以前,英国小麦的一般契约价格却为每夸特28先令。因此,白银价值在古代与现在相比,一定为3∶4的反比,即当时的3盎司白银与现在的4盎司白银能购得相同数量的劳动或商品。历史学家普林尼记载,塞伊阿斯①以6000塞斯特斯(合现今英币50镑)购买一只白夜莺献给女王阿格利皮纳,阿西尼阿斯·塞纳②以8000塞斯特斯(合现今英币66镑13先令4便士)购买一尾红鱼。这些奇贵的价格,尽管让我们惊讶不已,但在我们看来,仍然比其实际价格约低1/3。这两样东西的实际价格,即它

---

① 《自然史》,第10编,第29章。
② 《自然史》,第9编,第17章。

subsistence which was given away for them, was about one-third more than their nominal price is apt to express to us in the present times. Seius gave for the nightingale the command of a quantity of labour and subsistence equal to what 66*l*. 13*s*. 4*d*. would purchase in the present times; and Asinius Celer gave for the surmullet the command of a quantity equal to what 88*l*. 17*s*. 9*d*. $\frac{1}{3}$, would purchase. What occasioned the extravagance of those high prices was, not so much the abundance of silver, as the abundance of labour and subsistence, of which those Romans had the disposal, beyond what was necessary for their own use. The quantity of silver, of which they had the disposal, was a good deal less than what the command of the same quantity of labour and subsistence would have procured to them in the present times.

Second sort

(2) The sort which can be multiplied at will, e. g. cattle, poultry.

The second sort of rude produce of which the price rises in the progress of improvement, is that which human industry can multiply in proportion to the demand. It consists in those useful plants and animals, which, in uncultivated countries, nature produces with such profuse abundance, that they are of little or no value, and which, as cultivation advances, are therefore forced to give place to some more profitable produce. During a long period in the progress of improvement, the quantity of these is continually diminishing, while at the same time the demand for them is continually increasing. Their real value, therefore, the real quantity of labour which they will purchase or command, gradually rises, till at last it gets so high as to render them as profitable a produce as any thing else which human industry can raise upon the most fertile and best cultivated land. When it has got so high it cannot well go higher. If it did, more land and more industry would soon be employed to increase their quantity.

When the price of cattle, for example, rises so high that it is as profitable to cultivate land in order to raise food for them, as in order to raise food for man, it cannot well go higher. If it did,

们所能交换到的劳动和生活必需品的数量,比其名义价格在现时给我们表示的数量约多1/3。这就是说,就劳动和生活必需品的支配数量来说,塞伊阿斯为一只白夜莺而付出的等于现今66镑13先令4便士才能购买到的,阿西尼阿斯·塞纳为一尾红鱼而付出的等于现今88镑17先令91/3便士才能购买到的。这种价格之所以奇贵,不是因为白银数量非常充裕,而是因为罗马人可以支配的劳动和生活必需品非常充裕,超过了必要量。当时罗马人所拥有的白银数量,比相同劳动量和生活必需品量在当前所能交换到的白银数量要少得多。

第二类

随着社会进步而价格上升的第二类原生产物,是人类劳动可使之随需求的增加而增加的产物。这就是那些有用的动植物。当土地没有开垦时,自然界的生产物非常多,以致价值很小或根本没有价值。随着耕种的发展,它们就不得不让位给其他对人类更为有利的产物。在社会日益进步的长期过程中,这类产物的数量不断减少,而同时对它们的需求则继续增加。因此,其实际价值,即它们所能购买或支配的实际劳动量,逐渐上升,直到如此高度,以致与其他由人类劳动在最肥沃、耕种得最好的土地上产出的任何物品相比,也不分上下。但是,一旦达到这种高度,其实际价值就不能再增加了。如果超过了这个限度,那么不久就会有更多土地和劳动投入到这方面来进行生产。

例如,牲畜价格的上升程度,如果高到开垦土地用以生产牲畜饲料和用以生产人类食物一样有利可图时,就再也不能上升

(2)可以随意增加的原生产物,如牲畜、家禽。

<small>When It becomes profitable to cultivate land to yield food for cattle, the price of cattle cannot go higher.</small> more corn land would soon be turned into pasture. The extension of tillage, by diminishing the quantity of wild pasture, diminishes the quantity of butcher's-meat which the country naturally produces without labour or cultivation, and by increasing the number of those who have either corn, or, what comes to the same thing, the price of corn, to give in exchange for it, increases the demand. The price of butcher's-meat, therefore, and consequently of cattle, must gradually rise till it gets so high, that it becomes as profitable to employ the most fertile and best cultivated lands in raising food for them as in raising corn. But it must always be late in the progress of improvement before tillage can be so far extended as to raise the price of cattle to this height; and till it has got to this height, if the country is advancing at all, their price must be continually rising. There are, perhaps, some parts of Europe in which the price of cattle has not yet got to this height. It had not got to this height in any part of Scotland before the union. Had the Scotch cattle been always confined to the market of Scotland, in a country in which the quantity of land, which can be applied to no other purpose but the feeding of cattle, is so great in proportion to what can be applied to other purposes, it is scarce possible, perhaps, that their price could ever have risen so high as to render it profitable to cultivate land for the sake of feeding them. In England, the price of cattle, it has already been observed, seems, in the neighbourhood of London, to have got to this height about the beginning of the last century; but it was much later probably before it got to it through the greater part of the remoter counties; in some of which, perhaps, it may scarce yet have got to it. Of all the different substances, however, which compose this second sort of rude produce, cattle is, perhaps, that of which the price, in the progress of improvement, first rises to this height.

<small>It must go to this height in order to secure complete cultivation.</small> Till the price of cattle, indeed, has got to this height, it seems scarce possible that the greater part, even of those lands which are capable of the highest cultivation, can be completely cultivated. In all farms too distant from any town to carry manure from it, that is, in the far greater part of those of every extensive country, the quantity of well-cultivated land must be in proportion to the quantity of manure which the farm itself produces; and this again must be in proportion to the stock of cattle which are maintained upon it. The land is manured either by pasturing the cattle

第一篇 第十一章

了。如果再上升,不久就会有更多的谷田改成牧场。如果通过减少野生牧草的数量来扩张耕地,一方面会减少无需劳动培育或耕种而自然生产的鲜肉数量,另一方面因为拥有可以交换鲜肉的谷物或谷物替代品(两者具有相同意义)的人数增加了,进而导致对鲜肉需求的增加。于是,鲜肉价格,从而牲畜价格必然逐渐上升,直到如此高度,以致以最肥沃、耕种最好的土地种植牧草和生产谷物一样有利。但一定要到社会进步的后期,耕种才会如此扩大,使牲畜价格上升到这种程度。在没有达到这种高度以前,如果国家还在不断进步,牲畜价格一定会继续上升。现今的欧洲可能还有一些地区的牲畜价格尚未上升到这个高度。苏格兰在与英格兰合并以前,没有一个地方达到这个高度。苏格兰的土地,适宜畜牧的远远多于适宜其他用途的。所以,如果苏格兰的牲畜只局限于在苏格兰市场销售,则牲畜价格也许不会达到如此高度,以致耕种土地来种植牧草都变得有利可图。前面说过,就英格兰的牲畜价格来说,虽然伦敦附近的地方似乎在上世纪初就达到了这种高度,但大部分偏远地方可能很久以后才达到这种高度,而且也许还有少数地方至今尚未达到这种高度。但是,在第二类原生产物中,牲畜可能是其价格首先随社会进步而上升到这种高度的。

当耕地为提草有图,牲畜价格不上升时,畜牧得可供变利就再了。

在牲畜价格尚未达到这种高度之前,即使是适于深耕细作的土地,也一定有大部分不能得到完全耕种。土地辽阔的国家常有大部分农村土地远离城镇,以致难以把城镇的肥料运往农村。因此,耕种得好的土地数量一定和农自身所能生产的肥料量成比例,而后者又一定和农地所能维持的牲畜数量成比例。土地得以施肥的方式,或者是通过在土地上放牧牲畜得到粪肥,或者是通

必须达到这种高度,才能获得完全耕种。

upon it, or by feeding them in the stable, and from thence carrying out their dung to it. But unless the price of the cattle be sufficient to pay both the rent and profit of cultivated land, the farmer cannot afford to pasture them upon it; and he can still less afford to feed them in the stable. It is with the produce of improved and cultivated land only, that cattle can be fed in the stable; because to collect the scanty and scattered produce of waste and unimproved lands would require too much labour and be too expensive. If the price of the cattle, therefore, is not sufficient to pay for the produce of improved and cultivated land, when they are allowed to pasture it, that price will be still less sufficient to pay for that produce when it must be collected with a good deal of additional labour, and brought into the stable to them. In these circumstances, therefore, no more cattle can, with profit, be fed in the stable than what are necessary for tillage. But these can never afford manure enough for keeping constantly in good condition, all the lands which they are capable of cultivating. What they afford being insufficient for the whole farm, will naturally be reserved for the lands to which it can be most advantageously or conveniently applied; the most fertile, or those, perhaps, in the neighbourhood of the farm-yard. These, therefore, will be kept constantly in good condition and fit for tillage. The rest will, the greater part of them, be allowed to lie waste, producing scarce any thing but some miserable pasture, just sufficient to keep alive a few straggling, half-starved cattle; the farm, though much under-stocked in proportion to what would be necessary for its complete cultivation, being very frequently overstocked in proportion to its actual produce. A portion of this waste land, however, after having been pastured in this wretched manner for six or seven years together, may be ploughed up, when it will yield, perhaps, a poor crop or two of bad oats, or of some other coarse grain, and then, being entirely exhausted, it must be rested and pastured again as before, and another portion ploughed up to be in the same manner exhausted and rested again in its turn. Such accordingly was the general system of management all over the low country of Scotland before the union. The lands which were kept constantly well manured and in good condition, seldom exceeded a third or a fourth part of the whole farm, and sometimes did not amount to a fifth or a sixth part of it. The rest were never manured, but a certain portion of them was in its turn, notwithstanding, regularly

过在棚厩里饲养牲畜而后将其粪肥运到地里。但是,如果牲畜价格不够支付耕地的地租和利润,农场主就无力在土地上牧养牲畜,更无力搭棚设厩饲养牲畜。只有靠已经改良和耕种过的土地上的产物才能在棚厩里饲养牲畜,因为从荒芜和未经过改良的土地上割采稀少分散的草料,需要耗费非常多的劳动和费用。因此,如果在已经改良和耕种过的土地上牧养牲畜,而牲畜价格还不足以偿付该地生产草料的费用,那么,在棚厩里饲养牲畜时,草料的割采搬运要增加大量的劳动和费用,牲畜价格就更不够偿付生产草料的费用了。在这种情况下,在棚厩里饲养耕种所必需的牲畜还有点可行性,但要是再多养就无利可图了。可是,如果只饲养耕种所必需的牲畜,则它们提供的肥料又绝对不可能使全部可耕地保持良好状态。由于不够供给全部农地,肥料自然会被施用于最有利可图、最便于耕种的土地,即最肥沃而位于农家庭院附近的土地。结果,只有这一部分土地通常保持良好状态,而其余大部分土地则任其荒芜,最多只能生长些许可怜的小草,也仅能维持少数牲畜半饥半饱的生存。牲畜的数量,虽然与土地完全耕种所必需的数量相比还太少,但与土地实际所产的草料相比却往往又过多。一部分这样的荒芜地,在连续放牧六七年后,可能又重新耕种,或许也能产出一两季粗劣的燕麦或其他粗粮,以后则地力耗竭,必须再次像以前一样休耕放牧。于是,又转而耕种其他部分的土地,直到它们也同样地力耗竭,重新休耕。在与英格兰合并以前,苏格兰低地一带的土地大都采取这种经营方式。当时能够不断施肥和维持良好状态的土地,常常只有全部农地的 1/3 或 1/4,有时甚至不到 1/5 或 1/6。其余的土地则都不施肥,尽管其中还有一部分在依次轮流地耕种和休耕。所以,按照这种

cultivated and exhausted. Under this system of management, it is evident, even that part of the lands of Scotland which is capable of good cultivation, could produce but little in comparison of what it may be capable of producing. But how disadvantageous soever this system may appear, yet before the union the low price of cattle seems to have rendered it almost unavoidable. If, notwithstanding a great rise in their price, it still continues to prevail through a considerable part of the country, it is owing, in many places, no doubt, to ignorance and attachment to old customs, but in most places to the unavoidable obstructions which the natural course of things opposes to the immediate or speedy establishment of a better system: first, to the poverty of the tenants, to their not having yet had time to acquire a stock of cattle sufficient to cultivate their lands more completely, the same rise of price which would render it advantageous for them to maintain a greater stock, rendering it more difficult for them to acquire it; and, secondly, to their not having yet had time to put their lands in condition to maintain this greater stock properly, supposing they were capable of acquiring it. The increase of stock and the improvement of land are two events which must go hand in hand, and of which the one can nowhere much out-run the other. Without some increase of stock, there can be scarce any improvement of land, but there can be no considerable increase of stock but in consequence of a considerable improvement of land; because otherwise the land could not maintain it. These natural obstructions to the establishment of a better system, cannot be removed but by a long course of frugality and industry; and half a century or a century more, perhaps, must pass away before the old system, which is wearing out gradually, can be completely abolished through all the different parts of the country. Of all the commercial advantages, however, which Scotland has derived from the union with England, this rise in the price of cattle is, perhaps, the greatest. It has not only raised the value of all highland estates, but it has, perhaps, been the principal cause of the improvement of the low country.

<small>Consequently new colonies are poorly cultivated.</small> In all new colonies the great quantity of waste land, which can for many years be applied to no other purpose but the feeding of cattle, soon renders them extremely abundant, and in every thing great cheapness is the necessary consequence of great abundance. Though all the cattle of the European colonies in America were originally carried from Europe, they soon multiplied so much there, and became of so little value, that even horses were allowed to run wild in the woods

经营方式,在苏格兰,即使是本可进行良好耕种的土地,其产量与其完全可能达到的产量相比也要低得多。尽管这种经营方式很不利,但苏格兰在合并以前,因牲畜价格的低廉而几乎不得不采取这种经营方式。牲畜价格大大上升后,这种经营方式依然在苏格兰相当多的地区流行,那是因为许多地方的人民既愚昧且又循蹈旧习,而且大多数地方又存在反对迅速建立良好制度的不可避免的自然障碍。这些障碍可以大致分为两类:第一,由于租地人贫困以及还没有足够时间来获得足以充分耕种其土地的牲畜,所以,牲畜价格的上升,即既使他们饲养更多牲畜变得有利可图,同时也使他们难于获得更多牲畜;第二,由于租地人还没有时间去精心整治土地,即使有能力获得牲畜,他们也难以使土地能恰当地养活更多牲畜。总之,牲畜增加和土地改良这两件事情,必须同时进行,不能在时间顺序上相差太远。没有牲畜的增加,土地也无法改良;而土地没有大为改良,牲畜也不会显著增加,否则土地就不能维持大量增加的牲畜。只有经过长期的节约和勤劳,这些自然障碍才能铲除。或许必须经过半个世纪或一个世纪的时间,逐渐衰落的旧的经营方式才能在全国各地彻底废止。苏格兰在与英格兰合并所得到的一切商业利益中,可能以牲畜价格上升为最大好处。牲畜价格的上升,不但提高了苏格兰高地地产的价值,同时或许也成为其低地改进的主要原因。

在所有的新殖民地,大量荒芜的土地在多年内除饲养牲畜外不能做其他用途,因而牲畜不久就大量繁殖起来。对任何事物来说,极多则必然极其廉价。欧洲人的美洲殖民地上的一切牲畜,最初都是从欧洲运来,但很快就大量繁殖,以致价值变得极低,甚至马在森林里游荡也无人追寻。这些殖民地在开始建立之后,要

因此,新殖民地的耕种状况很差,

without any owner thinking it worth while to claim them. It must be a long time after the first establishment of such colonies, before it can become profitable to feed cattle upon the produce of cultivated land. The same causes, therefore, the want of manure, and the disproportion between the stock employed in cultivation, and the land which it is destined to cultivate, are likely to introduce there a system of husbandry not unlike that which still continues to take place in so many parts of Scotland. Mr. Kalm, the Swedish traveller, when he gives an account of the husbandry of some of the English colonies in North America, as he found it in 1749, observes, accordingly, that he can with difficulty discover there the character of the English nation, so well skilled in all the different branches of agriculture. They make scarce any manure for their corn fields, he says; but when one piece of ground has been exhausted by continual cropping, they clear and cultivate another piece of fresh land; and when that is exhausted, proceed to a third. Their cattle are allowed to wander through the woods and other uncultivated grounds, where they are half-starved; having long ago extirpated almost all the annual grasses by cropping them too early in the spring, before they had time to form their flowers, or to shed their seeds. [1]The annual grasses were, it seems, the best natural grasses in that part of North America; and when the Europeans first settled there, they used to grow very thick, and to rise three or four feet high. A piece of ground which, when he wrote, could not maintain one cow, would in former times, he was assured, have maintained four, each of which would have given four times the quantity of milk which that one was capable of giving. The poorness of the pasture had, in his opinion, occasioned the degradation of their cattle, which degenerated sensibly from one generation to another. They were probably not unlike that stunted breed which was common all over Scotland thirty or forty years ago, and which is now so much mended through the greater part of the low

---

[1] *Kalm's Travels*, vol. i. pp. 343, 344. [*Travels into North America, containing its natural history and a circumstantial account of its Plantations and Agriculture in general, with the civil, ecclesiastical and commercial state of the country, the manners of the inhabitants and several curious and important remarks on various subjects*, by Peter Kalm, Professor of Economy in the University of Aobo, in Swedish Finland, and member of the S. Royal Academy of Sciences. Translated by John Reinhold Forster, F. A. S, 3 vols. , 1770.]

使耕种土地以饲养牲畜变得有利可图,必须经过很长的时间才能办到。因此,同样的原因,肥料缺乏,以及用于耕种的投入品与用于耕种的土地不成比例,可能会导致那里采用苏格兰许多地区仍在继续实行的那种耕种方式。在叙述他于 1749 年在北美一些英国殖民地所看到的农业状况时,瑞典旅行家卡尔姆先生说,那里很难发现英格兰民族的特性,因为英格兰民族对于农业各个方面的事情都很娴熟。他又说,当地人很少给自己的谷田施肥,只是当一块地因连续收获而地力耗尽后就开垦、耕种另一块新地,而且到这块地又耗尽地力后再开辟第三块地。他们听任自己的牲畜在森林和荒地里游荡,听任其半饥半饱。每年生长的青草,由于在春天的时候就早早割采,往往还来不及开花或散布种子,就消灭殆尽①。牲畜因此常陷于半饥饿状态中。这种年生青草应该是北美地区最好的天然牧草。欧洲人在那里开始定居的时候,这种青草常常长得又密又高,而且往往高达三四英尺。卡尔姆先生明确指出,在他写这部游记时不能养活一头母牛的一块地,以前肯定可以养活四头母牛,而且,以前每头母牛产出的牛奶能够达到现在每头母牛四倍的水平。他认为,牧草缺乏是那里的牲畜之所以一代代日益退化的原因。这些牲畜或许很像三四十年前苏格兰各地所常见的那种矮小牪畜。那种矮小牪畜如今在苏格兰低地大部分地区已经得到很大的改良。这种改良,与其说是由于

---

① 《卡尔姆旅行记》,第 1 卷,第 343、344 页。该书全称为《北美旅行记:包括,其自然史、造林业和一般农业的详尽说明,该国民政、宗教、商业,居民习俗,一些关于若干问题的奇异而重要的说明》,作者为彼德·卡尔姆,瑞典属芬兰奥博大学经济学教授,皇家科学院院士。翻译者为约翰·莱因霍尔德·福斯特,二卷集,1770 年版。

country, not so much by a change of the breed, though that expedient has been employed in some places, as by a more plentiful method of feeding them.

<small>Cattle are the first of this second sort of rude produce to bring in the price necessary to secure cultivation,</small> Though it is late, therefore, in the progress of improvement before cattle can bring such a price as to render it profitable to cultivate land for the sake of feeding them; yet of all the different parts which compose this second sort of rude produce, they are perhaps the first which bring this price; because till they bring it, it seems impossible that improvement can be brought near even to that degree of perfection to which it has arrived in many parts of Europe.

<small>and venison is the last;</small> As cattle are among the first, so perhaps venison is among the last parts of this sort of rude produce which bring this price. The price of venison in Great Britain, how extravagant soever it may appear, is not near sufficient to compensate the expence of a deer park, as is well known to all those who have had any experience in the feeding of deer. If it was otherwise, the feeding of deer would soon become an article of common farming; in the same manner as the feeding of those small birds called Turdi was among the ancient Romans. Varro and Columella assure us that it was a most profitable article. ①The fattening of ortolans, birds of passage which arrive lean in the country, is said to be so in some parts of France. If venison continues in fashion, and the wealth and luxury of Great Britain increase as they have done for some time past, its price may very probably rise still higher than it is at present.

<small>other things are intermediate. such as poultry.</small> Between that period in the progress of improvement which brings to its height the price of so necessary an article as cattle, and that which brings to it the price of such a superfluity as venison, there is a very long interval, in the course of which many other sorts of rude produce gradually arrive at their highest price, some sooner and some later, according to different circumstances.

<small>Such as poultry,</small> Thus in every farm the offals of the barn and stables will maintain

---

① [Varro, *De re rustica*, iii. , 2, and Columella, *De re rustica*, viii. , 10, *ad fin.* , where Varro is quoted.]

改变了畜种,虽然有些地方曾经使用过这种方法,不如说是由于有了更充足的饲料。

因此,虽然牲畜价格,要到耕种状况改良的后期,才能上升到使耕种土地以饲养牲畜有利可图,但在这第二类原生产物中,或许只有牲畜才能首先达到这种价格,因为如果牲畜价格没有达到这个水平,则耕种状况改良的程度似乎也不可能接近欧洲许多地方如今已有的水平。牲畜是第二类原生产物中首先达到必要价格的产物,

第二类原生产物中,牲畜最先达到这种价格,而鹿肉或许是最后一批达到这种价格。有养鹿经验的人都知道,大不列颠的鹿肉价格,不管看起来有多么高,却实际上还不够补偿鹿园的开支。如果不是这样的话,养鹿不久就会成为普通农家都可以做的事情,就像古代罗马人饲养特蒂(Turdi)那种小鸟一样。瓦罗(Varro)和科卢梅拉(Columella)告诉我们,饲养特蒂极为有利可图①。据说,蒿雀这种候鸟飞到法国时很瘦弱,有些法国人把它们养肥就非常有利可图。因此,如果鹿肉仍然是流行食品,而大不列颠的财富与奢侈又像过去那样增长,则将来的鹿肉价格可能比现在还要高。鹿肉最后达到高价;

在改良进步的过程中,从牲畜这种必需品的价格上升到极限,到鹿肉这种奢侈品的价格上升到极限,两者之间有很长的时间跨度。在这个过程中,许多其他种类的原生产物,依据其具体情况或快或慢地逐渐达到其最高价格。其他产物也在这个过程中,

这样一来,每一个农场的谷仓和棚厩中的废料都能养活一定例如家禽,

---

① 瓦罗:《论乡间事》,第三编,第 2 章;科卢梅拉:《论乡间事》,第八编,第 10 章,引用了瓦罗的话。

a certain number of poultry. These, as they are fed with what would otherwise be lost, are a mere save-all; and as they cost the farmer scarce any thing, so he can afford to sell them for very little. Almost all that he gets is pure gain, and their price can scarce be so low as to discourage him from feeding this number. But in countries ill cultivated, and, therefore, but thinly inhabited, the poultry, which are thus raised without expence, are often fully sufficient to supply the whole demand. In this state of things, therefore, they are often as cheap as butcher's-meat, or any other sort of animal food. But the whole quantity of poultry, which the farm in this manner produces without expence, must always be much smaller than the whole quantity of butcher's-meat which is reared upon it; and in times of wealth and luxury what is rare, with only nearly equal merit, is always preferred to what is common. As wealth and luxury increase, therefore, in consequence of improvement and cultivation, the price of poultry gradually rises above that of butcher's-meat, till at last it gets so high that it becomes profitable to cultivate land for the sake of feeding them. When it has got to this height, it cannot well go higher. If it did, more land would soon be turned to this purpose. In several provinces of France, the feeding of poultry is considered as a very important article in rural Economy, and sufficiently profitable to encourage the farmer to raise a considerable quantity of Indian corn and buck-wheat for this purpose. A middling farmer will there sometimes have four hundred fowls in his yard. The feeding of poultry seems scarce yet to be generally considered as a matter of so much importance in England. They are certainly, however, dearer in England than in France, as England receives considerable supplies from France. In the progress of improvement, the period at which every particular sort of animal food is dearest, must naturally be that which immediately precedes the general practice of cultivating land for the sake of raising it. For some time before this practice becomes general, the scarcity must necessarily raise the price. After it has become general, new methods of feeding are commonly fallen upon, which enable the farmer to raise upon the same quantity of ground a much greater quantity of that particular sort of animal food. The plenty not only obliges him to sell cheaper, but in consequence of these improvements he can afford to sell cheaper; for if he could not afford it, the plenty would not be of long continuance. It has been probably in this manner that the introduction of clover, turnips, carrots, cabbages, &c. has contributed to sink the common price of butcher's meat in the London market somewhat below what it was about the beginning of the last century.

数量的家禽。这些家禽的饲养，只是利用行将丢弃的东西，并不需要特别的开支，所以，家禽通常卖得都很便宜。农场主的所得几乎全是纯收益，而价格也不会低到使他们不愿饲养那么多的程度。在耕种状况不佳并因而人口稀少的国家，像这样无需费用饲养的家禽往往就足以满足全部需求，因此，这种家禽就通常和鲜肉及其他一切肉食一样廉价。但是，用这种方法饲养的家禽，其总量一定比农场生产的鲜肉少得多。在富裕和奢华的时代，人们更为喜爱效用相差不多而数量较少的产物。所以，随着财富和奢侈性行为的增加，由于耕种状况的改善，家禽价格就逐渐上升并超过鲜肉价格，最终直到使耕种土地饲养家禽有利可图。家禽价格一旦达到这种高度，就不能再上升了，否则，更多的其他用途的土地就会改用来饲养家禽。在法国一些省份，家禽饲养被视为农村经济中非常重要的产业，其利润足以鼓励农场主为此而广种玉米和荞麦。有的中等农户在宅院里就养了 400 只家禽。家禽饲养在英格兰好像还没有被重视。可是，家禽价格在英格兰一定比在法国高，因为英格兰大量家禽来自于法国的供应。在耕种状况改善过程中，每一种肉食达到最高价格的时候，一定是在为生产这种肉食而普遍耕种土地之前。在这种做法通行以前，这些动物的价格必然会因其稀缺而上升。而在这种做法通行以后，通常就会找到新的饲养方法，使农场主能在相同面积的土地上生产出比以前更多的这种肉食。肉食的丰富产量，不但使农场主必须降低销售价格，而且也能够降低销售价格。因为如果不降价，这种多产状态也不能长期维持。也许就是这种原因，苜蓿、芜菁、胡萝卜、卷心菜等的引种，使得如今伦敦市场上鲜肉的一般价格比上世纪初期有所下降。

The hog, that finds his food among ordure, and greedily devours many things rejected by every other useful animal, is, like poultry, originally kept as a save-all. As long as the number of such animals, which can thus be reared at little or no expence, is fully sufficient to supply the demand, this sort of butcher's-meat comes to market at a much lower price than any other. But when the demand rises beyond what this quantity can supply, when it becomes necessary to raise food on purpose for feeding and fattening hogs, in the same manner as for feeding and fattening other cattle, the price necessarily rises, and becomes proportionably either higher or lower than that of other butcher's-meat, according as the nature of the country, and the state of its agriculture, happen to render the feeding of hogs more or less expensive than that of other cattle. In France, according to Mr. Buffon, the price of pork is nearly equal to that of beef. ① In most parts of Great Britain it is at present somewhat higher.

The great rise in the price both of hogs and poultry has in Great Britain been frequently imputed to the diminution of the number of cottagers and other small occupiers of land; an event which has in every part of Europe been the immediate forerunner of improvement and better cultivation, but which at the same time may have contributed to raise the price of those articles, both somewhat sooner and somewhat faster than it would otherwise have risen. As the poorest family can often maintain a cat or a dog, without any expence, so the poorest occupiers of land can commonly maintain a few poultry, or a sow and a few pigs, at very little. The little offals of their own table, their whey, skimmed milk and butter-milk, supply those animals with a part of their food, and they find the rest in the neighbouring fields without doing any sensible damage to any body. By diminishing the number of those small occupiers, therefore, the quantity of this sort of provisions which is thus produced at little or no expence, must certainly have been a good deal diminished, and their price must consequently have been raised both sooner and faster than it would otherwise have risen. Sooner or later, however, in the progress of improvement, it must at any rate have risen to the utmost height to which it is capable of rising; or to the price which pays the labour and expence of cultivating the land which furnishes them with food as well as these are

---

① [*Histotre Naturelle*, vol. v. (1755), p. 122.]

猪是贪食的动物。它以粪便和其他一切有用动物所嫌忌的东西为食。因此,与家禽一样,猪的饲养起先不过是为了废物利用。在这样不花钱或少花钱饲养猪的数量能充分满足需求时,猪肉的市场价格必然比其他鲜肉要低得多。但是,一旦需求超过所能供应的数量,换句话说,养猪如果同饲养其他牲畜一样必须专门为其生产饲料,那么猪的价格必然上升。在具体的自然条件和农业状况下,养猪比饲养其他牲畜所需费用的多与少,决定猪肉价格将比其他各种鲜肉价格的昂贵或低廉。据布丰先生说,法国的猪肉价格几乎与牛肉价格相同①。在大不列颠大部分地区,现在猪肉却比牛肉稍贵。

关于大不列颠猪和家禽价格的高涨,常常有人归因于佃农和其他小土地占有者的人数减少。这种人数的减少,是欧洲各地技术改良和耕种进步的前奏,同时,又使猪和家禽的价格上升得更早更快一些。一个最贫穷的家庭,往往不花分文就能养活一只猫或一条狗。一个最贫穷的土地占有者,也往往花费无几就能养活几只家禽或一头母猪和几头小猪。他们把餐桌上吃剩的东西、奶浆、奶渣等,当作这些动物的一部分食料,而其余的食料则任其在附近田野里自行寻找,而不会明显地损害其他人。因为小土地占有者人数减少,这些不花分文或花费很少而饲养的动物,其数量必然大大减少,同时,其价格也因而必然比其数量没有减少时上升得更早更快。但是,在改良的过程中,这些动物的价格迟早会达到可能上升的最高限度,换句话说,迟早会达到这样高的价格,以致就耕种土地所使用的劳动和费用来说,为饲养这些动物而耕

---

① 《自然史》,第 5 卷(1755 年),第 122 页。

paid upon the greater part of other cultivated land.

milk, butter, and cheese.

The business of the dairy, like the feeding of hogs and poultry, is originally carried on as a save-all. The cattle necessarily kept upon the farm, produce more milk than either the rearing of their own young, or the consumption of the farmer's family requires; and they produce most at one particular season. But of all the productions of land, milk is perhaps the most perishable. In the warm season, when it is most abundant, it will scarce keep four-and-twenty hours. The farmer, by making it into fresh butter, stores a small part of it for a week: by making it into salt butter, for a year: and by making it into cheese, he stores a much greater part of it for several years. Part of all these is reserved for the use of his own family. The rest goes to market, in order to find the best price which is to be had, and which can scarce be so low as to discourage him from sending thither whatever is over and above the use of his own family. If it is very low, indeed, he will be likely to manage his dairy in a very slovenly and dirty manner, and will scarce perhaps think it worth while to have a particular room or building on purpose for it, but will suffer the business to be carried on amidst the smoke, filth, and nastiness of his own kitchen; as was the case of almost all the farmers dairies in Scotland thirty or forty years ago, and as is the case of many of them still. The same causes which gradually raise the price of butcher's-meat, the increase of the demand, and, in consequence of the improvement of the country, the diminution of the quantity which can be fed at little or no expence, raise, in the same manner, that of the produce of the dairy, of which the price naturally connects with that of butcher's-meat, or with the expence of feeding cattle. The increase of price pays for more labour, care, and cleanliness. The dairy becomes more worthy of the farmer's attention, and the quality of its produce gradually improves. The price at last gets so high that it becomes worth while to employ some of the most fertile and best cultivated lands in feeding cattle merely for the purpose of the dairy; and when it has got to this height, it cannot well go higher. If it did, more land would soon be turned to this purpose. It seems to have got to this height through the greater part of England, where much good land is commonly employed in this manner. If you except the neighbourhood of a few considerable towns, it seems not yet to have got to this height anywhere in Scotland, where common farmers seldom employ much good land in raising

种的土地与大部分其他耕地所支付的报酬一样。

制乳业像饲养猪和家禽一样,最初也是为了废物利用。农场饲养的必要的牲畜所产的奶,平常都超过幼畜哺育和农场主自家消费的需要量,而且在某一个季节产得特别多。可是,牛奶也许是土地生产物中最容易变质的。牛奶在产量最高的温暖季节很难保存24小时。于是,农场主把一小部分牛奶制成新鲜黄油,能保存一星期;一部分牛奶制成咸黄油,能保存一年;一大部分牛奶制成干乳酪,能保存几年。所有这些东西,农场主通常保存一部分留给自己用,其余部分则都运往市场,只求卖得最好的价钱。市场价格不可能低到使农场主不愿把自家消费不完的东西送到市场销售。如果市场价格过低,农场主对于乳制品作业就可能会搞得马马虎虎、不干不净,乃至于也不置备专门作坊,只是在烟熏火燎、污秽脏乱的厨房中进行。实际上,在苏格兰,在三四十年前,几乎所有农场主的乳制品作业都是这样,直到现在,还有许多农场主仍然是这种情形。导致鲜肉价格逐渐上升的原因,即对鲜肉需求的增加,以及由于农村状况的改善而使利用废物饲养的牲畜数量的减少,也同样会使乳制品的价格上升起来。乳制品的价格当然与鲜肉价格或牲畜饲养费用有着天然的联系。价格增高,就能够补偿更多的劳动,也能够促进人们关心工作、注意卫生。乳制品业就更值得农场主重视,其产品质量也就日益提高。最后,乳制品价格上升到如此高度,以致即使以最好的耕地为乳制品业而饲养牲畜都能获利。可是,价格一旦达到这种高度,就再也不能上升了,否则不久就会有更多的土地转作这种用途。英格兰大部分地区的乳制品价格好像已经达到这种高度,所以,那里有许多好地转而饲养牲畜。在苏格兰,除了几个大城市周围附近

牛奶、黄油和乳酪。

food for cattle merely for the purpose of the dairy. The price of the produce, though it has risen very considerably within these few years, is probably still too low to admit of it. The inferiority of the quality, indeed, compared with that of the produce of English dairies, is fully equal to that of the price. But this inferiority of quality is, perhaps, rather the effect of this lowness of price than the cause of it. Though the quality was much better, the greater part of what is brought to market could not, I apprehend, in the present circumstances of the country, be disposed of at a much better price; and the present price, it is probable, would not pay the expence of the land and labour necessary for producing a much better quality. Through the greater part of England, notwithstanding the superiority of price, the dairy is not reckoned a more profitable employment of land than the raising of corn, or the fattening of cattle, the two great objects of agriculture. Through the greater part of Scotland, therefore, it cannot yet be even so profitable.

<small>The rise of price, being necessary for good cultivation, should be regarded with satisfaction.</small> The lands of no country, it is evident, can ever be completely cultivated and improved, till once the price of every produce, which human industry is obliged to raise upon them, has got so high as to pay for the expence of complete improvement and cultivation. In order to do this, the price of each particular produce must be sufficient, first, to pay the rent of good corn land, as it is that which regulates the rent of the greater part of other cultivated land; and secondly, to pay the labour and expence of the farmer as well as they are commonly paid upon good corn-land; or, in other words, to replace with the ordinary profits the stock which he employs about it. This rise in the price of each particular produce, must evidently be previous to the improvement and cultivation of the land which is destined for raising it. Gain is the end of all improvement, and nothing could deserve that name of which loss was to be the necessary consequence. But loss must be the necessary consequence of improving land for the sake of a produce of which the price could never bring back the expence. If the complete improvement and cultivation of the country be, as it

的地区外，其余各地好像都还没有达到这种高度，所以，普通农场主很少为了乳制品而以好地种植牲畜草料。最近几年，乳制品价格确实上升很多，但仍然还太低，还不足以为此而使用好地种植牲畜草料。诚然，与英格兰乳制品相比，苏格兰乳制品质量上的低劣恰好与其价格上的低廉相称。可是，质量低劣或许是价格低廉的结果，而不是价格低廉的原因。我认为，即使苏格兰乳制品的质量更好一些，但在目前情况下，大部分进入市场的乳制品仍不能卖得更好的价钱。现在的价格，或许还不够补偿生产质量优良的乳制品所必需的土地和劳动的费用。在英格兰大部分地区，尽管乳制品价格很高，但与种植谷物和饲养牲畜这两种主要的农业项目相比，乳制品业仍不能被视为一种比较有利的土地利用途径。所以，在苏格兰大部分地区，乳制品业甚至还不能像在英格兰那样有利可图。

很显然，不管是哪一个国家，如果其必须由人类劳动在土地上生产的一切产物的价格不足以补偿土地改良费用和耕种费用，则该国的土地绝不会完全得到耕种和改良。要使全国土地完全得到耕种和改良，每一种产物的价格必须满足两个条件：第一，要足以支付好庄稼地的地租，因为其他大部分耕地的地租都依据好庄稼地的地租而定；第二，要足以补偿农场主所付出的劳动和费用，就像好庄稼地通常所提供的报酬一样。换句话说，农场主必须从每一种产物的价格中，取回其投入的资本，并获得资本的正常利润。每一种产物的价格上涨，显然必须先于生产这种产物的土地的改良和耕种。获利是一切改良的目的，结果必然是损失的改良算不上改良。如果由改良而生产的物品价格不足以补偿改良的费用，那么改良的结果就必然是损失。因此，如果全国土地

<small>价格上升是良好耕种的必要条件。</small>

most certainly is, the greatest of all public advantages, this rise in the price of all those different sorts of rude produce, instead of being considered as a public calamity, ought to be regarded as the necessary forerunner and attendant of the greatest of all public advantages.

<small>It is due not to a fall of silver but to a rise in the real price of the produce.</small>   This rise too in the nominal or money-price of all those different sorts of rude produce has been the effect, not of any degradation in the value of silver, but of a rise in their real price. They have become worth, not only a greater quantity of silver, but a greater quantity of labour and subsistence than before. As it costs a greater quantity of labour and subsistence to bring them to market, so when they are brought thither, they represent or are equivalent to a greater quantity.

Third Sort

<small>(3) The sort in regard to which the efficacy of industry is limited or uncertain,</small>   The third and last sort of rude produce, of which the price naturally rises in the progress of improvement, is that in which the efficacy of human industry, in augmenting the quantity, is either limited or uncertain. Though the real price of this sort of rude produce, therefore, naturally tends to rise in the progress of improvement, yet, according as different accidents happen to render the efforts of human industry more or less successful in augmenting the quantity, it may happen sometimes even to fall, sometimes to continue the same in very different periods of improvement, and sometimes to rise more or less in the same period.

<small>e. g. wool and hides, which are appendages to other sorts of produce.</small>   There are some sorts of rude produce which nature has rendered a kind of appendages to other sorts; so that the quantity of the one which any country can afford, is necessarily limited by that of the other. The quantity of wool or of raw hides, for example, which any country can afford, is necessarily limited by the number of great and small cattle that are kept in it. The state of its improvement, and the nature of its agriculture, again necessarily determine this number.

The same causes, which, in the progress of improvement, gradually raise the price of butcher's-meat, should have the same effect, it may be thought, upon the prices of wool and raw

的改良与耕种是最大的公共利益,而绝大多数情况下确实如此,则这一类原生产物的价格上涨,就不能看作是一种公共灾难,而应看作是最大的公共利益必要的先驱和伴随物。

上述所有原生产物的名义价格或货币价格的上涨,不是白银价值下降的结果,而是这些产物自身实际价格上升的结果。这些原生产物不但比以前值更多的白银,而且比以前值更多的劳动和生活必需品。由于把它们送往市场需要花费更多的劳动和生活必需品,因此投入市场后,它们就代表更多的劳动和生活必需品,或者说在价值上等于更多的劳动和生活必需品。

这不是白银价值下降结果,而是这些产物实际价格上升的结果。

第三类

第三类即最后一类原生产物,其价格随着改良程度的增进而自然上升,人类劳动的力量可以使之数量增加但效果有限或不确定。因此,这类原生产物的实际价格,虽然有随改良的进步而上升的自然趋势,但由于各种偶然事件使人类增加产量的努力所取得的成就有大有小,所以有时甚至会下降,有时在不同时期保持不变,而有时又会在同一时期里或多或少地上升。

(3) 人类劳动力受到限制或确定一类产物生物。

某些原生产物的生产以其他原生产物的生产为转移。因此,一个国家所能提供的前一类原生产物量,必然受到其所能提供的后一类原生产物量的限制。例如,一个国家所能提供的羊毛或生皮,必然受到该国所保有的大小牲畜数量的限制;它所保有的大小牲畜数量,又必然受到该国改良状况和农业性质的限制。

例如羊毛生皮,它们是其他产物的附属物。

也许有人说,在改良的过程中,使牛羊肉价格逐渐上升的原因,也同样会使羊毛和生皮的价格按几乎相同的比例上升。如果

<small>Wool and hides in early times have a larger market open to them than butcher's-meat.</small> hides, and raise them too nearly in the same proportion. It probably would be so, if in the rude beginnings of improvement the market for the latter commodities was confined within as narrow bounds as that for the former. But the extent of their respective markets is commonly extremely different.

The market for butcher's-meat is almost every-where confined to the country which produces it. Ireland, and some part of British A- merica indeed, carry on a considerable trade in salt provisions; but they are, I believe, the only countries in the commercial world which do so, or which export to other countries any considerable part of their butcher's-meat.

The market for wool and raw hides, on the contrary, is in the rude beginnings of improvement very seldom confined to the country which produces them. They can easily be transported to distant coun- tries, wool without any preparation, and raw hides with very little: and as they are the materials of many manufactures, the industry of other countries may occasion a demand for them, though that of the country which produces them might not occasion any.

<small>In thinly inhabited countries the wool and hide are more valuable in proportion to the carcase.</small> In countries ill cultivated, and therefore but thinly inhabited, the price of the wool and the hide bears always a much greater proportion to that of the whole beast, than in countries where, improvement and population being further advanced, there is more demand for butcher's-meat. Mr. Hume observes, that in the Saxon times, the fleece was estimated at two-fifths of the value of the whole sheep, and that this was much above the proportion of its present estimation. ①In some provinces of Spain, I have been assured, the sheep is frequently killed merely for the sake of the fleece and the tallow. The carcase is often left to rot upon the ground, or to be devoured by beasts and birds of prey. If this sometimes happens even in Spain, it happens almost constantly in Chili, at Buenos Ayres,② and in many other parts of Span- ish America, where the horned cattle are almost constantly killed merely for the sake of the hide and the tallow. This too used to happen almost

---

① [*History*, ed. of 1773, vol. i. , p. 226.]

② [Juan and Ulloa, *Voyage historique*, 2de ptie, liv. i. , chap. v. , vol. i. , p. 552.]

在进行改良的初期,毛皮市场像鲜肉市场一样局限于狭窄范围,则前面所说的情形也许会真实地发生。可是,它们的市场范围通常极不相同。

<small>在改良初期,毛皮市场比鲜肉市场更大。</small>

鲜肉市场几乎在哪里都是局限于鲜肉的生产国之内。诚然,爱尔兰和英属美洲的一些地方在经营着大规模的腌制品贸易。但我相信,在如今的商业世界中,从事这种贸易的,换句话说,以本国大部分鲜肉输往其他国家的,只有这两个地方。

相反,毛皮市场在改良开始的时候就很少局限于毛皮的生产国之内。羊毛不需要经过加工,生皮只需要略为加工,就可以很容易地出口到遥远的国家。由于毛皮是许多制造品的原料,所以,即使其生产国的产业对它们没有需求,其他国家的产业也可能对它们有需求。

在耕种状况不佳并因而人口稀少的国家,毛皮价格在一头牲畜的全部价格中所占的部分,总是比在耕种状况不断改善、人口不断增加而对鲜肉有较大需求的国家大得多。据休谟先生观察,在撒克逊[1]时代,羊毛价格就约占一头羊的价格的 2/5,远远超过现今羊毛价格在全羊价格中所占的比例①。据我得到的确切信息,在西班牙的一些省份,宰羊往往只是为了取得羊毛和羊脂,而羊的尸体则常常听其在地上腐烂,或让肉食鸟兽吃掉。这种事情,如果在西班牙是有时发生,那么在智利、布宜诺斯艾利斯②、西属美洲的其他许多地方,就几乎是习以为常的现象了。那些地方

<small>在人口稀少的国家,毛皮比兽肉更有价值。</small>

---

① 《英格兰史》,1773 年,第 1 卷,第 226 页。
② 胡安和乌洛阿:《航海史》,第 1 卷,第五章,第 552 页。
〔1〕撒克逊(Saxon),西部德意志民族中的一支,居住在德国北部,在公元 5 世纪和 6 世纪与盎格鲁人和朱特人一起入侵大不列颠。

constantly in Hispaniola, while it was infested by the Buccaneers, and before the settlement, improvement, and populousness of the French plantations (which now extend round the coast of almost the whole western half of the island) had given some value to the cattle of the Spaniards, who still continue to possess, not only the eastern part of the coast, but the whole inland and mountainous part of the country.

<small>In the progress of improvement the wool and hide should rise, though not so much as the carcase</small>   Though in the progress of improvement and population, the price of the whole beast necessarily rises, yet the price of the carcase is likely to be much more affected by this rise than that of the wool and the hide. The market for the carcase, being in the rude state of society confined always to the country which produces it, must necessarily be extended in proportion to the improvement and population of that country. But the market for the wool and the hides even of a barbarous country often extending to the whole commercial world, it can very seldom be enlarged in the same proportion. The state of the whole commercial world can seldom be much affected by the improvement of any particular country; and the market for such commodities may remain the same, or very nearly the same, after such improvements, as before. It should, however, in the natural course of things rather upon the whole be somewhat extended in consequence of them. If the manufactures, especially, of which those commodities are the materials, should ever come to flourish in the country, the market, though it might not be much enlarged, would at least

往往只是为了取得兽皮、兽脂而不断宰杀有角牲畜。伊斯帕尼奥拉岛[1]（Hispaniola）也几乎经常发生这种事情。当该岛经常受到海盗侵扰，而法国人的种植园（现在几乎已延伸到该岛的全部西部海岸）的安定、改良和人口状况，还没有改善到足以使西班牙人的牲畜具有若干价值的时候，那里才发生这种事情。西班牙现今仍不仅继续占有该岛的东部海岸，而且占有该岛的全部内陆地区和山区。

随着社会的进步和人口的增长，整个一头牲畜的价格必然上升。不过，这种价格上升对兽肉价格的影响比对毛皮价格的影响更大。兽肉市场在原始的社会状态下总是局限于其产出国之内，所以其必然随着社会进步和人口增长而成比例地扩大。但是，即使原来是在野蛮的国家，毛皮市场也往往会扩展到整个商业世界，其也就很少再随着社会进步和人口增长而同比例地扩大。整个商业世界的状况很少会因某个国家的状况改善而受到显著影响。所以，在社会进步、人口增加之后，这种商品的市场可能仍然与以前完全相同或几乎相同。不过，按照事物发展的自然趋势，这种市场也会由于社会进步而略有扩大。特别是，如果一个国家以这些商品为原料的制造业日益发达，那么这些商品的市场，即

（在社会进步过程中，价格应该上升，尽管不像兽肉那么多。毛皮价格应上升。）

---

[1] 伊斯帕尼奥拉岛（Hispaniola），拉丁美洲西印度群岛中部，古巴西部的西印度群岛中的一个岛屿，为海地和多米尼加共和国所在地。哥伦布1492年发现了该岛，最初它被叫作埃斯帕尼奥拉岛。岛的西部（现在的海地）于1697年被西班牙割让给法国。

be brought much nearer to the place of growth than before; and the price of those materials might at least be increased by what had usually been the expence of transporting them to distant countries. Though it might not rise therefore in the same proportion as that of butcher's-meat, it ought naturally to rise somewhat, and it ought certainly not to fall.

<small>But in England wool has fallen since 1339,</small>

In England, however, notwithstanding the flourishing state of its woollen manufacture, the price of English wool has fallen very considerably since the time of Edward III. There are many authentic records which demonstrate that during the reign of that prince (towards the middle of the fourteenth century, or about 1339) what was reckoned the moderate and reasonable price of the tod or twenty-eight pounds of English wool was not less than ten shillings of the money of those times, ①containing, at the rate of twenty-pence the ounce, six ounces of silver Tower-weight, equal to about thirty shillings of our present money. In the present times, one-and-twenty shillings the tod may be reckoned a good price for very good English wool. The money-price of wool, therefore, in the time of Edward III, was to its money-price in the present times as ten to seven. The superiority of its real price was still greater. At the rate of six shillings and eightpence the quarter, ten shillings was in those ancient times the price of twelve bushels of wheat. At the rate of twenty-eight shillings the quarter, one-and-twenty shillings is in the present times the price of six bushels only. The proportion between the real prices of ancient and modern times, therefore, is as twelve to six, or as two to one. In those ancient times a tod of wool would have purchased twice the quantity of subsistence which it will purchase at present; and consequently twice the quantity of labour, if the real recompence of labour had been the same in both periods.

<small>This has been caused by artificial regulations.</small>

This degradation both in the real and nominal value of wool, could never have happened in consequence of the natural course

---

① See Smith's *Memoirs of Wool*, vol. i. c. 5, 6, and 7; also, vol. ii. c. 176. [Ed. 1 does not give the volumes and chapters. The work was *Chronicon Rusticum-Commerciale, or Memoirs of Wool, etc.* , by John Smith, and published 1747;]

使扩大不是很多,也至少会转移到比以前更接近于产地的地方,而这些商品的价格也至少会按所节省运费的通常程度而提高。因此,毛皮价格虽然不能与兽肉价格按照相同比例上升,也自然会上升一些,而绝不应该下降。

不过,在英格兰,尽管毛织品制造业很繁荣,但羊毛价格却自爱德华三世以来已经大大下降。许多可靠的记录表明,在爱德华三世时代(14世纪中叶或1339年左右),英格兰羊毛一托德[1](即28磅)的合理适中价格不下于当时的货币10先令①。当时的货币10先令,含有陶衡银6盎司,以每盎司合20便士计算,约等于现时的货币30先令。现在每托德21先令算是英国最优良羊毛的好价钱。这样,爱德华三世时代羊毛的货币价格与现时羊毛货币价格的比例,为10∶7。就实际价格来说,前者的优越性更大。按每夸特麦价6先令8便士计算,10先令在那时候可以购买12蒲式耳小麦。按每夸特麦价28先令计算,现在21先令只能购买6蒲式耳小麦。因此,那时候羊毛的实际价格对于现在羊毛的实际价格的比例,应当是12∶6,即2∶1。这就是说,那时候一托德羊毛所能购买的生活必需品,在数量上相当于现在一托德羊毛所能购买的生活必需品的二倍。如果这两个时代的劳动实际报酬相等,则那时候一托德羊毛所能购买的劳动量也相当于现在的二倍。

> 但在英格兰,羊毛价格自1339年以来已经下降。

羊毛实际价格和名义价格的下降,绝不会是自然产生的结

> 这是由于人为的规定。

---

① 参见约翰·史密斯:《羊毛研究报告》,1747年版,第一卷,第5、6、7章;以及第二卷,第176章。

[1] 托德:羊毛的重量单位,尤指1托德等于28磅(12.7公斤)的托德。

of things. It has accordingly been the effect of violence and artifice: First, of the absolute prohibition of exporting wool from England;① Secondly, of the permission of importing it from Spain duty free; Thirdly, of the prohibition of exporting it from Ireland to any other country but England. In consequence of these regulations, the market for English wool, instead of being somewhat extended in consequence of the improvement of England, has been confined to the home market, where the wool of several other countries is allowed to come into competition with it, and where that of Ireland is forced into competition with it. As the woollen manufactures too of Ireland are fully as much discouraged as is consistent with justice and fair dealing, the Irish can work up but a small part of their own wool at home, and are, therefore, obliged to send a greater proportion of it to Great Britain, the only market they are allowed.

The real price of hides at present is somewhat lower than in the fifteenth century,
I have not been able to find any such authentic records concerning the price of raw hides in ancient times. Wool was commonly paid as a subsidy to the king, and its valuation in that subsidy ascertains, at least in some degree, what was its ordinary price. But this seems not to have been the case with raw hides. Fleetwood, however, from an account in 1425, between the prior of Burcester Oxford and one of his canons, gives us their price, at least as it was stated, upon that particular occasion; viz. five ox hides at twelve shillings; five cow hides at seven shillings and three pence; thirty-six sheep skins of two years old at nine shillings; sixteen calves skins at two shillings. ② In 1425, twelve shillings contained about the same quantity of silver as four-and-twenty shillings of our present money. An ox hide, therefore, was in this account valued at the same quantity of silver as 4s. $\frac{4}{5}$ ths of our present money. Its nominal price was a good deal lower than at present. But at the rate of six shillings and eight-pence the quarter, twelve shillings would in those times have purchased fourteen bushels and four-fifths of a bushel of wheat, which, at three and six-pence the bushel, would in the present times cost 51s. 4d. An ox hide, therefore, would in those times have

---

① [See below, vol. ii. , p. 146, and Smith's *Memoirs of Wool*, vol. i. , pp. 159, 170, 182.]

② [*Chronicon preciosum*, ed. of 1707, p. 100]

果。这是暴力和人为的结果:第一,是绝对禁止英格兰羊毛出口的结果①;第二,是准许西班牙羊毛免税进口的结果;第三,是禁止爱尔兰向英格兰以外的任何国家出口羊毛的结果。由于这些规定,英格兰羊毛市场,就只能局限于国内,而不能随社会进步而扩展了。在英格兰市场上,其他几个国家的羊毛被允许进入参与竞争,爱尔兰羊毛也被迫参与竞争。另外,由于爱尔兰毛织品制造业遭到不公正、不公平的待遇,爱尔兰人只能在本国加工利用一小部分自产羊毛,而不得不把大部分羊毛输往大不列颠这个唯一准许进入的市场。

关于古代的生皮价格,我没有找到任何可靠的记录。羊毛通常是作为对国王的贡品输纳的。羊毛在输纳时所评定的价格至少在一定程度上是其当时的正常价格。生皮的情况似乎不是这样。不过,弗里特伍德曾根据1425年牛津伯塞斯特修道院副院长与该院某牧师之间的账单,告诉了我们生皮至少在那种特殊场合的价格:五张公牛皮值12先令;五张母牛皮值7先令3便士;36张两岁羊皮值9先令;16张小牛皮值二先令②。在1425年时,12先令所含的白银大约与现时的英币24先令所含的白银一样多。因此,根据这个账单,一张公牛皮价格与现时的英币4.8先令所价值的白银一样多。它的名义价格比现在要低得多,但当时12先令,按每夸特6先令8便士计算,可购买小麦14.8蒲式耳。这些小麦,在现今按每蒲式耳3先令6便士计算,却要值51先令4

现在生皮的实际价格比15世纪略低,

---

① 参阅后面,第二篇。以及参见约翰·史密斯:《羊毛研究报告》,第一卷,第159、170、182页。

② 《宝贵的纪年考证》,1707年版,第100页。

purchased as much corn as ten shillings and three-pence would purchase at present. Its real value was equal to ten shillings and three-pence of our present money. In those ancient times, when the cattle were half starved during the greater part of the winter, we cannot suppose that they were of a very large size. An ox hide which weighs four stone of sixteen pounds averdupois, is not in the present times reckoned a bad one; and in those ancient times would probably have been reckoned a very good one. But at half a crown the stone, which at this moment (February 1773) I understand to be the common price, such a hide would at present cost only ten shillings. Though its nominal price, therefore, is higher in the present than it was in those ancient times, its real price, the real quantity of subsistence which it will purchase or command, is rather somewhat lower. The price of cow hides, as stated in the above account, is nearly in the common proportion to that of ox hides. That of sheep skins is a good deal above it. They had probably been sold with the wool. That of calves skins, on the contrary, is greatly below it. In countries where the price of cattle is very low, the calves, which are not intended to be reared in order to keep up the stock, are generally killed very young; as was the case in Scotland twenty or thirty years ago. It saves the milk, which their price would not pay for. Their skins, therefore, are commonly good for little.

The price of raw hides is a good deal lower at present than it was a few years ago; owing probably to the taking off the duty upon seal skins, and to the allowing, for a limited time, the importation of raw hides from Ireland and from the plantations duty free, which was done in 1769. ①Take the whole of the present century at an average, their real price has probably been somewhat higher than it was in those ancient times. The nature of the commodity renders it not quite so proper for being transported to distant markets as wool. It suffers more by keeping. A salted hide is reckoned inferior to a fresh one, and sells for a lower price. This circumstance must necessarily

---

① [9 Geo. Ⅲ., c. 39, for five years; continued by 14 Geo. Ⅲ., c. 86, and 21 Geo. Ⅲ., c. 29.]

便士。因此,当时一张公牛皮与现在10先令3便士能购买到相同数量的小麦,即其实际价值等于现今英币10先令3便士。在古时候,牲畜在冬季的大部分时间里处于半饥饿状态,因此我们不能设想它们具有肥大的身躯。一张重量四石即常衡16磅的公牛皮,在今天可能被视为中等牛皮,在古代或许要被视为上等牛皮。我知道,每石半克朗,只是今天,即1773年2月牛皮的普通价格。按这价格,这重四石的一张公牛皮不过只值现时的英币10先令。因此,虽然公牛皮的名义价格在现时比古代高,但其实际价格,即所能购买或支配的生活必需品的实际量,在现时比古代低。在上述账单中,母牛皮价格对公牛皮价格大致保持通常的比例。羊皮价格则大大超过这种比例。羊皮也许是和羊毛一起销售的。相反,小牛皮价格则大大低于这种比例。在牲畜价格非常低廉的国家中,不是为了延续畜种而饲养的小牛,一般都在很小的时候宰杀,就像苏格兰二三十年前的做法一样。小牛皮价格通常不够补偿小牛所消费的牛奶价格,所以,宰杀小牛可以节省牛奶。小牛皮的价格也因此很低。

  生皮价格现在比几年前要低得多。这或许是由于海豹皮的关税废止了,并于1769年[①]准许在限定时期内从爱尔兰及其他殖民地免税进口生皮。但从本世纪平均来看,生皮的实际价格大概要比古时候略高。生皮和羊毛比较,其性质就更不宜于运往远方市场,其保存起来所易于受到的损害也比羊毛大。用盐腌制的生皮,通常被认为品质不如新鲜生皮,所以其售价将更低。这种情

---

① 乔治三世九年第39号法令,限定5年;乔治三世十四年第86号法令,以及乔治三世二十一年第29号法令,继续实行。

but their average price during the present century is probably higher. They are not so easily transported as wool, and tanners have not been so much favoured by legislation as clothiers.

have some tendency to sink the price of raw hides produced in a country which does not manufacture them, but is obliged to export them; and comparatively to raise that of those produced in a country which does manufacture them. It must have some tendency to sink their price in a barbarous, and to raise it in an improved and manufacturing country. It must have had some tendency therefore to sink it in ancient, and to raise it in modern times. Our tanners besides have not been quite so successful as our clothiers, in convincing the wisdom of the nation, that the safety of the commonwealth depends upon the prosperity of their particular manufacture. They have accordingly been much less favoured. The exportation of raw hides has, indeed, been prohibited, and declared a nuisance:①but their importation from foreign countries has been subjected to a duty;②and though this duty has been taken off from those of Ireland and the plantations (for the limited time of five years only), yet Ireland has not been confined to the market of Great Britain for the sale of its surplus hides, or of those which are not manufactured at home. The hides of common cattle have but within these few years been put among the enumerated commodities which the plantations can send no-where but to the mother country; neither has the commerce of Ireland been in this case oppressed hitherto, in order to support the manufactures of Great Britain.

Regulations which sink the price of wool or hides in an improved country raise the price of meat, but not in an unimproved country.

Whatever regulations tend to sink the price either of wool or of raw hides below what it naturally would be, must, in an improved and cultivated country, have some tendency to raise the price of butcher's-meat. The price both of the great and small cattle, which are fed on improved and cultivated land, must be sufficient to pay the rent which the landlord, and the profit which the farmer has reason to expect from improved and cultivated land. If it is not, they will soon cease to feed them. Whatever part of this price, therefore, is not paid by the wool and the hide, must be paid by the carcase. The less there is paid for the one, the more must be paid for the other. In what manner this price is to be divided upon the different parts of the beast, is indifferent to the

① [By 5 Eliz., c. 22; 8 Eliz., c. 14; 18 Eliz., c. 9; 13 and 14 Car. II., c. 7,]

② [9 Ann., c. 11.]

第一篇 第十一章

况,必定会使生皮价格在能自行加工的产出国有上升的趋势,而在不能自行加工而只得向国外出口的产出国有下降的趋势。生皮价格在文明程度较低的国家有下降的趋势,在进步而制造业发达的国家有上升的趋势。因此,生皮价格在古代有下降的趋势,在现代有上升的趋势。另外,英国制革业,并不能像毛织业那样,使人相信国家安全依存于这种制造业的繁荣,因而像后者那样受到国民的重视。尽管生皮的出口被禁止了,并被宣布是一种令人讨厌的行为①,但由国外进口的生皮却已课税②。由爱尔兰及各殖民地进口的生皮关税,虽然一度废除(仅限 5 年),可是,爱尔兰出售剩余的生皮,即不能在爱尔兰本土自行加工的生皮,也不一定要局限于大不列颠这个市场。在这几年中,各殖民地普通牲畜的生皮,被列入只许在母国销售而不能在别处贩卖的商品项目中。在这一方面,爱尔兰的商业也不曾因要支持大不列颠制造业而受到压制。

在进步和文明的国家里,无论任何规定,只要目的在于降低毛皮价格,就必然有提高兽肉价格的倾向。农场主在改良的土地上饲养的牲畜,其价格必须足以支付给地主有理由希望得自这种土地的地租和农场主有理由希望得自这种土地的利润,否则他们就将不再饲养。因此,凡是通过毛皮价格还不能支付的那一部分,就必须由兽肉价格来支付。一方面支付得少,另一方面就必定支付得多,两者此消彼长。地主只要获取地租,农场主只要获

----

① 伊丽莎白五年第 22 号法令;伊丽莎白八年,第 14 号法令;伊丽莎白十八年,第 9 号法令;查理二世十三、十四年第 7 号法令。
② 安妮女王九年第 11 号法令。

landlords and farmers, provided it is all paid to them. In an improved and cultivated country, therefore, their interest as landlords and farmers cannot be much affected by such regulations, though their interest as consumers may, by the rise in the price of provisions. ①It would be quite otherwise, however, in an unimproved and uncultivated country, where the greater part of the lands could be applied to no other purpose but the feeding of cattle, and where the wool and the hide made the principal part of the value of those cattle. Their interest as landlords and farmers would in this case be very deeply affected by such regulations, and their interest as consumers very little. The fall in the price of the wool and the hide, would not in this case raise the price of the carcase; because the greater part of the lands of the country being applicable to no other purpose but the feeding of cattle, the same number would still continue to be fed. The same quantity of butcher's-meat would still come to market. The demand for it would be no greater than before. Its price, therefore, would be the same as before. The whole price of cattle would fall, and along with it both the rent and the profit of all those lands of which cattle was the principal produce, that is, of the greater part of the lands of the country. The perpetual prohibition of the exportation of wool, which is commonly, but very falsely, ascribed to Edward Ⅲ, ②would, in the then circumstances of the country, have been the most destructive regulation which could well have been thought of. It would not only have reduced the actual value of the greater part of the lands of the kingdom, but by reducing the price of the most important species of small cattle, it would have retarded very much its subsequent improvement.

The Union sank the price of Scotch wool, while it raised the price of Scotch meat.

The wool of Scotland fell very considerably in its price in consequence

① 1[This passage, from the beginning of the paragraph, is quoted at length below, vol. ii.]

② [John Smith, *Memoirs of Wool*, vol. i. , p. 25, explains that the words 'It shall be felony to carry away any wool out of the realm until it be otherwise ordained' do not imply a perpetual prohibition.]

取利润,至于毛、皮、肉的价格分别在一头牲畜的全部价格中占到多大比例,他们无暇关注。在进步和文明的国家里,地主和农场主的利益绝不会受到这些规定的多大影响,尽管他们作为消费者可能会由于食品价格上升而受到一些影响①。但是,在社会不进步、耕种不发达的国家里,情形就完全不一样。在这种国家里,土地大部分都用来饲养牲畜,除此以外,别无其他用途,而牲畜价格主要由毛皮部分构成,肉只不过占极少的部分。在这种情况下,他们作为地主和农场主就将受到上述规定的很大影响,而作为消费者受到的影响则极为有限。在这种情况下,毛皮价格的下降并不会引起肉价的上升,因为该国大部分土地除饲养牲畜外别无他用,所以,即使毛皮价格下降,也只好继续饲养原来数量的牲畜。鲜肉将仍然以同一数量供应市场,而鲜肉的需求不会大于以前,因此,鲜肉价格也不会比以前更高。肉价保持不变,毛皮价格下降,于是,整个一头牲畜的价格就下降,接着,以牲畜为主要产物的全部土地,即该国大部分土地的地租和利润也因而下降。因此,永久禁止羊毛出口的规定,在当时的情况下,成为最具有破坏性的规定,而这种规定通常被错误地认为是爱德华三世制定的②。这个规定的实行不但会降低国家大部分土地的实际价值,而且使最重要的小牲畜的价格下降,因而在很大程度上延缓土地的进一步改良。

自从苏格兰与英格兰合并以后,苏格兰羊毛价格明显下降。与英格兰的合并降低了苏格兰羊毛价格,并提高了它的鲜肉价格。

---

① 这一段,从开头到此处,在后面第二篇中被全部引用。
② 约翰·斯密:《羊毛研究报告》,第1卷,第25页,说明"直到做出其他规定以前,从帝国输出羊毛是重罪"的话并不意味着永久禁止。

of the union with England, by which it was excluded from the great market of Europe, and confined to the narrow one of Great Britain. The value of the greater part of the lands in the southern counties of Scotland, which are chiefly a sheep country, would have been very deeply affected by this event, had not the rise in the price of butcher's-meat fully compensated the fall in the price of wool.

<small>The efficacy of industry in increasing wool and hides is both limited and uncertain.</small>   As the efficacy of human industry, in increasing the quantity either of wool or of raw hides, is limited, so far as it depends upon the produce of the country where it is exerted; so it is uncertain so far as it depends upon the produce of other countries. It so far depends, not so much upon the quantity which they produce, as upon that which they do not manufacture; and upon the restraints which they may or may not think proper to impose upon the exportation of this sort of rude produce. These circumstances, as they are altogether independent of domestic industry, so they necessarily render the efficacy of its efforts more or less uncertain. In multiplying this sort of rude produce, therefore, the efficacy of human industry is not only limited, but uncertain.

<small>The same thing is true of fish, which naturally rise in the progress of improvement.</small>   In multiplying another very important sort of rude produce, the quantity of fish that is brought to market, it is likewise both limited and uncertain. It is limited by the local situation of the country, by the proximity or distance of its different provinces from the sea, by the number of its lakes and rivers, and by what may be called the fertility or barrenness of those seas, lakes and rivers, as to this sort of rude produce. As population increases, as the annual produce of the land and labour of the country grows greater and greater, there come to be more buyers of fish, and those buyers too have a greater quantity and variety of other goods, or, what is the same thing, the price of a greater quantity and variety of other goods, to buy with. But it will generally be impossible to supply the great and extended market without employing a quantity of labour greater than in proportion to what had been requisite for supplying the narrow and confined one. A market which, from requiring only one thousand, comes to require annually ten thousand ton of fish, can seldom be supplied without employing more than ten times the quantity of labour which had before been sufficient to supply it. The fish must generally be sought for at a greater distance, larger vessels must be employed, and more expensive machinery of every kind made use of. The real price of this commodity, therefore, naturally rises in the progress of improvement. It has

因为苏格兰羊毛自合并时起就与欧洲大市场失去了联系,而只局限于大不列颠这个狭小市场中。如果不是鲜肉价格的上升充分补偿了羊毛价格的下降,那么,苏格兰南部各郡主要用于养羊业的大部分土地的价值,必然会深受这次合并的影响。

人类为增加羊毛或生皮的产量而做出的努力,就其要依赖于本国牲畜的产量来说,其功效必然受到一定限制,就其要依赖于外国牲畜的产量来说,其功效又必然难以确定。关于后者,与其说要依赖于外国出产的羊毛和生皮的数量,倒不如说要依赖于外国不自行加工的羊毛和生皮的数量,以及外国对于这些原生产物的出口是否认为应加以限制。这些情况都与本国的劳动毫不相关。所以,人类劳动在这方面所取得的实效,不但受到限制,而且不能确定。

_{劳动增加羊毛生皮产量的实效受到限制,且不确定。}

人类劳动增加另一种非常重要的原生产物即鱼类的上市量所取得的效果,也是既受到限制而且又不能确定。这方面的努力,必然要受当地地理状况的限制,例如距离海洋的远近,内地江河湖沼的多少,海洋江河湖沼产出量的丰富与否等。当该国人口、土地和劳动年产物增多的时候,鱼的购买者必然增多,而且,这些购买者拥有更大量的各种其他商品,换句话说,拥有更大量的各种其他商品的替代物来进行购买。但是,为了供应这种扩大的市场所投入的劳动量,如果没有增多到超过市场扩大的比例,那就不能满足这种扩大的需要。例如,原来每年只需要一千吨鱼的市场,如果扩大到需要一万吨鱼,那么,为供应这个市场而增加的劳动量,不超过十倍,就不能满足需要。在这种情况下,鱼类一般要到较远的地方去捕获,而且必须使用较大的渔船,必须使用价格较高的捕鱼工具。因此,这种商品的实际价格自然会随着社

_{鱼类价格也一样会在社会状况改善的过程中自然上升。}

— 539 —

accordingly done so, I believe, more or less in every country.

<small>The connexion of success in fishing with the state of improvement is uncertain.</small> Though the success of a particular day's fishing may be a very uncertain matter, yet, the local situation of the country being supposed, the general efficacy of industry in bringing a certain quantity of fish to market, taking the course of a year, or of several years together, it may perhaps be thought, is certain enough; and it, no doubt, is so. As it depends more, however, upon the local situation of the country, than upon the state of its wealth and industry; as upon this account it may in different countries be the same in very different periods of improvement, and very different in the same period; its connection with the state of improvement is uncertain, and it is of this sort of uncertainty that I am here speaking.

<small>In increasing minerals the efficacy of industry is not limited but uncertain.</small> In increasing the quantity of the different minerals and metals which are drawn from the bowels of the earth, that of the more precious ones particularly, the efficacy of human industry seems not to be limited, but to be altogether uncertain.

<small>The quantity of the precious metals in a country depends on its power of purchasing and the fertility of the mines.</small> The quantity of the precious metals which is to be found in any country is not limited by any thing in its local situation, such as the fertility or barrenness of its own mines. Those metals frequently abound in countries which possess no mines. Their quantity in every particular country seems to depend upon two different circumstances; first, upon its power of purchasing, upon the state of its industry, upon the annual produce of its land and labour, in consequence of which it can afford to employ a greater or a smaller quantity of labour and subsistence in bringing or purchasing such superfluities as gold and silver, either from its own mines or from those of other countries; and, secondly, upon the fertility or barrenness of the mines which may happen at any particular time to supply the commercial world with those metals. The quantity of those metals in the countries most remote from the mines, must be more or less affected by this fertility or barrenness, on account of the easy and cheap transportation of those metals, of their small bulk and great value. Their quantity in China and Indostan must have been more or less affected by the abundance of the mines of America.

<small>So far as it depends on the former circumstance the real price is likely to rise with improvement;</small> So far as their quantity in any particular country depends upon the former of those two circumstances (the power of purchasing), their real price, like that of all other luxuries and superfluities, is

会状况的改善而上升。我相信,各国的情况多少都是这样。

每天的捕鱼量是难以确定的。但假定一个国家的地方情况不变,那么就一年或数年来说,人类捕鱼努力的一般功效相当确定,而实际情况也确实是这样。可是,由于这功效更多地取决于一国的地理状况,而不是财富和劳动状况,所以,它在社会状况改善的程度非常不同的两个国家,却可能是相同的;而在社会状况改善的程度相同的两个国家,却可能大不相同。捕鱼的功效与社会改善状况的关系很不确定。我在这里所要讨论的就是这种不确定性。

> 捕鱼功效的改善与社会状况的联系是不确定的。

在增加由地下采掘的各种矿物和金属特别是贵金属的数量时,人类劳动的功效似乎不受限制,但完全是不确定的。

> 在增加矿产方面,劳动功效不受限制,但不确定。

一个国家所有贵金属量的多少,并不受该国地理状况的限制,例如自身矿藏的丰裕或贫瘠。没有矿山的国家往往拥有大量贵金属。无论什么国家,其所拥有的贵金属的多少,看来取决于以下两种情况。第一,取决于该国的购买力,取决于其产业状态,取决于其土地和劳动的年产物。因为,这些因素决定该国能使用多少的劳动和生活资料,去开采本国矿山或从其他国家的矿山购买黄金白银这样的非必需品。第二,取决于在一定时期内以黄金白银供应世界商业的矿山的丰裕或贫瘠。因为黄金白银运输方便、运费低廉,而且体积小价值大,所以,即使离矿山很远的国家,其黄金白银量也必然要多少受这种矿山丰瘠程度的影响。中国、印度斯坦的黄金白银量,必然多少受到美洲矿山丰裕的影响。

> 一个国家的贵金属量取决于它的购买力和矿山的丰裕程度。

就一个国家的黄金白银量必须取决于上述两种情况的前一种情况(购买力)来说,黄金白银的实际价格,与其他一切奢侈品、非必需品的实际价格一样,可能随该国财富及改良状况的增进而

> 就前一种情况而言,实际价格可能随着社会状况的改善而上升;

likely to rise with the wealth and improvement of the country, and to fall with its poverty and depression. Countries which have a great quantity of labour and subsistence to spare, can afford to purchase any particular quantity of those metals at the expence of a greater quantity of labour and subsistence, than countries which have less to spare.

<small>so far as it depends on the latter circumstance the real price will vary with the fertility of the mines,</small> So far as their quantity in any particular country depends upon the latter of those two circumstances (the fertility or barrenness of the mines which happen to supply the commercial world) their real price, the real quantity of labour and subsistence which they will purchase or exchange for, will, no doubt, sink more or less in proportion to the fertility, and rise in proportion to the barrenness, of those mines.

<small>which has no connexion with the state of industry.</small> The fertility or barrenness of the mines, however, which may happen at any particular time to supply the commercial world, is a circumstance which, it is evident, may have no sort of connection with the state of industry in a particular country. It seems even to have no very necessary connection with that of the world in general. As arts and commerce, indeed, gradually spread themselves over a greater and a greater part of the earth, the search for new mines, being extended over a wider surface, may have somewhat a better chance for being successful, than when confined within narrower bounds. The discovery of new mines, however, as the old ones come to be gradually exhausted, is a matter of the greatest uncertainty, and such as no human skill or industry can ensure. All indications, it is acknowledged, are doubtful, and the actual discovery and successful working of a new mine can alone ascertain the reality of its value, or even of its existence. In this search there seem to be no certain limits either to the possible success, or to the possible disappointment of human industry. In the course of a century or two, it is possible that new mines may be discovered more fertile than any that have ever yet been known; and it is just equally possible that the most fertile mine then known may be more barren than any that was wrought before the discovery of the mines of America. Whether the one or the other of those two events may happen to take place, is of very little importance to the real wealth and prosperity of the world, to the real value of the annual produce of the land and labour of mankind. Its nominal value, the quantity of gold and silver by which this annual produce could be expressed or

上升,也可能随该国的贫困与衰退而下降。因为,持有多量剩余劳动与生活资料的国家,和只持有少量剩余劳动与生活资料的国家相比,在购买一定数量的这种金属时,必然能支付较大数量的劳动与生活资料。

就一个国家的黄金白银量必须取决于上述两种情况的后一情况(以黄金白银供给商业世界的各矿山的丰瘠情况)来说,黄金白银的实际价格,换句话说,它们所能购买或交换的劳动和生活资料的实际数量,必然按照那矿山的丰瘠情况而或多或少地成比例升降。

<small>取决于后一种情况,它的实际价格随着矿山丰瘠情况而变化。</small>

但是,在一定时期内供应商业世界的矿山,究竟是丰裕,还是贫瘠,与某一特定国家的产业状态显然没有任何联系,而且通常与世界的产业状态似乎也没有十分必要的联系。诚然,当技艺和商业逐渐向世界更广的范围扩展时,寻找新矿山也随之扩大到更广的地面,而发现新矿的机会或许比局限于狭窄地区的时候要大。可是,当旧矿山逐渐枯竭的时候,能否发现新矿山是最没有把握的事,而且绝非人类的技能和勤劳所能保证。众所周知,只有迹象的事情是不可靠的。没有实际发现,没有采掘成功,就不能确定新矿山的现实价值,甚至也不能确定新矿山的存在。在探寻新矿山的时候,人类劳动成功或不成功的可能性都似乎无限大。在今后一两个世纪的时间里,也许能发现比任何已知矿山更为丰裕的新矿山,同样可能的是,那时候最多产的矿山也许比美洲各矿山发现以前的任何矿山还要贫瘠。不管这两种事情究竟是哪一种发生,它们对于世界的实际财富和繁荣,换句话说,对于土地和人类劳动的年产物的实际价值,都无关紧要。这些年产物的名义价值,即表明或代表这些年产物的黄金和白银的数量,无

<small>它与产业状态没有联系。</small>

represented, would, no doubt, be very different; but its real value, the real quantity of labour which it could purchase or command, would be precisely the same. A shilling might in the one case represent no more labour than a penny does at present; and a penny in the other might represent as much as a shilling does now. But in the one case he who had a shilling in his pocket, would be no richer than he who has a penny at present; and in the other he who had a penny would be just as rich as he who has a shilling now. The cheapness and abundance of gold and silver plate, would be the sole advantage which the world could derive from the one event, and the dearness and scarcity of those trifling superfluities the only inconveniency it could suffer from the other.

Conclusion of the Digression concerning the Variations in the Value of Silver

The high value of the precious metals is no proof of poverty and barbarism,

The greater part of the writers who have collected the money prices of things in ancient times, seem to have considered the low money price of corn, and of goods in general, or, in other words, the high value of gold and silver, as a proof, not only of the scarcity of those metals, but of the poverty and barbarism of the country at the time when it took place. This notion is connected with the system of political economy which represents national wealth as consisting in the abundance, and national poverty in the scarcity, of gold and silver; a system which I shall endeavour to explain and examine at great length in the fourth book of this enquiry. I shall only observe at present, that the high value of the precious metals can be no proof of the poverty or barbarism of any particular country at the time when it took place. It is a proof only of the barrenness of the mines which happened at that time to supply the commercial world. A poor country, as it cannot afford to buy more, so it can as little afford to pay dearer for gold and silver than a rich one; and the value of those metals, therefore, is not likely to be higher in the former than in the latter. In China, a country much richer than any part of Europe, the value of the precious metals is much higher than in any part of Europe. As the wealth of Europe, indeed, has increased greatly since the discovery of the mines of America, so the value of gold and silver has gradually diminished. This diminution of their value, however, has not been owing to the increase of the real wealth of Europe, of the annual produce of its land and labour, but to the accidental discovery of more

疑会有极大的差异,而其实际价值,即其所能购买或支配的实际劳动量,却完全一样。在前一种情况下,1先令所代表的劳动可能不超过如今1便士所代表的劳动。在后一种情况下,1便士所代表的劳动可能和如今1先令所代表的一样多。但是,在前一种情况下,拥有1先令的人并不比如今拥有1便士的人富,在后一种情况下,拥有1便士的人也并不比如今拥有1先令的人穷。人类从前一种情况所得到的唯一好处,是金银器皿的低廉与充裕,而从后一种情况所遭受的唯一不便,是那些无关紧要的非必需品的昂贵与稀缺。

关于白银价值变动的结论

大部分搜集古代物价资料的学者似乎都认为,谷物和一般物品的货币价格的低廉,换句话说,金银价值的高昂,不仅证明了这些金属的稀缺性,而且也证明了当时国家处于贫穷和野蛮的状态。这种观点与认为国家富裕就是金银富足以及国家贫穷就是金银稀缺的政治经济学体系是分不开的。关于这个体系,我将在第四篇作详细的说明和探讨。在此我只想说明,金银价值的高昂,只是证明当时供应商业世界的矿山贫瘠,绝不能证明金银昂贵国家的贫穷或野蛮。贫国由于没有能力购买那么多的金银,也就不可能比富国为金银支付更高的价格。所以,这些金属的价值在穷国绝不会比富国更高。中国比欧洲任何国家都富裕,但在中国贵金属的价值却比欧洲各国高得多。诚然,自从美洲发现矿山以来,欧洲的财富已经大幅增长,同时金银的价值也逐渐降低。但是金银价值的降低不是由于欧洲实际财富的增长,或欧洲土地

贵金属价值高并不是贫穷和野蛮的证明,

abundant mines than any that were known before. The increase of the quantity of gold and silver in Europe, and the increase of its manufactures and agriculture, are two events which, though they have happened nearly about the same time, yet have arisen from very different causes, and have scarce any natural connection with one another. The one has arisen from a mere accident, in which neither prudence nor policy either had or could have any share: The other from the fall of the feudal system, and from the establishment of a government which afforded to industry the only encouragement which it requires, some tolerable security that it shall enjoy the fruits of its own labour. Poland, where the feudal system still continues to take place, is at this day as beggarly a country as it was before the discovery of America. The money price of corn, however, has risen; the real value of the precious metals has fallen in Poland, in the same manner as in other parts of Europe. Their quantity, therefore, must have increased there as in other places, and nearly in the same proportion to the annual produce of its land and labour. This increase of the quantity of those metals, however, has not, it seems, increased that annual produce, has neither improved the manufactures and agriculture of the country, nor mended the circumstances of its inhabitants. Spain and Portugal, the countries which possess the mines, are, after Poland, perhaps, the two most beggarly countries in Europe. The value of the precious metals, however, must be lower in Spain and Portugal than in any other part of Europe; as they come from those countries to all other parts of Europe, loaded, not only with a freight and an insurance, but with the expence of smuggling, their exportation being either prohibited, or subjected to a duty. In proportion to the annual produce of the land and labour, therefore, their quantity must be greater in those countries than in any other part of Europe: Those countries, however, are poorer than the greater part of Europe. Though the feudal system has been abolished in Spain and Portugal, it has not been succeeded by a much better.

As the low value of gold and silver, therefore, is no proof of the wealth and flourishing state of the country where it takes place; so neither is their high value, or the low money price either of goods in general, or of corn in particular, any proof of its poverty and barbarism.

和劳动的年产量的增长,而是由于前所未有的丰裕矿山的偶然发现。欧洲金银数量的增加与制造业及农业的发达,虽然是几乎同时发生的两件事情,但它们产生的原因却非常不同,彼此间没有任何自然的联系。金银数量的增加只是偶然事件,谨慎多思和国家政策既没有也不可能在其中起任何作用。制造业和农业的发达则是由于封建制度的崩溃以及新政府的建立。后者对劳动提供了所必需的唯一的鼓励,即它能相当程度地保证每个人享有自身的劳动成果。如今波兰仍残存着封建制度,它同美洲发现以前同样赤贫。不过,像在欧洲其他地方一样,在波兰,谷物的货币价格已经上升,金银的实际价值已经下降。所以,同其他地方一样,那里贵金属数量增加了,并且是与土地和劳动的年产量以相似的比例增加的。然而,这些贵金属数量的增加看起来并没有增加该国的年产量,也没有改良其制造业和农业,更没有改善其居民的境况。西班牙和葡萄牙这两个拥有矿山的国家,也许是欧洲仅次于波兰最赤贫的国家了。可是,在西班牙和葡萄牙,贵金属的价值比欧洲任何国家都低,因为贵金属是从这两个国家运往欧洲各地的,不仅要支付运费和保险费,还要负担走私的费用,这是由于两国金银的出口是被禁止的或需课以重税。所以,就贵金属数量与土地和劳动的年产物相比来说,贵金属数量在这两个国家一定比欧洲其他各国都多。可是,这两个国家却比欧洲其他各国都穷。封建制度虽然在这两个国家已经被废除,但取而代之的并不是更好的制度。

正如金银价值的低廉不能证明一个国家的富裕和繁荣一样,金银价值的高昂,或者一般物品尤其是谷物的货币价格的低廉,也不能证明一个国家的贫穷和野蛮。

but the low price of cattle, poultry, game, &c., is a proof of poverty or barbarism.

But though the low money price either of goods in general, or of corn in particular, be no proof of the poverty or barbarism of the times, the low money price of some particular sorts of goods, such as cattle, poultry, game of all kinds, &c. in proportion to that of corn, is a most decisive one. It clearly demonstrates, first, their great abundance in proportion to that of corn, and consequently the great extent of the land which they occupied in proportion to what was occupied by corn; and, secondly, the low value of this land in proportion to that of corn land, and consequently the uncultivated and unimproved state of the far greater part of the lands of the country. It clearly demonstrates that the stock and population of the country did not bear the same proportion to the extent of its territory, which they commonly do in civilized countries, and that society was at that time, and in that country, but in its infancy. From the high or low money price either of goods in general, or of corn in particular, we can infer only that the mines which at that time happened to supply the commercial world with gold and silver, were fertile or barren, not that the country was rich or poor. But from the high or low money price of some sorts of goods in proportion to that of others, we can infer, with a degree of probability that approaches almost to certainty, that it was rich or poor, that the greater part of its lands were improved or unimproved, and that it was either in a more or less barbarous state, or in a more or less civilized one.

A rise of price due entirely to degradation of silver would affect all goods equally, but corn has risen much less than other provisions.

Any rise in the money price of goods which proceeded altogether from the degradation of the value of silver, would affect all sorts of goods equally, and raise their price universally a third, or a fourth, or a fifth part higher, according as silver happened to lose a third, or a fourth, or a fifth part of its former value. ①But the rise in the price of provisions, which has been the subject of so much reasoning and conversation, does not affect all sorts of provisions equally. Taking the course of the present century at an average, the price of corn, it is acknowledged, even by those who account for this rise by the degradation of the value of silver, has risen much less than that of some other sorts of provisions. The rise in the price of those other sorts of provisions, therefore, cannot be owing altogether to the degradation of the value of silver. Some other causes must be taken into the account, and those which have been above assigned, will, perhaps, without having recourse to the supposed degradation of the value of silver, sufficiently explain this rise in those

---

① [The arithmetic is slightly at fault. It should be, ' happened to lose a fourth, a fifth, or a sixth part of its former value '.]

尽管一般商品尤其是谷物的货币价格的低廉不能证明一国的贫穷或野蛮,而与谷物低廉的货币价格成比例的某些特殊种类物品如牲畜、家禽和各种猎物的低廉的货币价格却是决定性的证明。它明显地证明了两个事实:第一,牲畜比谷物更丰富,因而牲畜与谷物相比所占土地面积更大;第二,畜牧用地的价值比庄稼用地的价值更低,因而该国大部分土地 45 还没有开垦和改良。这两点分析表明,就资金和人口与其领土面积的比例来说,这类国家与文明国家不同,因而证明这类国家社会处于幼稚阶段。从一般商品尤其是谷物的货币价格的高低,我们只能推断出那时为商业世界供应金银的矿山的丰瘠程度,而不能据此推断该国的贫富程度。但是,从某些商品与其他商品的货币价格比例的高低,我们可以几乎准确地推断出,该国是富裕的还是贫困的,其大部分土地是否经过改良,其社会处于何种程度的野蛮状态,或者处于何种程度的文明状态。

如果商品货币价格上升完全是由于白银价值的降低,那么所有各种商品将会受到同等程度的影响。例如,如果白银价值降低了1/3,或者 1/4、1/5,那么一切商品价格必然普遍上升 1/3,或者 1/4、1/5①。但是,一直众说纷纭的各种食物价格的上涨,对所有各种食物会产生不同程度的影响。以本世纪平均水平来看,谷物价格的上升比例大大低于其他食物价格的上升比例,这是人们公认的,即使那些将这种上升归因于白银价值降低的人也是如此。因此,其他食物价格的上升不能完全归因于白银价值的降低,必须考虑其他原因。也许不需要假定白银价值降低,以上所提到的

旁注:牲畜、家禽、猎物等价格低廉是贫穷或野蛮的证明。

旁注:由白银价值下降造成的价格上升,将同等地影响所有的商品,但谷物价格比其他物品上升得少。

---

① 这里的数字略有错误,应为"价值比以前降低1/4、1/5或1/6"。

particular sorts of provisions of which the price has actually risen in proportion to that of corn.

<small>and has indeed been somewhat lower in 1701-64 than in 1637-1700</small> As to the price of corn itself, it has, during the sixty-four first years of the present century, and before the late extraordinary course of bad seasons, been somewhat lower than it was during the sixty-four last years of the preceding century. This fact is attested, not only by the accounts of Windsor market, but by the public fiars of all the different counties of Scotland, and by the accounts of several different markets in France, which have been collected with great diligence and fidelity by Mr. Messance,①and by Mr. Duprède St. Maur. The evidence is more complete than could well have been expected in a matter which is naturally so very difficult to be ascertained.

<small>while its recent high price has been due only to bad seasons.</small> As to the high price of corn during these last ten or twelve years, it can be sufficiently accounted for from the badness of the seasons, without supposing any degradation in the value of silver.

The opinion, therefore, that silver is continually sinking in its value, seems not to be founded upon any good observations, either upon the prices of corn, or upon those of other provisions.

<small>The distinction between a rise of prices and a fall in the value of silver is not useless:</small> The same quantity of silver, it may, perhaps, be said, will in the present times, even according to the account which has been here given, purchase a much smaller quantity of several sorts of provisions than it would have done during some part of the last century; and to ascertain whether this change be owing to a rise in the value of those goods, or to a fall in the value of silver, is only to establish a vain and useless distinction, which can be of no sort of service to the man who has only a certain quantity of silver to go to market with, or a certain fixed revenue in money. I certainly do not pretend that the knowledge of this distinction will enable him to buy cheaper. It may not, however, upon that account be altogether useless.

<small>it affords an easy proof of the prosperity of the country,</small> It may be of some use to the public by affording an easy proof of the prosperous condition of the country. If the rise in the price of some sorts of provisions be owing altogether to a fall in the

---

① [Recherches sur la Population, pp. 293-304.]

原因就足以解释,为什么那些食物价格的涨幅高于谷物价格的涨幅。

就谷物价格来说,其在本世纪头 64 年间以及最近歉收的非常时期之前一直略低于上世纪后 64 年的水平。英国温莎市场的账目,苏格兰各郡的法定谷价调查表,以及麦桑斯先生①和杜普雷·得·圣莫尔先生尽力而详实地搜集的法国几个不同市场的账目,都证明了这个事实。对一件本来非常难以确证的事情,这些证据比我们所期望的要充分得多。

<small>价格在 1701—1764 年确实比在 1637—1700 年低一些,</small>

至于最近 10 年或 12 年的谷物价格高昂,年成不好就足以解释,而不必推想到白银价值下降上。

<small>它最近的价格高昂只是由于年成不好。</small>

因此,认为白银价值一直在下降的看法似乎不是建立在正确的观察上。既没有观察谷物的价格,也没有观察其他食物的价格。

也许可以说,根据这里提供的记录,现在等量白银可购买的几种食物的数量,比上世纪有些年份能购买到的数量要少。要明确这种变化是由于这些商品价格的上升还是由于白银价值的下降,只是一种徒劳无用的区分。这种区分对于只有一定数量白银或者只有一定数量货币收入的人来说毫无帮助。我不敢断言,知道这种区分就能以便宜的价格买到商品。但也不能说,这种区分因此就毫无用处。

<small>对价格上升和白银价值下降区分并非无用的:</small>

这种区分很容易证明一国的繁荣程度。这也许对公众有些用处。如果某些食物价格的上升完全是由于白银价值的下降,就

<small>它很容易证明国家的繁荣,</small>

---

① 《人口调查》,第 293～304 页。

value of silver, it is owing to a circumstance from which nothing can be inferred but the fertility of the American mines. The real wealth of the country, the annual produce of its land and labour, may, notwithstanding this cir. cumstance, be either gradually declining, as in Portugal and Poland; or gradually advancing, as in most other parts of Europe. But if this rise in the price of some sorts of provisions be owing to a rise in the real value of the land which produces them, to its increased fertility; or, in consequence of more extended improvement and good cultivation, to its having been rendered fit for producing corn; it is owing to a circumstance which indicates in the clearest manner the prosperous and advancing state of the country. The land constitutes by far the greatest, the most important, and the most durable part of the wealth of every extensive country. It may surely be of some use, or, at least, it may give some satisfaction to the Public, to have so decisive a proof of the increasing value of by far the greatest, the most important, and the most durable part of its wealth.

and may be of use in regulating the wages of the inferior servants of the state. It may too be of some use to the Public in regulating the pecuniary reward of some of its inferior servants. If this rise in the price of some sorts of provisions be owing to a fall in the value of silver, their pecuniary reward, provided it was not too large before, ought certainly to be augmented in proportion to the extent of this fall. If it is not augmented, their real recompence will evidently be so much diminished. But if this rise of price is owing to the increased value, in consequence of the improved fertility of the land which produces such provisions, it becomes a much nicer matter to judge either in what proportion any pecuniary reward ought to be augmented, or whether it ought to be augmented at all. The extension of improvement and cultivation, as it necessarily raises more or less, in proportion to the price of corn, that of every sort of animal food, so it as necessarily lowers that of, I believe, every sort of vegetable food. It raises the price of animal food; because a great part of the land which produces it, being rendered fit for producing corn, must afford to the landlord and farmer the rent and profit of corn land. It lowers the price of vegetable food; because, by increasing the fertility of the land, it increases its abundance. The improvements of agriculture too introduce many sorts of vegetable food, which, requiring less

将处于这样一种情况,即由此只能得出美洲矿山丰裕多产的结论。在这种情况下,一个国家的实际财富,即土地和劳动的年产物,或者像葡萄牙和波兰一样逐渐减少,或者像欧洲其他大部分地方那样逐渐增加。某些种食物价格的上升,是由于生产它们的土地的实际价值提高了,即由于该土地肥力增强了,或者由于进行了更广泛的改良和良好耕种使土地变得更适于谷物生长。如果是这样一种情况,那就清楚地表明该国正处于繁荣和进步的状态。土地是一切大国最大的、最重要的、最持久的国家财富。能为一国财富中最大、最重要、最持久部分的价值有否提高提供决定性的证据,这种区分对公众就有些用处,至少能使公众感到满足。

在规定某些低级雇员的货币报酬时,这种区分对公众也是有某些用处的。如果某些种食物价格的上升是由于白银价值的下降,如果雇工的货币报酬以前不是太高,那么货币报酬肯定就应按照白银价值下降的比例予以增加。如果不增加,他们的实际报酬将明显同比例的减少。但如果食物价格的上升是由于生产它们的土地经过改良更加肥沃了,使得土地价格提高,那么就很难判断应按什么比例增加其货币报酬或者是否要增加其报酬。改良和耕种的扩大,必然按谷物价格的提高比例或多或少地提高每一种肉食的价格。我相信,这必然会降低每一种植物性食物的价格。之所以提高了肉食的价格,是因为生产肉食的土地已改良得适合于生产谷物,而这些土地必须能为地主和农场主提供谷物用地的地租和利润。之所以降低了植物性食物的价格,是因为通过增加土地肥力提高了土地的丰产程度。农业的改良还引进了许多植物性食物的新品种,它们比谷物需要的土地更少,需要的劳

在规定一个国家低级雇工的工资时可能有用。

land and not more labour than corn, come much cheaper to market. Such are potatoes and maize, or what is called Indian corn, the two most important improvements which the agriculture of Europe, perhaps, which Europe itself, has received from the great extension of its commerce and navigation. Many sorts of vegetable food, besides, which in the rude state of agriculture are confined to the kitchen-garden, and raised only by the spade, come in its improved state to be introduced into common fields, and to be raised by the plough: such as turnips, carrots, cabbages, &c. If in the progress of improvement, therefore, the real price of one species of food necessarily rises, that of another as necessarily falls, and it becomes a matter of more nicety to judge how far the rise in the one may be compensated by the fall in the other. When the real price of butcher's-meat has once got to its height (which, with regard to every sort, except, perhaps, that of hogs fesh, it seems to have done through a great part of England more than a century ago), any rise which can afterwards happen in that of any other sort of animal food, cannot much affect the circumstances of the inferior ranks of people. The circumstances of the poor through a great part of England cannot surely be so much distressed by any rise in the price of poultry, fish, wild-fowl, or venison, as they must be relieved by the fall in that of potatoes.

The poor are more distressed by the artificial rise of some manufactures than by the natural rise of rude produce other than corn.

In the present season of scarcity the high price of corn no doubt distresses the poor. But in times of moderate plenty, when corn is at its ordinary or average price, the natural rise in the price of any other sort of rude produce cannot much affect them. They suffer more, perhaps, by the artificial rise which has been occasioned by taxes in the price of some manufactured commodities; as of salt, soap, leather, candles, malt, beer, and ale, &c.

Effects of the Progress of Improvement upon the real Price of Manufactures

But the natural effect of improvement is to diminish the price of manufactures.

IT is the natural effect of improvement, however, to diminish gradually the real price of almost all manufactures. That of the manufacturing workmanship diminishes, perhaps, in all of them without exception. In consequence of better machinery, of greater dexterity,

动也不会更多,市场价格也便宜些,如马铃薯和玉米或所谓印度小麦都属于此类。它们是欧洲农业,或者说欧洲本身,从商业和航运的扩张中获得的两个极其重要的改良。此外,在原始农业状态下,许多植物性食物品种仅限于菜园里栽种和用锄头来培植,而在改良农业状态下,这些植物已被引进到普通田地里栽植和用犁培植,如芜青、胡萝卜、卷心菜等都属于此类食物。因此,在改良的进程中,如果某一食物的实际价格必然上升,另一种食物的实际价格必然下降,那就更难以判断前者的上升能在多大程度上被后者的下降所抵消。也许除了猪肉外,似乎早在一个多世纪前,英格兰大部分地区每种鲜肉的价格都已经达到最高限度。一旦鲜肉的价格上升到最高限度,其后,任何其他肉食的涨价都不会对下层人民的境况产生太大影响。英格兰大部分地区穷人的境况,不会因家禽、鱼类、野禽或鹿肉价格的上升而陷入太大的困苦,因为他们一定能从马铃薯价格的下降中得到补偿。

在目前的歉收年份,谷价高昂肯定会使穷人陷于困苦。但在一般的丰年,当谷物处于一般价格或平均价格水平时,其他任何原生产物价格的自然上涨都不会对穷人有太大的影响。他们或许由于食盐、肥皂、皮革、蜡烛、麦芽、啤酒、麦酒等某些制造品伴随着课税的人为涨价而感到痛苦。

穷人受到某些制造品价格上升的困扰,比以谷物以外的原生产物价格的自然上升更大。

改良进程对制造品实际价格的影响

但是,改良自然而然地会导致几乎所有制造品的实际价格逐渐降低。在改良进程中,也许几乎所有制造业的费用都会降低。由于机器更完善、技术更熟练以及劳动分工更适当,所有这些改

但是,改良的自然影响是降低制造品的价格。

and of a more proper division and distribution of work, all of which are the natural effects of improvement, a much smaller quantity of labour becomes requisite for executing any particular piece of work; and though, in consequence of the flourishing circumstances of the society, the real price of labour should rise very considerably, yet the great diminution of the quantity will generally much more than compensate the greatest rise which can happen in the price.

<small>In a few manufactures the rise in the price of raw material counterbalances improvement in execution,</small> There are, indeed, a few manufactures, in which the necessary rise in the real price of the rude materials will more than compensate all the advantages which improvement can introduce into the execution of the work. In carpenters and joiners work, and in the coarser sort of cabinet work, the necessary rise in the real price of barren timber, in consequence of the improvement of land, will more than compensate all the advantages which can be derived from the best machinery, the greatest dexterity, and the most proper division and distribution of work.

<small>but in other cases price falls considerably.</small> But in all cases in which the real price of the rude materials either does not rise at all, or does not rise very much, that of the manufactured commodity sinks very considerably.

<small>Since 1600 this has been most remarkable in manufactures made of the coarser metals.</small> This diminution of price has, in the course of the present and preceding century, been most remarkable in those manufactures of which the materials are the coarser metals. A better movement of a watch, than about the middle of the last century could have been bought for twenty pounds, may now perhaps be had for twenty shillings. In the work of cutlers and locksmiths, in all the toys[①] which are made of the coarser metals, and in all those goods which are commonly known by the name of Birmingham and Sheffield ware, there has been, during the same period, a very great reduction of price, though not altogether so great as in watch-work. It has, however, been sufficient to astonish the workmen of every other part of Europe, who in many cases acknowledge that they can produce no work of equal goodness for double, or even for triple the price. There are perhaps no manufactures in which the division of labour can be carried further, or in which the machinery employed admits of a greater variety of improvements, than those of which the materials are the coarser metals.

<small>Clothing has not fallen much in the same period.</small> In the clothing manufacture there has, during the same period, been no such sensible reduction of price. The price of superfine cloth, I have been assured, on the contrary, has, within these five-and-twenty or thirty years, risen somewhat in proportion to its quality;

① [Lectures, pp. 159, 164.]

良的自然结果，使从事任何一项具体工作所需的劳动量大大减少。同时，尽管社会的繁荣会大幅度提高劳动的实际价格，但所需劳动量的大量减少通常能绰绰有余地抵补价格中劳动价格的上涨。

诚然，有些制造品，改良生产所带来的好处远远不足以抵补原材料实际价格的必然上升带来的影响。对于许多木工来说，在制作精细家具的工作中，木材的实际价格因土地改良必然上升，这种上升足以抵消最好的机器、最熟练的技术、最恰当的分工所带来的全部好处而有余。

<small>少数制造品原材料价格上升了消其具体操作的改良，</small>

但在原材料的实际价格根本没有上升或上升不多的情况下，制造品的实际价格会大幅下降。

<small>但在其情况下价格下降很多。</small>

在本世纪和上世纪，以低廉金属为原料的制造品价格下降得最为显著。一只较好的手表，上世纪中叶可能要卖 20 镑，如今可能只需 20 先令就能买到。在同一时期，刀匠和锁匠的所有制造品、所有用低廉金属制成的玩具①以及所有冠以伯明翰和雪菲尔德之名的制造品，价格都大为下降。尽管这些制造品的价格下降幅度不像手表那么大，但也足以使欧洲其他各地的工人感到震惊。这些工人在许多场合都承认，他们用两倍甚至三倍的价钱，也生产不出同样优质的产品。也许没有一种制造业，能比以低廉金属为原材料的制造业所进行的劳动分工更细致，或者使用改良程度更大的机器。

<small>自 1600 年来，以低廉金属做原料的制造品价格下降为最显著。</small>

在同一时期，毛织业就没有出现过这样显著的降价。相反，在最近 25 年或 30 年里，最上等毛织物价格相对于其质量来说还

<small>在同一时期，一衣格没有多大下降，</small>

---

① 《关于法律、警察、岁入及军备的演讲》，第 159、164 页。

owing, it was said, to a considerable rise in the price of the material, which consists altogether of Spanish wool. That of the Yorkshire cloth, which is made altogether of English wool, is said indeed, during the course of the present century, to have fallen a good deal in proportion to its quality. Quality, however, is so very disputable a matter, that I look upon all information of this kind as somewhat uncertain. In the clothing manufacture, the division of labour is nearly the same now as it was a century ago, and the machinery employed is not very different. There may, however, have been some small improvements in both, which may have occasioned some reduction of price.

<small>but very considerably since the fifteenth century</small> But the reduction will appear much more sensible and undeniable, if we compare the price of this manufacture in the present times with what it was in a much remoter period, towards the end of the fifteenth century, when the labour was probably much less subdivided, and the machinery employed much more imperfect, than it is at present.

<small>Fine cloth has fallen to less than one-third of its price in 1487.</small> In 1487, being the 4th of Henry VII. it was enacted, that "whosoever shall sell by retail a broad yard of the finest scarlet grained, or of other grained cloth of the finest making, above sixteen shillings, " shall forfeit forty shillings for every yard so sold. " Sixteen shillings, therefore, containing about the same quantity of silver as four-and-twenty shillings of our present money, was, at that time, reckoned not an unreasonable price for a yard of the finest cloth; ① and as this is a sumptuary law, such cloth, it is probable, had usually been sold somewhat dearer. A guinea may be reckoned the highest price in the present times. Even though the quality of the cloths, therefore, should be supposed equal, and that of the present times is most probably much superior, yet, even upon this supposition, the money price of the finest cloth appears to have been considerably reduced since the end of the fifteenth century. But its real price has been much more reduced. Six shillings and eight-pence was then, and long afterwards, reckoned the average price of a quarter of wheat. Sixteen shillings, therefore, was the price of two quarters and more than three bushels of wheat. Valuing a quarter of wheat in the present times at eight-and-twenty shillings, the real price of a yard of fine cloth must, in those times, have been equal to at least three pounds six shillings and sixpence of our present money. The man who bought it must have parted with the command of a quantity of labour and subsistence equal to what that sum would

---

① [C. 8.]

略有上升。据说这是因为原材料价格大幅上升,而这些原材料完全是西班牙羊毛。的确,据说本世纪完全用英格兰羊毛织成的约克郡呢绒的价格相对于其质量来说已经大幅下降。不过质量是个非常有争议的问题,我认为这类信息都未必确实。毛织业中现在的劳动分工与一个世纪前几乎一样,所使用机器也没有多大不同。不过,劳动分工和机器可能都有些小的改进,使得毛织品价格有一定幅度的下降。

但是,如果我们把这种制造品现在的价格与更远的 15 世纪末的价格相比较,则其价格下降看起来就非常明显和无可厚非。当时,劳动分工或许远没有今天细致,机器也远没有今天完善。 但自从 15 世纪以来下降价很多。

1487 年,即亨利七世四年颁布的法律①规定:"凡零售最上等红花呢或其他上等花呢每码售价超过 16 先令者,所售每码罚款 40 先令。"所以,16 先令含银量大约与现时的货币 24 先令相同,当时被视作一码上等呢绒的合理价格。由于此项法律意在禁止奢侈,因此这种呢绒通常售价可能要略高些。如今一几尼就算是呢绒的最高价格了。即使假定质量一样,自 15 世纪末以来,最上等呢绒的货币价格也已经大幅下降,而其实际价格降幅更大,何况现在的呢绒质量可能比过去要好得多。6 先令 8 便士,在当时以及随后的一段时期里,被认为是一夸特小麦的平均价格。所以,16 先令就是 2 夸特 3 蒲式耳多小麦的价格。如果现在以 1 夸特 28 先令来估算小麦的价格,当时一码最上等呢绒的实际价格至少等于现时的货币 3 镑 6 先令 6 便士。购买一码上等呢绒的人,就必须放弃他现在 3 镑 6 先令 6 便士所能支配的劳动和生活 上等布料比 1487 年降价将近 1/3。

---

① 第 8 号法令。

国民财富的性质与原理

purchase in the present times.

<small>and coarse cloth has fallen to less than one half of its price in 1463.</small>

The reduction in the real price of the coarse manufacture, though considerable, has not been so great as in that of the fine.

In 1463, being the 3d of Edward Ⅳ. it was enacted, that "no servant in husbandry, nor common labourer, nor servant to any artificer inhabiting out of a city or burgh, shall use or wear in their clothing "any cloth above two shillings the broad yard. " In the 3d of Edward Ⅳ. two shillings contained very nearly the same quantity of silver as four of our present money. But the Yorkshire cloth which is now sold at four shillings the yard, is probably much superior to any that was then made for the wearing of the very poorest order of common servants. Even the money price of their clothing, therefore, may, in proportion to the quality, be somewhat cheaper in the present than it was in those ancient times. The real price is certainly a good deal cheaper. Ten-pence was then reckoned what is called the moderate and reasonable price of a bushel of wheat. Two shillings, therefore, was the price of two bushels and near two pecks of wheat, which in the present times, at three shillings and sixpence the bushel, would be worth eight shillings and nine-pence. For a yard of this cloth the poor servant must have parted with the power of purchasing a quantity of subsistence equal to what eight shillings and nine-pence would purchase in the present times. This is a sumptuary law too, restraining the luxury and extravagance of the poor. Their clothing, therefore, had commonly been much more expensive. ①

<small>Hose have fallen very considerably since 1463,</small>

The same order of people are, by the same law, prohibited from wearing hose, of which the price should exceed fourteen-pence the pair, equal to about eight-and-twenty pence of our present money. But fourteen-pence was in those times the price of a bushel and near two pecks of wheat; which, in the present times, at three and sixpence the bushel, would cost five shillings and three-pence. We should in the present times consider this as a very high price for a pair of stockings to a servant of the poorest and lowest order. He must, however, in those times have paid what was really equivalent to this price for them.

<small>when they were made of common cloth.</small>

In the time of Edward Ⅳ. the art of knitting stockings was probably not known in any part of Europe. Their hose were made of

---

① [C. 5]

资料的数量。

粗呢的实际价格虽然也下降很多，但还没有上等呢绒下降得多。

粗呢价格比1463年下降将近一半。

1463年，即爱德华四世三年颁布的法律①规定："凡农业雇工、普通工人以及住在城镇之外的工匠所雇用的工人，都不得穿用每码2先令以上的衣料。"在爱德华四世三年，2先令的含银量与现时的货币4先令的含银量相同。但现在每码售价4先令的约克郡呢，恐怕比当时普通雇工中最穷困的人所穿的任何衣料要好得多。可见，这些人所穿衣服的货币价格相对于其质量来说比从前略低，其实际价格肯定也低得更多。当时10便士被视作1蒲式耳小麦适中而合理的价格，则两先令就是约2蒲式耳2配克小麦的合理价格。按现在每蒲式耳合3先令6便士计算，当时的两先令现在要值8先令9便士。为了购买1码这种呢料，穷困的雇工要舍弃购买相当于今天8先令9便士所能购买的生活资料的数量。此项禁止奢侈的法律限制穷人的奢侈和浪费。可见，当时他们的衣服比现在要昂贵得多。

这一项法令还规定，禁止该阶层的人民穿价格超过14便士（约合现时的货币28便士）的长袜。当时14便士是1蒲式耳2配克小麦的价格，以现在每蒲式耳3先令6便十计算，现在要值5先令6便士。在今天看来，这个价格应该是最贫贱阶层的雇工买长袜的非常高的价格。不过，当时为了一双长袜，他必须支付出实际等于这一价格的东西。

长袜价格自1463年以来下降很多，当时长袜是由普通布料做成。

在爱德华四世时代，欧洲各地可能都不知道编制长袜的技

---

① 第5号法令。

common cloth, which may have been one of the causes of their dearness. The first person that wore stockings in England is said to have been Queen Elizabeth. She received them as a present from the Spanish ambassador. ①

<small>The machinery for making cloth has been much improved, which explains the fall of price.</small>

Both in the coarse and in the fine woollen manufacture, the machinery employed was much more imperfect in those ancient, than it is in the present times. It has since received three very capital improvements, besides, probably, many smaller ones of which it may be difficult to ascertain either the number or the importance. The three capital improvements are: first, The exchange of the rock and spindle for the spinning-wheel, which, with the same quantity of labour, will perform more than double the quantity of work. Secondly, the use of several very ingenious machines which facilitate and abridge in a still greater proportion the winding of the worsted and woollen yarn, or the proper arrangement of the warp and woof before they are put into the loom; an operation which, previous to the inventions of those machines, must have been extremely tedious and troublesome. Thirdly, The employment of the fulling mill for thickening the cloth, instead of treading it in water. Neither wind nor water mills of any kind were known in England so early as the beginning of the sixteenth century, nor, so far as I know, in any other part of Europe north of the Alps. They had been introduced into Italy some time before.

The consideration of these circumstances may, perhaps, in some measure explain to us why the real price both of the coarse and of the fine manufacture, was so much higher in those ancient, than it is in the present times. It cost a greater quantity of labour to bring the goods to market. When they were brought thither, therefore, they must have purchased or exchanged for the price of a greater quantity.

The coarse manufacture probably was, in those ancient times, carried on in England, in the same manner as it always has been in countries where arts and manufactures are in their infancy. It was probably a houshold manufacture, in which every different part of the work was occasionally performed by all the different members of almost every private family; but so as to be their work only when they had nothing else to do, and not to be the principal business from

---

① ['Dr. Howell in his History of the World, vol. ii. , p. 222]

术。当时所穿的长袜,都是用普通呢绒制成。这可能是长袜昂贵的原因之一。据说英格兰第一个穿长袜的人是伊丽莎白女王。那是西班牙大使赠送给她的礼物①。

无论是粗精毛织业,古代所用机器都远不如现代的那样完善。此后,毛织业所用机器曾经历了三次重大改良,此外或许还有许多难以确定数目和重要性的小改良。三次重大改良是:第一,以纺条、纺锤代替纺轮,其结果,等量劳动能完成两倍以上的工作量。第二,使用多种精妙机器,极大地方便和简化了绒线、毛线的卷绕,也就是缩短了经纬线放入纺机前进行适当安排的时间。这道工序在这些机器发明之前是极其单调、烦琐的工作。第三,采用漂布机浆洗呢绒,代替以往在水中踩踏使其厚实的方法。在16世纪初,英格兰各地还不知道有水车或风车,据我所了解的情况,当时阿尔卑斯山以北的欧洲地区也无人知道。它们不久前才被引进意大利。(制造布料的机器已经改进很大)

这些情况也许可以在一定程度上向我们说明,为什么粗精毛织品的实际价格在古代都比现在高那么多。当时把商品运送到市场也许要花费大量的劳动。所以,在这些商品被送到市场后,就必须购买或交换更多商品的货币价格。(这解释了价格下降的原因)

英格兰古代的粗纺业经营方式,可能与工艺和制造都处于幼稚阶段的其他国家一样。它可能是一种家庭制造业,工作的各部分由每一家庭的不同成员偶尔完成,而且这只是他们通常没有别的工作可做时才做的工作,并不是他们赚取大部分生活资料的工

---

① 豪威尔博士:《世界历史》,第2卷,第222页。

_{The coarse manufacture was a household one, but the fine was carried on in Flanders by people who subsisted on it, and was subject to customs duty,} which any of them derived the greater part of their subsistence. The work which is performed in this manner, it has already been observed, comes always much cheaper to market than that which is the principal or sole fund of the workman's subsistence. The fine manufacture, on the other hand, was not in those times carried on in England, but in the rich and commercial country of Flanders; and it was probably conducted then, in the same manner as now, by people who derived the whole, or the principal part of their subsistence from it. It was besides a foreign manufacture, and must have paid some duty, the ancient custom of tonnage and poundage at least, to the king. This duty, indeed, would not probably be very great. It was not then the policy of Europe to restrain, by high duties, the importation of foreign manufactures, but rather to encourage it, in order that merchants might be enabled to supply, at as easy a rate as possible, the great men with the convenieneies and luxuries which they wanted, and which the industry of their own country could not afford them.

_{which explains why the coarse was in those times lower in proportion to the fine.} The consideration of these circumstances may perhaps in some measure explain to us why, in those ancient times, the real price of the coarse manufacture was, in proportion to that of the fine, so much lower than in the present times.

作。前面已经指出，与作为职业工人生活资料主要或唯一来源的产品相比，以这种方式完成的产品其价格要便宜得多。另一方面，当时英格兰还没有精纺业，只有富裕的、商业繁荣的佛兰德斯才经营，而且当时那里可能只有完全依赖或主要依赖纺织业为生的人才以与现在相同的方式从事精纺业。此外，当时佛兰德斯细呢是一种外国货，必须向国王缴纳某些赋税，至少要缴纳以往通行的吨税和镑税等关税。当然，这种赋税可能不会很重。当时欧洲国家的政策不是以高关税限制进口外国制造品，而是鼓励进口，以便使商人以尽可能低的价格供应达官显贵需要而本国又无力生产的便利品和奢侈品。

粗纺业是一种家庭业，精纺业在佛兰德斯以此为生的人从事，而且要缴纳关税。

这些情况可能在某种程度上向我们说明，为什么古代粗呢的实际价格与细呢的实际价格相比大大低于现在的价格。

这说明为什么当时粗呢价格比细呢价格低。

Conclusion Of The Chapter.

<small>Every improvement in the circumstances of society raises rent.</small> I shall conclude this very long chapter with observing that every improvement in the circumstances of the society tends either directly or indirectly to raise the real rent of land, to increase the real wealth of the landlord, his power of purchasing the labour, or the produce of the labour of other people.

<small>Extension of improvement and cultivation raises it directly,</small> The extension of improvement and cultivation tends to raise it directly. The landlord's share of the produce necessarily increases with the increase of the produce.

<small>and so does the rise in the price of cattle, &c.</small> That rise in the real price of those parts of the rude produce of land, which is first the effect of extended improvement and cultivation, and afterwards the cause of their being still further extended, the rise in the price of cattle, for example, tends too to raise the rent of land directly, and in a still greater proportion. The real value of the landlord's share, his real command of the labour of other people, not only rises with the real value of the produce, but the proportion of his share to the whole produce rises with it. That produce, after the rise in its real price, requires no more labour to collect it than before. A smaller proportion of it will, therefore, be sufficient to replace, with the ordinary profit, the stock which employs that labour. A greater proportion of it must, consequently, belong to the landlord.

<small>Improvements which reduce the price of manufactures raise it indirectly,</small> All those improvements in the productive powers of labour, which tend directly to reduce the real price of manufactures, tend indirectly to raise the real rent of land. The landlord exchanges that part of his rude produce, which is over and above his own consumption, or what comes to the same thing, the price of that part of it, for manufactured produce. Whatever reduces the real price of the latter, raises that of the former. An equal quantity of the former becomes thereby equivalent to a greater quantity of the latter; and the landlord is enabled to purchase a greater quantity of the

本章的结论

我将以下述观点结束这冗长的一章:社会状况每次改良都直接或间接地倾向于提高土地的实际地租,增加地主的实际财富即增加地主对他人劳动或劳动产品的购买力。

改良和耕种的扩大会直接提高实际地租。地主在产品中所占有的份额必然随产量的增长而增大。

有一部分土地原生产物,其实际价格的上升是土地改良和耕种扩大的结果,随后又是改良和耕种进一步扩大的原因。例如,牲畜价格的提高,也会直接并且以更大比例提高地租。地主所占份额的实际价值,即他对他人劳动的实际支配能力,不仅随着产品的实际价值而上升,而且他的份额占全部产品的比例也随之提高。这种产品在实际价值提高之后,并不需要比以前更多的劳动获取它。所以,其中较小的比例就足以补偿雇用这种劳动的资本及平均利润。于是,产品中较大的比例必然属于地主。

劳动生产力中的所有这些进步,都趋向于直接降低制造品的实际价格,间接提高土地的实际地租。地主用自己消费后剩余的那部分原生产物,或者说是用剩余的原生产物的价格,去交换制成品。任何因素降低了后者的实际价格都必然提高前者的实际价格。因为,等量的原生产物相当于更多数量的制成品,而地主

conveniencies, ornaments, or luxuries, which he has occasion for.

and so does every increase in the quantity of useful labour employed.
Every increase in the real wealth of the society, every increase in the quantity of useful labour employed within it, tends indirectly to raise the real rent of land. A certain proportion of this labour naturally goes to the land. A greater number of men and cattle are employed in its cultivation, the produce increases with the increase of the stock which is thus employed in raising it, and the rent increases with the produce.

The contrary circumstances lower rent.
The contrary circumstances, the neglect of cultivation and improvement, the fall in the real price of any part of the rude produce of land, the rise in the real price of manufactures from the decay of manufacturing art and industry, the declension of the real wealth of the society, all tend, on the other hand, to lower the real rent of land, to reduce the real wealth of the landlord, to diminish his power of purchasing either the labour, or the produce of the labour of other people.

There are three parts of produce and three original orders of society.
The whole annual produce of the land and labour of every country, or what comes to the same thing, the whole price of that annual produce, naturally divides itself, it has already been observed, into three parts; the rent of land, the wages of labour, and the profits of stock; and constitutes a revenue to three different orders of people; to those who live by rent, to those who live by wages, and to those who live by profit. These are the three great, original and constituent orders of every civilized society, from whose revenue that of every other order is ultimately derived.

The interest of the proprietors of land is inseparably connected with the general interest of the society.
The interest of the first of those three great orders, it appears from what has been just now said, is strictly and inseparably connected with the general interest of the society. Whatever either promotes or obstructs the one, necessarily promotes or obstructs the other. When the public deliberates concerning any regulation of commerce or police, the proprietors of land never can mislead it, with a view to promote the interest of their own particular order; at least, if they have any tolerable knowledge of that interest. They are, indeed, too often defective in this tolerable knowledge. They are the only one of the three orders whose revenue costs them neither labour nor care, but comes to them, as it were, of its own accord, and independent of any plan or project of their own. That indolence, which is the natural effect of the ease and security of their situation,

本章的结论

便能购买更多便利品、装饰品和奢侈品。

社会实际财富的任何增加,投入其中的有用劳动量的任何增加,都趋向于会间接提高土地实际地租。这种增加的劳动量自然有一定比例流向土地。更多的人和牲畜用于耕种,其产物随着投入生产的资本的增加而增加,而地租也随着产物的增加而增加。

雇佣的有用劳动的数量增加也是这样。

至于相反的情况,例如,忽视耕种和改良,任何一部分土地原生产物实际价格的下降,制造品的实际价格由于制造技术和产业的衰落而上升,社会实际财富减少,所有这些事情,都倾向于降低土地的实际地租,减少地主的实际财富,削弱他对于他人的劳动或他人劳动产品的购买力。

相反的情况会降低地租。

前面已经提到,每一国家土地和劳动的全部年产物,或者说,年产物的全部价格,自然而然的分解为三部分,即土地的地租、劳动的工资以及资本的利润。这三部分构成三个不同阶层人们的收入,即靠地租生活的人的收入、靠工资生活的人的收入以及靠利润生活的人的收入。这三个阶层是组成每一个文明社会的重要的基本阶层。任何其他阶层的收入都最终来自于这三个阶层的收入。

三种产品和三个阶层是基本社会阶层。

由此可见,这三大阶层中的第一阶层,即地主阶层的利益与社会的整体利益密切相关而不可分离。凡是促进或妨碍其中一种利益的事情,必然促进或妨碍另一种利益。当公众商讨关于商业及政治的规定时,土地所有者为了促进本阶层的利益,是从来不会起误导作用的,至少在他们对这种利益关系还有一定认识的时候应该这样。当然,他们常常是缺乏这种认识。他们是这三个阶层中的一个特殊阶层。他们获取收入,既不需要费力,也不需要劳神,而仿佛是不依靠自己的任何计划和筹算而自然取得。他

土地所有者的利益和社会整体利益不可分割联系在一起。

— 569 —

| 国民财富的性质与原理 |

renders them too often, not only ignorant, but incapable of that application of mind which is necessary in order to foresee and understand the conesquences of any public regulation.

So also is that of those who live by wages. The interest of the second order, that of those who live by wages, is as strictly connected with the interest of the society as that of the first. The wages of the labourer, it has already been shewn, are never so high as when the demand for labour is continually rising, or when the quantity employed is every year increasing considerably. When this real wealth of the society becomes stationary, his wages are soon reduced to what is barely enough to enable him to bring up a family, or to continue the race of labourers. When the society declines, they fall even below this. The order of proprietors may, perhaps, gain more by the prosperity of the society, than that of labourers: but there is no order that suffers so cruelly from its decline. But though the interest of the labourer is strictly connected with that of the society, he is incapable either of comprehending that interest, or of understanding its connexion with his own. His condition leaves him no time to receive the necessary information, and his education and habits are commonly such as to render him unfit to judge even though he was fully informed. In the public deliberations, therefore, his voice is little heard and less regarded, except upon some particular occasions, when his clamour is animated, set on, and supported by his employers, not for his, but their own particular purposes.

but the interest of those who live by profit has not the same connexion with the general interest of the society. His employers constitute the third order, that of those who live by profit. It is the stock that is employed for the sake of profit, which puts into motion the greater part of the useful labour of every society. The plans and projects of the employers of stock regulate and direct all the most important operations of labour, and profit is the end proposed by all those plans and projects. But the rate of profit does not, like rent and wages, rise with the prosperity, and fall with the declension, of the society. On the contrary, it is naturally low in rich, and high in poor countries, and it is always highest in the countries which are going fastest to ruin. The interest of this third order, therefore, has not the same connexion with the general interest of the society as that of the

本章的结论

们舒适而安全的境况产生的自然结果就是懒惰。这常常使他们不但无知,而且也没有动脑筋去预见和理解任何公共规定的后果的能力。

第二阶层即靠工资为生的阶层,与第一阶层的人一样,其利益紧密地与社会利益联系在一起。如前所述,当劳动的需求不断增长时,或者当所雇用的劳动量逐年大幅度增长时,劳动者的工资才会达到最高。当社会实际财富处于不增不减的状态时,劳动者的工资就会降低到仅能养家糊口、延续香火的水平。当社会衰落的时候,其工资甚至还要低于这个水平。当社会繁荣的时候,土地所有者阶层所得可能多于劳动者阶层。但当社会衰落的时候,没有哪一个阶层所遭受的痛苦比劳动者阶层更大。尽管劳动者的利益与社会的利益紧密联系在一起,但劳动者却既不能理解这种社会利益,也不能理解社会利益与自身利益的联系程度。他们的境况使他们没有时间去接受必须的信息,何况即使得到了充分的信息,所受的教育和习惯一般也使他们不善于判断。所以,在公众讨论时,他们的声音几乎听不到,或者很少受到重视,除非在某些情况下,他们的叫嚷才受到雇主们的鼓动、怂恿和支持,但不是为了达到他们的目的,而是为了雇主们自己的目的。

> 靠工资生活的人的利益也是这样。

雇主们构成第三阶层,他们靠利润为生。推动社会大部分有用劳动的正是追逐利润而投入的资本。资本使用者的规划和设计调控和支配着所有重要的劳动活动,而利润是所有这些规划和设计要达到的目标。但是,利润率与地租及工资不同,它不随社会的繁荣而上升,也不随社会的衰落而下降。相反,它在富裕国家自然而然的低,在贫穷国家自然而然的高,而且总是在迅速趋于没落的国家最高。所以,第三阶层的利益不像其他两个阶层那

> 靠利润生活的人的利益与整个社会利益没有联系。

other two. Merchants and master manufacturers are, in this order, the two classes of people who commonly employ the largest capitals, and who by their wealth draw to themselves the greatest share of the public consideration. As during their whole lives they are engaged in plans and projects, they have frequently more acuteness of understanding than the greater part of country gentlemen. As their thoughts, however, are commonly exercised rather about the interest of their own particular branch of business, than about that of the society, their judgment, even when given with the greatest candour (which it has not been upon every occasion), is much more to be depended upon with regard to the former of those two objects, than with regard to the latter, Their superiority over the country gentleman is, not so much in their knowledge of the public interest, as in their having a better knowledge of their own interest than he has of his. It is by this superior knowledge of their own interest that they have frequently imposed upon his generosity, and persuaded him to give up both his own interest and that of the public, from a very simple but honest conviction, that their interest, and not his, was the interest of the public. The interest of the dealers, however, in any particular branch of trade or manufactures, is always in some respects different from, and even opposite to, that of the public. To widen the market and to narrow the competition, is always the interest of the dealers. To widen the market may frequently be agreeable enough to the interest of the public; but to narrow the competition must always be against it, and can serve only to enable the dealers, by raising their profits above what they naturally would be, to levy, for their own benefit, an absurd tax upon the rest of their fellow-citizens. The proposal of any new law or regulation of commerce which comes from this order, ought always to be listened to with great precaution, and ought never to be adopted till after having been long and carefully examined, not only with the most scrupulous, but with the most suspicious attention. It comes from an order of men, whose interest is never exactly the same with that of the public, who have generally an interest to deceive and even to oppress the public, and who accordingly have, upon many occasions, both deceived and oppressed it.

本章的结论

样与社会整体利益有紧密联系。在这个阶层中，商人和工场主一般是投入资本最多的两大类人，因其财富而备受尊重。他们终日从事规划与设计，所以常常比大部分乡绅具有更敏锐的理解力。不过，由于他们通常思考的是自己具体业务的利益，而不是社会的利益，所以，他们的判断即使是以最大限度的公正做出的（并非总是如此），也更多地取决于关于他们自身利益的考虑，而很少取决于关于社会利益的考虑。他们比乡绅高明的地方，不在于他们更了解公共利益，而在于他们对自身利益的认识更深刻。正是由于更了解自身利益，他们常常利用乡绅们的慷慨，以一个极其简单而又诚实的信念，即他们的而不是乡绅的利益才是公共利益，说服乡绅们放弃自己和公共的利益。不过，在商业和制造业的任何部门，商人的利益总是在某些方面与公共利益不同，甚至相对立。扩张市场和减少竞争总是商人的利益所在。扩张市场往往与公共利益相一致，可是减少竞争则与公共利益相违背，只会使商人的利润超过应有的自然水平，从而使他们为了自身利益给其他的同胞带来不合情理的负担。因此，对于这一阶层提出的关于任何商业的新的法律和规定的建议，必须十分谨慎地去听取，并且不经过长期、细致、全面的认真考察绝不能轻易采纳。因为这个阶层的人们的利益从来不与公共利益完全一致，他们往往出于自身利益热衷于欺骗、甚至压迫公众，而且在许多情况下也确实欺骗和压迫了公众。

Years XII	Price of the Quarter of Wheat each Year①	Average of the different Prices of the same Year	The average Price of each Year in Money of the present Times②
	£. s. d.	£. s. d.	£. s. d.
1202	— 12 —	— — —	1 16 —
1205	{— 12 — — 13 4 — 15 —}	— 13 5	2 — 3
1223	— 12 —	— — —	1 16 —
1237	— 3 4	— — —	— 10 —
1243	— 2 —	— — —	— 6 —
1244	— 2 —	— — —	— 6 —
1246	— 16 —	— — —	2 8 —
1247	— 13 4	— — —	2 — —
1257	1 4 —	— — —	3 12 —
1258	{1 — — — 15 — — 16 —}	— 17 —	2 11 —
1270	{4 16 — 6 8 —}	5 12 —	16 16 —
1286	{— 2 8 — 16 —}	— 9 4	1 8 —
Total Average Price			35 9 3 2 19 1¼

---

① [As is explained above, P. 185 the prices from 1202 to 1597 are collected from Fleetwood (*Chronicon Preciosum*, 1707, pp. 77-124), and from 1598 to 1601 they are from the Eton College account without any reduction for the size of the Windsor quarter or the quality of the wheat, and consequently identical with those given in the table on p. 255 below, as to which see note.]

② [In the reduction of the ancient money to the eighteenth century standard the table in Martin Folkes (*Table of English Silver Coins*, 1745, p. 142) appears to have been followed. Approximate figures are aimed at (e.g., the factor 3 does duty both for 2. 906 and 2. 871), and the error is not always uniform, e.g., between 1464 and 1497 some of the sums appear to have been multiplied by the approximate $1\frac{1}{2}$ and others by the exact 1. 55.]

本章的结论

年　度 （共 12 年）	各年度每夸特 小麦的价格[1]			同一年度各种 价格的平均数			换算为现时货币后各 年度的平均价格[2]		
	镑	先令	便士	镑	先令	便士	镑	先令	便士
1202	—	12	—	—	—	—	1	16	—
1205	{ — 12 — — 13 4 — 15 — }			—	13	5	2	—	3
1223	—	12	—				1	16	—
1237	—	3	—				—	10	—
1243	—	2	—				—	6	—
1244	—	2	—				—	6	—
1246	—	16	—				2	8	—
1247	—	13	4				2	—	—
1257	1	4	—				3	12	—
1258	{ 1 — — — 15 — — 16 — }			—	17	—	2	11	—
1270	{ 4 16 — 6 8 — }			5	12	—	16	16	—
1286	{ — 2 8 — 16 — }			—	9	—	1	8	—
合　计							35	9	3
平均价格							2	19	$1\frac{1}{4}$

① 正如前面第 185 页所说的，1202～1597 年的价格依据弗利特伍德的记载（《宝贵的纪年考证》，1707 年，第 77～124 页）；1598～1601 年的价格依据伊顿公学的记载，对温莎夸特的大小和小麦的质量没有加以修订，因而与第 256 页的表格完全一致。

② 在将古代货币换算为 18 世纪的标准时，似乎是按照马丁·福克斯（《英格兰银币表》，1745 年，第 142 页）的表。采用了近似值（例如用 3 代替 2.906 和 2.872），误差不完全相同，例如，1467～1494 年似乎是用 1.5 的近似值去乘的，其他年份则是用 1.55 去乘的。

国民财富的性质与原理

Years XII	Price of the Quarter of Wheat each Year	Average of the different Prices of the same Year	The average Price of each Year in Money of the present Times
	£ . s. d.	£ . s. d.	£ . s. d.
1287	— 3 4	— — —	— 10 —
1288	⎧ — — 8 ⎫ ⎪ — 1 — ⎪ ⎪ — 1 4 ⎪ ⎨ — 1 6 ⎬ ⎪ — 1 8 ⎪ ⎪ — 2 — ⎪ ⎪ — 3 4 ⎪ ⎩ — 9 4 ⎭	— 3 1/4 ③	— 9 3/4
1289	⎧ — 12 — ⎫ ⎪ — 6 — ⎪ ⎨ — 2 — ⎬ ⎪ — 10 8 ⎪ ⎩ 1 — — ⎭	— 10 $1\frac{2}{4}$	1 10 $4\frac{2}{4}$ ④
1290	— 16 — ①	— — —	2 8 —
1294	— 16 —	— — —	2 8 —
1302	— 4 —	— — —	— 12 —
1309	— 7 2	— — —	1 1 6
1315	1 — —	— — —	3 — —

本章的结论

年　度 (共12年)	各年度小麦每夸特的价格	同一年度各种价格的平均数	换算为现时货币后各年度的平均价格
	镑　先令　便士	镑　先令　便士	镑　先令　便士
1287	—　3　4	—　—　—	—　10　—
	—　—　8		
	—　1　—		
	—　1　4		
1288	—　1　6	—　3　1/4 ③	—　9　3/4
	—　1　8		
	—　2　—		
	—　3　4		
	—　9　4		
	—　12　—		
	—　6　—		
1289	—　2　—	—　10　$1\frac{2}{4}$	1　10　$4\frac{2}{4}$ ④
	—　10　8		
	1　—　—		
1290	—　16　— ①	—　—　—	2　8　—
1294	—　16　—	—　—　—	2　8　—
1302	—　4　—	—　—　—	—　12　—
1309	—　7　2	—　—　—	1　1　6
1315	1　—　—	—　—　—	3　—　—

577

国民财富的性质与原理

Years XII	Price of the Quarter of Wheat each Year			Average of the different Prices of the same Year			The average Price of each Year in Money of the present Times		
	£	s.	d.	£	s.	d.	£	s.	d.
1316	$\begin{cases} 1 & — & — \\ 1 & 10 & — \\ 1 & 12 & — \\ 2 & — & — \end{cases}$			1	10	6	4	11	6
1317	$\begin{cases} 2 & 4 & — \\ — & 14 & — \\ 2 & 13 & —② \\ 4 & — & — \end{cases}$			1	19	6	5	18	6
1336	—	6	8	—	—	—	—	6	—
	—	2	—						
1338	—	3	4	—	—	—	—	10	—
Total Average Price							23	4	11 $\frac{1}{4}$
							1	18	8

① [This should be 2s. 7 $\frac{1}{4}$d. The mistake is evidently due to the 3s. 4d. belonging to the year 1287 having been erroneously added in.]

② [Sic in all editions. More convenient to the unpractised eye in adding up than '$\frac{1}{2}$'.]

③ ['And sometime xxs. as H. Knighton. —Fleetwood, *Chronicon Preciosum*, p. 82.]

④ [Miscopied: it is £ 213s. 4d. in Fleetwood, *op. cit.*, p. 92.]

本章的结论

年　度 （共12年）	各年度小麦每夸特的价格	同一年度各种价格的平均数	换算为现时货币后各年度的平均价格
	镑　先令　便士	镑　先令　便士	镑　先令　便士
1316	⎧ 1　—　—　⎫ ⎪ 1　10　— ⎪ ⎨ 1　12　—　⎬ ⎩ 2　—　—　⎭	1　10　6	4　11　6
1317	⎧ 2　4　—　⎫ ⎪ —　14　— ⎪ ⎨ 2　13　—②⎬ ⎩ 4　—　—　⎭	1　19　6	5　18　6
1336	—　6　8 —　2　—	—　—　—	—　6　—
1338	—　3　4	—　—　—	—　10　—
合计 平均价格			23　4　11$\frac{1}{4}$ 1　18　8

---

① 应为2先令7$\frac{1}{4}$便士。错误很明显，因为1287年的3先令4便士被错误地加进去了。

② 各版都是这样。2/4应为1/2。

③ 弗利特伍德的《宝贵的纪年考证》，第82页；"有时为20先令，如H. 佘顿所言。"

④ 抄写错误。弗利特伍德，上引书，第92页，为2镑13先令4便士。

国民财富的性质与原理

Years XII	Price of the Quarter of Wheat each Year			Average of the different Prices of the same year			The avarage Price of each Year in Money of the present Times		
	£.	s.	d.	£.	s.	d.	£.	s.	d.
1339	—	9	—	—	—	—	1	7	—
1349	—	2	—	—	—	—	—	5	2
1359	1	6	8	—	—	—	3	2	2
1361	—	2	1	—	—	—	—	4	8
1363	—	15	—	—	—	—	1	15	—
1369	1	—	—	1	2	—	2	9	4①
1379	$\begin{cases} 1 & 4 & —\\ — & 4 & — \end{cases}$			—	—	—	—	9	4
1387	—	2	—	—	—	—	—	4	8
1390	$\begin{cases} — & 13 & 4\\ — & 14 & —\\ — & 16 & — \end{cases}$ — 16 —			— 14 5 — 3 10			1	13	7
1401	$\begin{cases} — & 4 & 4\frac{1}{4}\\ — & 3 & 4 \end{cases}$						1	17	4
1407							—	8	11
1416	— 16 —			— — —			1	12	—
Average Price							15 1	9 5	4 $9\frac{1}{3}$

本章的结论

年　度 （共 12 年）	各年度小麦每夸特的价格	同一年度各种价格的平均数	换算为现时货币后各年度的平均价格
	镑　先令　便士	镑　先令　便士	镑　先令　便士
1339	—　9　—	—　—　—	1　7　—
1349	—　2　—	—　—　—	—　5　2
1359	1　6　8	—　—　—	3　2　2
1361	—　2　1	—　—　—	—　4　8
1363	—　15　—	—　—　—	1　15　—
1369	1　—　—	1　2　—	2　9　4①
1379	$\begin{cases} 1 \ \ 4 \ \ - \\ - \ \ 4 \ \ - \end{cases}$	—　—　—	—　9　4
1387	—　2　—	—　—　—	—　4　8
1390	$\begin{cases} - \ \ 13 \ \ 4 \\ - \ \ 14 \ \ - \\ - \ \ 16 \ \ - \end{cases}$ —　16　—	—　14　5	1　13　7
1401	$\begin{cases} - \ \ 4 \ \ 4\frac{1}{4} \\ - \ \ 3 \ \ 4 \end{cases}$	—　3　10	1　17　4
1407			—　8　11
1416	—16　—	—　—　—	1　12　—
合计 平均价格			15　9　4 1　5　9$\frac{1}{3}$

581

Years XII	Price of the Quarter of Wheat each Year			Average of the different Prices of the same Year			The average Price of each Year in Money of the present Times		
	£	s.	d.	£	s.	d.	£	s.	d.
1423	—	8	—	—	—	—	—	16	—
1425	—	4	—	—	—	—	—	8	—
1434	1	6	8	—	—	—	2	13	4
1435	—	5	4	—	—	—	—	10	8
1439	{1 — — / 1 6 8}			1	3	4	2	6	8
1440	1	4	—	—	—	—	2	8	—
1444	{— 4 4 / — 4 —}			—	4	2	—	8	4
1445	—	4	6	—	—	—	—	9	—
1447	—	8	—	—	—	—	—	16	—
1448	—	6	8	—	—	—	—	13	4
1449	—	5	—	—	—	—	—	10	—
1451	—	8	—	—	—	—	—	16	—
Total							12	15	4
Average Price							1	1	$3\frac{1}{2}$

---

① [Obviously a mistake for £ 2 11s. 4d.]

本章的结论

年　度 （共12年）	各年度小麦每夸特的价格	同一年度各种价格的平均数	换算为现时货币后各年度的平均价格
	镑　先令　便士	镑　先令　便士	镑　先令　便士
1423	—　8　—	—　—　—	—　16　—
1425	—　4　—	—　—　—	—　8　—
1434	1　6　8	—　—　—	2　13　4
1435	—　5　4	—　—　—	—　10　8
1439	{1　—　— 1　6　8}	1　3　4	2　6　8
1440	1　4　—	—　—　—	2　8　—
1444	[—　4　4	—　4　2	—　8　4
1445	—　4　—]		—　9　—
1447	—　4　6	—　—　—	—　16　—
1448	—　8　—	—　—　—	—　13　4
1449	—　6　8	—　—　—	—　10　—
1451	—　5　—	—　—　—	—　16　—
合　计	—　8　—	—　—　—	12　15　4
平均价格			1　1　3$\frac{1}{2}$

---

① 显然是2英镑11先令2便士之误。

Years XII	Price of the Quarter of Wheat each Year			Average of the different Prices of the same Year			The average Price of each Year in Money of the present Times		
	£	s.	d.	£	s.	d.	£	s.	d.
1453	—	5	4	—	—	—	—	10	8
1455	—	1	2	—	—	—	—	2	4
1457	—	7	8	—	—	—	—	15	4
1459	—	5	—	—	—	—	—	10	—
1460	—	8	—	—	—	—	—	16	—
1463	{ — 2 — / — 1 8 }			—	1	10	—	3	8
1464	—	6	8	—	—	—	—	10	—
1486	1	4	—	—	—	—	1	17	—
1491	—	14	8	—	—	—	1	2	—
1494	—	4	—	—	—	—	—	6	—
1495	—	3	4	—	—	—	—	5	—
1497	1	—	—	—	—	—	1	11	—
Total							8	9	—
Average Price							—	14	1

本章的结论

年　度 (共 12 年)	各年度小麦每夸特的价格	同一年度各种价格的平均数	换算为现时货币后各年度的平均价格
	镑　先令　便士	镑　先令　便士	镑　先令　便士
1453	—　5　4	—　—　—	—　10　8
1455	—　1　2	—　—　—	—　2　4
1457	—　7　8	—　—　—	—　15　4
1459	—　5　—	—　—　—	—　10　—
1460	—　8　—	—　—　—	—　16　—
1463	{—　2　— —　1　8}	—　1　10	—　3　8
1464	—　6　8	—　—　—	—　10　—
1486	1　4　—	—　—　—	1　17　—
1491	—　14　8	—　—　—	1　2　—
1494	—　4　—	—　—　—	—　6　—
1495	—　3　4	—　—　—	—　5　—
1497	1　—　—	—　—　—	1　11　—
合　计			8　9　—
平均价格			—　14　1

国民财富的性质与原理

Years XII	Price of the Quarter of Wheat each Year			Average of the different Prices of the same Year			The average Price of each Year in Money of the present Times		
	£	s.	d.	£	s.	d.	£	s.	d.
1499	—	4	—	—	—	—	—	8	—
1504	—	5	8	—	—	—	—	8	6
1521	1	—	—	—	—	—	1	10	—
1551	—	8	—	—	—	—	—	2	—
1553	—	8	—	—	—	—	—	8	—
1554	—	8	—	—	—	—	—	8	—
1555	—	8	—	—	—	—	—	8	—
1556	—	8	—	—	—	—	—	8	—
1557	⎧ — 4 —			—	17	$8\frac{1}{2}$①	—	17	$8\frac{1}{2}$
	⎪ — 5 —								
1558	⎨ — 8 —			—	—	—	—	8	—
1559	⎩ 2 13 4			—	—	—	—	8	—
1560	—	8	—	—	—	—	—	8	—
Total	—	8	—				6	0	$2\frac{1}{2}$
Average Price	—	8	—				—	10	$0\frac{5}{12}$②

① [This should be 17 s. 7d. here and in the next column.]

② [This should obviously be 10s. $\frac{5}{24}$d.]

本章的结论

年　度 (共12年)	各年度小麦每夸特的价格	同一年度各种价格的平均数	换算为现时货币后各年度的平均价格
	镑　先令　便士	镑　先令　便士	镑　先令　便士
1499	—　4　—	—　—　—	—　8　—
1504	—　5　8	—　—　—	—　8　6
1521	1　—　—	—　—　—	1　10　—
1551	—　8　—	—　—　—	—　2　—
1553	—　8　—		—　8　—
1554	—　8　—	—　—　—	—　8　—
1555	—　8　—	—　—　—	—　8　—
1556	—　8　—	—　—　—	—　8　—
1557		—　17　8$\frac{1}{2}$①	—　17　8$\frac{1}{2}$
	⎧ —　4　— ⎫ ⎨ —　5　— ⎬ ⎩ —　8　— ⎭ 　2　13　4	—　—　—	
1558	—　8　—		—　8　—
1559	—　8　—		—　8　—
1560	—　8　—	—　—　—	—　8　—
合　计			6　0　2$\frac{1}{2}$
平均价格			—　10　0$\frac{5}{12}$②

① 本行及下一行都应为17先令7便士。
② 显然应为10先令5/24便士。

国民财富的性质与原理

Years XII	Price of the Quarter of Wheat each Year			Average of the different Prices of the same Year			The average Price of each Year in Money of the present Times		
	£	s.	d.	£	s.	d.	£	s.	d.
1561	—	8	—	—	—	—	—	8	—
1562	—	8	—	—	—	—	—	8	—
1574	{2 1	16 4	— —}	2	—	—	2	—	—
1587	3	4	—	—	—	—	3	4	—
1594	2	16	—	—	—	—	2	16	—
1595	2	13	—①	—	—	—	2	13	—
1596	4	—	—	—	—	—	4	—	—
1597	{5 4	4 —	— —}	4	12	—	4	12	—
1598	2	16	8	—	—	—	2	16	8
1599	1	19	2	—	—	—	1	19	2
1600	1	17	8	—	—	—	1	17	8
1601	1	14	10	—	—	—	1	14	10
Total							28	9	4
Average Price							2	7	$5\frac{1}{3}$

---

① [Miscopied: it is £ 2 13s. 4d. in Fleetwood, *Chronicon Preciosum*, p. 123.]

本章的结论

年　度 （共12年）	各年度小麦每夸特的价格	同一年度各种价格的平均数	换算为现时货币后各年度的平均价格
	镑　先令　便士	镑　先令　便士	镑　先令　便士
1561	—　8　—	—　—　—	—　8　—
1562	—　8　—	—　—　—	—　8　—
1574	{2　16　— 　1　4　—}	2　—　— —　—　—	2　—　—
1587	3　4　—	—　—　—	3　4　—
1594	2　16　—	—　—　—	2　16　—
1595	2　13　—①	—　—　—	2　13　—
1596	4　—　—	—　—　—	4　—　—
1597	{5　4　— 　4　—　—}	4　12　—	4　12　—
1598	2　16　8	—　—　—	2　16　8
1599	1　19　2	—　—　—	1　19　8
1600	1　17　8	—	1　17　8
1601	1　14　10	—　—　—	1　14　10
合　计			28　9　4
平均价格			2　7　5$\frac{1}{3}$

① 抄写错误。弗利特伍德的《宝贵的纪年考证》第82页为2镑13先令4便士。

国民财富的性质与原理

Prices of the Quarter of nine Bushels of the best or highest priced Wheat at Windsor Market, on Lady-Day and Michaelmas, from 1595 to 1764, both inclusive; the Price of each Year being the Medium between the highest Prices of those Two Market-days. ①

Years	Wheat per quarter			Years	Wheat per quarter		
	£	s.	d.		£	s.	d.
1595	2	0	0	1609	2	10	0
1596	2	8	0	1610	1	15	10
1597	3	9	6	1611	1	18	8
1598	2	16	8	1612	2	2	4
1599	1	19	2	1613	2	8	8
1600	1	17	8	1614	2	1	$8\frac{1}{2}$
1601	1	14	10	1615	1	18	8
1602	1	9	4	1616	2	0	4
1603	1	15	4	1617	2	8	8
1604	1	10	8	1618	2	6	8
1605	1	15	10	1619	1	15	4
1606	1	13	0	1620	1	10	8
1607	1	16	8	Total	54	0	$6\frac{1}{2}$
1608	2	16	8	Average Price	2	1	$6\frac{9}{13}$

---

① [The list of prices, but not the division into periods, is apparently copied from Charles Smith (Tracts on the Corn Trade, 1766, pp. 97-102, cp. pp. 43, 104), who, however, states that it had been previously published, p. 96.]

本章的结论

温莎市场1595~1764年(两年包括在内)报喜节和米迦勒节每夸特(九蒲式耳)最好或最贵小麦的价格。每个价格是各年两个节日最高价格的平均数。①

年　度 (共26年)	每夸特 小麦的价格	年　度	每夸特小麦的价格
	镑　先令　便士		镑　先令　便士
1595	2　0　0	1609	2　10　0
1596	2　8　0	1610	1　15　10
1597	3　9　6	1611	1　18　8
1598	2　16　8	1612	2　2　4
1599	1　19　2	1613	2　8　8
1600	1　17　8	1614	2　1　$8\frac{1}{2}$
1601	1　14　10	1615	1　18　8
1602	1　9　4	1616	2　0　4
1603	1　15　4	1617	2　8　8
1604	1　10　8	1618	2　6　8
1605	1　15　10	1619	1　15　4
1606	1　13　0	1620	1　10　8
1607	1　16　8	合　计	54　0　$6\frac{1}{2}$
1608	2　16　8	平均价格	2　1　$6\frac{9}{13}$

---

① 价格表,不包括进行时期划分,显然是抄自查理·史密斯:《谷物贸易论丛》,1766年,第97~102页。但他说数字以前发表过,第96页。

Years	Wheat Per quarter			Years	Wheat per quarter		
	£	s.	d.		£	s.	d.
1621	1	10	4	1630	2	15	8
1622	2	18	8	1631	3	8	0
1623	2	12	0	1632	2	13	4
1624	2	8	0	1633	2	18	0
1625	2	12	0	1634	2	16	0
1626	2	9	4	1635	2	16	0
1627	1	16	0	1636	2	16	8
1628	1	8	0	Total	40	0	0
1629	2	2	0	Average Price	2	10	0

本章的结论

年　度 （共16年）	每夸特小麦的价格	年　度	每夸特小麦的价格
	镑　先令　便士		镑　先令　便士
1621	1　10　4	1630	2　15　8
1622	2　18　8	1631	3　8　0
1623	2　12　0	1632	2　13　4
1624	2　8　0	1633	2　18　0
1625	2　12　0	1634	2　16　0
1626	2　9　4	1635	2　16　0
1627	1　16　0	1636	2　16　8
1628	1　8　0	合　计	40　0　0
1629	2　2　0	平均价格	2　10　0

国民财富的性质与原理

Years	Wheat per quarter			Years
	£.	s.	d.	
1637	3	13	0	1659
1638	2	17	4	1660
1639	2	4	10	1661
1640	2	4	8	1662
1641	2	8	0	1663
1642 } wanting in the account. The year 1646 supplied by Bishop Fleetwood.	0	0	0	1664
1643	0	0	0	1665
1644	0	0	0	1666
1645	0	0	0	1667
1646	2	8	0	1668
1647	3	13	8	1669
1648	4	5	0	1670
				Brought over
1649	4	0	0	1671
1650	3	16	8	1672
1651	3	13	4	1673
1652	2	9	6	1674
1653	1	15	6	1675
1654	1	6	0	1676
1655	1	13	4	1677
1656	2	3	0	1678
1657	2	6	8	1679
1658	3	5	0	1680

本章的结论

年 度 (共64年)	每夸特 小麦的价格			年 度
	镑	先令	便士	
1637	3	13	0	1659
1638	2	17	4	1660
1639	2	4	10	1661
1640	2	4	8	1662
1641	2	8	0	1663
1642[1]	0	0	0	1664
1643	0	0	0	1665
1644	0	0	0	1666
1645	0	0	0	1667
1646[2]	2	8	0	1668
1647	3	13	8	1669
1648	4	5	0	1970
1649	4	0	0	1671
1650	3	16	8	1672
1651	3	13	4	1673
1652	2	9	6	1674
1653	1	15	6	1675
1654	1	6	0	1676
1655	1	13	4	1677
1656	2	3	0	1678
1657	2	6	8	1679
1658	3	5	0	1680

[1] 表中缺少1642~1645年的数字。
[2] 1646年的数字由弗利特伍德主教提供。

Wheat per quarter			Years	Wheat per quarter		
£.	s.	d.		£.	s.	d.
3	6	0	1681	2	6	8
2	16	6	1682	2	4	0
3	10	0	1683	2	0	0
3	14	0	1684	2	4	0
2	17	0	1685	2	6	8
2	0	6	1686	1	14	0
2	9	4	1687	1	5	2
1	16	0	1688	2	6	0
1	16	0	1689	1	10	0
2	0	0	1690	1	14	8
2	4	4	1691	1	14	0
2	1	8	1992	2	6	8
2	2	0	1693	3	7	8
2	1	0	1694	3	4	0
2	6	8	1695	2	13	0
3	8	8	1696	3	11	0
3	4	8	1697	3	0	0
1	18	0	1698	3	8	4
2	2	0	1699	3	4	0
2	19	0	1700	2	0	0
3	0	0	Total	153	1	8
2	5	0	Average Price	2	1	$0\frac{1}{3}$

本章的结论

每夸特小麦的价格			年 度	每夸特小麦的价格		
镑	先令	便士		镑	先令	便士
3	6	0	1681	2	6	8
2	16	6	1682	2	4	0
3	10	0	1683	2	0	0
3	14	0	1684	2	4	0
2	17	0	1685	2	6	8
2	0	6	1686	1	14	0
2	9	4	1687	1	5	2
1	16	0	1688	2	6	0
1	16	0	1689	1	10	0
2	0	0	1690	1	14	8
2	4	4	1691	1	14	0
2	1	8	1992	2	6	8
2	2	0	1693	3	7	8
2	6	8	1694	3	4	0
3	8	8	1695	2	13	0
3	4	8	1696	3	11	0
1	18	0	1697	3	0	0
2	2	0	1698	3	8	4
2	19	0	1699	3	4	0
3	0	0	16700	2	0	0
2	5	0	合 计	153	1	8
			平均价格	2	1	1/3

国民财富的性质与原理

Years	Wheat per quarter			Years
	£.	s.	d.	
1701	1	17	8	1723
1702	1	9	6	1724
1703	1	16	0	1725
1704	2	6	6	1726
1705	1	10	0	1727
1706	1	6	0	1728
1707	1	8	6	1729
1708	2	1	6	1730
1709	3	18	6	1731
1710	3	18	0	1732
1711	2	14	0	1733
1712	2	6	4	1734
1713	2	11	0	1735
1714	2	10	4	1736
1715	2	3	0	1737
1716	2	8	0	1738
1717	2	5	8	1739
1718	1	18	10	1740
1719	1	15	0	1741
1720	1	17	0	1742
1721	1	17	6	1743
1722	1	16	0	1744

本章的结论

年　度 (共64年)	每夸特小麦的价格			年　度
	镑	先令	便士	
1701	1	17	8	1723
1702	1	9	6	1724
1703	1	16	0	1725
1704	2	6	6	1726
1705	1	10	0	1727
1706	1	6	0	1728
1707	1	8	6	1729
1708	2	1	6	1730
1709	3	18	6	1731
1710	3	18	0	1732
1711	2	14	0	1733
1712	2	6	4	1734
1713	2	1	0	1735
1714	2	10	4	1736
1715	2	3	0	1737
1716	2	8	0	1738
1717	2	5	8	1739
1718	1	18	10	1740
1719	1	15	0	1741
1720	1	17	0	1742
1721	1	17	6	1743
1722	1	16	0	1744

国民财富的性质与原理

Wheat per quarter			Years	Wheat per quarter		
£.	s.	d.		£.	s.	d.
1	14	8	1745	1	7	6
1	17	0	1746	1	19	0
2	8	6	1747	1	14	10
2	6	0	1748	1	17	0
2	2	0	1749	1	17	0
2	14	6	1750	1	12	6
2	6	10	1751	1	18	6
1	16	6	1752	2	1	10
1	12	10	1753	2	4	8
1	6	8	1754	1	14	8
1	8	4	1755	1	13	10
1	18	10	1756	2	5	3
2	3	0	1757	3	0	0
2	0	4	1758	2	10	0
1	18	0	1759	1	19	10
1	15	6	1760	1	16	6
1	18	6	1761	1	10	3
2	10	8	1762	1	19	0
2	6	8	1763	2	0	9
1	14	0	1764	2	6	9
1	4	10	Total	129	13	6
1	4	10	Average Price	2	0	$6\frac{19}{32}$①

① [This should be $\frac{9}{32}$.]

本章的结论

每夸特小麦的价格			年　度	每夸特小麦的价格		
镑	先令	便士		镑	先令	便士
1	14	8	1745	1	7	6
1	17	0	1746	1	19	0
2	8	6	1747	1	14	10
2	6	0	1748	1	17	0
2	2	0	1749	1	17	0
2	14	6	1750	1	12	6
2	6	10	1751	1	18	6
1	16	6	1752	2	1	10
1	12	10	1753	2	4	8
1	6	8	1754	1	14	8
1	8	4	1755	1	13	10
1	18	10	1756	2	5	3
2	3	0	1757	3	0	0
2	0	4	1758	2	10	0
1	18	0	1759	1	19	10
1	15	6	1760	1	16	6
1	18	6	1761	1	10	3
2	10	8	1762	1	19	0
2	6	8	1763	2	0	9
1	14	0	1764	2	6	9
1	4	10	合　计	129	3	6
1	4	10	平均价格	2	0	$6\frac{19}{32}$ ①

---

① 应为 9/32。

国民财富的性质与原理

Years	Wheat per quarter			Years	Wheat per quarter		
	£	s.	d.		£	s.	d.
1731	1	12	10	1741	2	6	8
1732	1	6	8	1742	1	14	0
1733	1	8	4	1743	1	4	10
1734	1	18	10	1744	1	4	10
1735	2	3	0	1745	1	7	6
1736	2	0	4	1746	1	19	0
1737	1	18	0	1747	1	14	10
1738	1	15	6	1748	1	17	0
1739	1	18	6	1749	1	17	0
1740	2	10	8	1750	1	12	6
Total	18	12	8	Total	16	18	2
Average Price	1	17	$3\frac{1}{5}$	Average Price	1	13	$9\frac{4}{5}$

本章的结论

年　度 （共 10 年）	每夸特 小麦的价格			年　度 （共 10 年）	每夸特小麦的价格		
	镑	先令	便士		镑	先令	便士
1731	1	12	10	1741	2	6	8
1732	1	6	8	1742	1	14	0
1733	1	8	4	1743	1	4	10
1734	1	18	10	1744	1	4	10
1735	2	3	0	1745	1	7	6
1736	2	0	4	1746	1	19	0
1737	1	18	6	1747	1	14	10
1738	1	15	6	1748	1	17	0
1739	1	18	6	1749	1	17	0
1740	2	10	8	1750	1	12	6
合　计	18	12	8	合　计	16	18	2
平均价格	1	17	3/5	平均价格	1	13	$9^{4}/5$

BOOK II

Of The Nature, Accumulation, And Employment Of Stock

INTRODUCTION

<small>In the rude state of society stock is unnecessary.</small>   In that rude state of society in which there is no division of labour, in which exchanges are seldom made, and in which every man provides every thing for himself, it is not necessary that any stock should be accumulated or stored up beforehand, in order to carry on the business of the society. Every man endeavours to supply by his own industry his own occasional wants as they occur. When he is hungry, he goes to the forest to hunt; when his coat is worn out, he clothes himself with the skin of the first large animal he kills: and when his hut begins to go to ruin, he repairs it, as well as he can, with the trees and the turf that are nearest it.

<small>Division of labour makes it necessary.</small>   But when the division of labour has once been thoroughly introduced, the produce of a man's own labour can supply but a very small part of his occasional wants. The far greater part of them are supplied by the produce of other mens labour, which he purchases with the produce, or, what is the same thing, with the price of the produce of his own. But this purchase cannot be made till such time as the produce of his own labour has not only been completed, but sold. A stock of goods of different kinds, therefore, must be stored up somewhere sufficient to maintain him, and to supply him with the materials and tools of his work, till such time, at least, as both these events can be brought about. A weaver cannot apply himself entirely to his peculiar business, unless there is beforehand stored up somewhere, either in his own possession or in that of some other person, a stock sufficient to maintain him, and to supply him with the materials and tools of his work, till he has not only completed but sold his web. This accumulation must, evidently, be previous to his applying his in-

第二篇 论资财的性质及其蓄积和用途

绪 论

在没有分工,交换很少,自己所需要的一切物品都由自己供给的原始社会状态下,要经营社会事业,不需要预先积累或储备财货。人人都力图依靠自己的劳动来满足自身随时发生的需要。饿了就到森林去打猎充饥;衣服破旧了,便使用他所狩猎的最大兽类皮革来当衣服穿;房屋快要坍塌了,便就近采伐树枝和草皮,尽其所能地来加以修缮。_{在原始社会状态下,并不需要财货。}

在完全实行劳动分工之后,一个人自己劳动的产物,仅仅能够满足自身随时发生的需要的极小一部分。其他大部分需要必须依靠其他人的劳动产出来供给。这种产出必须由购买获得。购买的手段也就是他自己的产出,或者说,他自己产出的价格。但在购买以前,不仅自己劳动产出的生产已经完成,并且已经卖掉;所以至少在这两件事情能够办到以前,必须先在某个地方储备各种各样的货物,足以维持他的生活,并提供材料和工具供他使用。例如,在纺织业工作的人在织物尚未完成、尚未卖掉以前,如果不是在自己手中或他人手中有所积累足以维持他的生活,并给他提供材料和工具,他就织不出任何东西。很明显,这种储备必_{分工使财货储存很有必要。}

dustry for so long a time to such a peculiar business. ①

<small>Accumulation of stock and division of labour advance together.</small> As the accumulation of stock must, in the nature of things, be previous to the division of labour, so labour can be more and more subdivided in proportion only as stock is previously more and more accumulated. The quantity of materials which the same number of people can work up, increases in a great proportion as labour comes to be more and more subdivided; and as the operations of each workman are gradually reduced to a greater degree of simplicity, a variety of new machines come to be invented for facilitating and abridging those operations. As the division of labour advances, therefore, in order to give constant employment to an equal number of workmen, an equal stock of provisions, and a greater stock of materials and tools than what would have been necessary in a ruder state of things, must be accumulated beforehand. But the number of workmen in every branch of business generally increases with the division of labour in that branch, or rather it is the increase of their number which enables them to class and subdivide themselves in this manner.

<small>Accumulation causes the same quantity of industry to produce more.</small> As the accumulation of stock is previously necessary for carrying on this great improvement in the productive powers of labour, so that accumulation naturally leads to this improvement. The person who employs his stock in maintaining labour, necessarily wishes to employ it in such a manner as to produce as great a quantity of work as possible. He endeavours, therefore, both to make among his workmen the most proper distribution of employment, and to furnish them with the best machines which he can either invent or afford to purchase. His abilities in both these respects are generally in proportion to the extent of his stock, or to the number of people whom it can employ. The quantity of industry, therefore, not only increases in every country with the increase of the stock which employs it, but, in consequence of that increase, the same quantity of industry produces a much greater quantity of work.

Such are in general the effects of the increase of stock upon industry and its productive powers.

In the following book I have endeavoured to explain the nature of stock, the effects of its accumulation into capitals of different kinds, and the effects of the different employments of those capitals. This book is divided into five chapters. In the first chapter, I have endeav-

---

① [*Lectures*, p. 181.]

第二篇 绪　论

须非在他开始从事这项具体职业很久以前完成不可。①

就事物的性质来说,财货的积累必须在劳动分工以前;这样预先储备的财货愈丰富,分工就能按比例地愈加细密;而分工愈细密,相同数量的工人所能够加工的材料,就能按更大的比例增加。每个工人所从事的操作的繁简程度逐渐趋向更加简单,便有各种新机械发明使操作更为简便迅速。所以,当劳动分工取得进步时,在雇用工人数目不变情况下,所必须事先储备的食物供应,与在分工没有取得进步时相同;而必须事先储备的材料和工具,却要比在分工没有这样进步时所需要的数量要多。况且,一种行业分工越是细密,它的工人人数往往越是增加;更确切地说,正是工人人数的增加使他们分工能够越来越细密。〔分工和财货积累同时取得进步。〕

要大幅度地提高劳动生产力,预先储备财货是绝对必要的。而这种积累,也自然会导致这种劳动生产力的提高。使用积累雇用劳动的人,自然希望这种方法尽量使产出数量最大化。所以,他会努力做到:给他所雇用的工人分配的职务是最适当的分配,给工人所备的机械是最先进的。但在这两方面,他的能力如何,往往要看他能拥有多少财货,看他能雇用多少工人。所以,在每一国家里,产业的数量不仅随着兴办产业的财货的增加而增加,而且由于财货增加的结果,同等规模产业所能生产的产品也会大幅增加。〔财货的积累使同样数量的产业能够生产更多的产出。〕

这就是财货增加对产业和生产能力带来的影响。

我在本篇所要说明的是:财货的性质怎样？财货蓄积对各种资本的影响怎样？资本用途不同,其影响又是怎样？本篇共分五

---

① 《关于法律、警察、岁入及军备的演讲》,第181页。

<small>This Book treats of the nature of stock, the effects of its accumulation, and its different employments.</small> oured to show what are the different parts or branches into which the stock, either of an individual, or of a great society, naturally divides itself. In the second, I have endeavoured to explain the nature and operation of money considered as a particular branch of the general stock of the society. The stock which is accumulated into a capital, may either be employed by the person to whom it belongs, or it may be lent to some other person. In the third and fourth chapters, I have endeavoured to examine the manner in which it operates in both these situations. The fifth and last chapter treats of the different effects which the different employments of capital immediately produce upon the quantity both of national industry, and of the annual produce of land and labour.

第二篇 绪 论

本篇对财货的性质、积累的效果以及对财货的不同使用方法进行论述。

章。我们知道,一个人或一个大社会的资财,自然会分成几个不同部门或分支;所以在第一章,我要说明这些部门是什么。我们把货币看作是社会总财货的一个特殊部门。在第二章我要讨论货币的性质和作用。积累为资本的财货,要么由所有者自己使用,要么贷于其他人使用;所以在第三章和第四章,我要就这两种情形加以讨论。第五章所要讨论的是,资本的不同用途,对国民产出水平及土地和劳动的年产出数量会直接发生什么不同的影响。

CHAPTER I

Of The Division Of Stock

<small>A man does not think of obtaining revenue from a small stock.</small> When the stock which a man possesses is no more than sufficient to maintain him for a few days or a few weeks, he seldom thinks of deriving any revenue from it. He consumes it as sparingly as he can, and endeavours by his labour to acquire something which may supply its place before it be consumed altogether. His revenue is, in this case, derived from his labour only. This is the state of the greater part of the labouring poor in all countries.

<small>but when he has more than enough for immediate consumption, he endeavours to derive a revenue from the rest,</small> But when he possesses stock sufficient to maintain him for months or years, he naturally endeavours to derive a revenue from the greater part of it; reserving only so much for his immediate consumption as may maintain him till this revenue begins to come in. His whole stock, therefore, is distinguished into two parts. That part which, he expects, is to afford him this revenue, is called his capital. The other is that which supplies his immediate consumption; and which consists either, first, in that portion of his whole stock which was originally reserved for this purpose; or, secondly, in his revenue, from whatever source derived, as it gradually comes in; or, thirdly, in such things as had been purchased by either of these in former years, and which are not yet entirely consumed; such as a stock of clothes, household furniture, and the like. In one, or other, or all of these three articles, consists the stock which men commonly reserve for their own immediate consumption.

There are two different ways in which a capital may be employed so as to yield a revenue or profit to its employer.

<small>using it either as (1) circulating capital,</small> First, it may be employed in raising, manufacturing, or purchasing goods, and selling them again with a profit. The capital employed in this manner yields no revenue or profit to its employer, while it either remains in his possession, or continues in the same shape. The goods of the merchant yield him no revenue or profit till

— 610 —

第一章 论财货的划分

一个人所拥有的财货,如果仅仅能够维持他数日或几个星期的生活,他就很少想从这笔财货中赚取收入。他将慎之又慎地消费它,并且希望在用完它之前,能够依靠自身的劳动,取得一些东西来做补充。在这种情况下,他的收入完全来源于他的劳动。这就是各国大部分贫穷劳动者的生活状态。

一个人从很小数量的财货中取得收入。

他所有的财货,如果足够维持他数月或数年的生活,他自然希望这笔财货有一大部分可以提供收入;他将仅保留一个适当部分,作为没有取得收入以前的消费来维持他的生活。他的全部财货就分成两部分。他希望从中取得收入的部分,称为资本;另一部分,则供给目前消费,其中包含三项东西:(1)原为这一目的而保留的那部分财货;(2)逐渐取得的收入,不论来源如何;(3)以前使用以上两项购进但至今尚未用完的物品,如被服、家具等等。为目前的消费而保留的财货,或包含三项其一,或三项其二,或三项全有。

超前所费的量,但当消费数时,他就想设法从剩余财货获取收入。

为投资者提供收入或利润的资本使用方法,有两种:

第一,资本可用来生产、制造或购买物品,然后再卖出去以取得利润。这样使用的资本,为所有者持有或保持原状时,对于投资者来说不能提供任何收入或利润。商人的货物,在没有卖出换

(1)要么通过使用流动资本。

he sells them for money, and the money yields him as little till it is again exchanged for goods. His capital is continually going from him in one shape, and returning to him in another, and it is only by means of such circulation, or successive exchanges, that it can yield him any profit. Such capitals, therefore, may very properly be called circulating capitals.

<small>or (2) fixed capital</small>
Secondly, it may be employed in the improvement of land, in the purchase of useful machines and instruments of trade, or in suchlike things as yield a revenue or profit without changing masters, or circulating any further. Such capitals, therefore, may very properly be called fixed capitals.

<small>Different proportions of fixed and circulating capital are required in different trades.</small>
Different occupations require very different proportions between the fixed and circulating capitals employed in them.

The capital of a merchant, for example, is altogether a circulating capital. He has occasion for no machines or instruments of trade, unless his shop, or warehouse, be considered as such.

Some part of the capital of every master artificer or manufacturer must be fixed in the instruments of his trade. This part, however, is very small in some, and very great in others. A master taylor requires no other instruments of trade but a parcel of needles. Those of the master shoemaker are a little, though but a very little, more expensive. Those of the weaver rise a good deal above those of the shoemaker. The far greater part of the capital of all such master artificers, however, is circulated, either in the wages of their workmen, or in the price of their materials, and repaid with a profit by the price of the work.

In other works a much greater fixed capital is required. In a great iron-work, for example, the furnace for melting the ore, the forge, the slitt-mill, are instruments of trade which cannot be erected without a very great expence. In coal-works, and mines of every kind, the machinery necessary both for drawing out the water and for other purposes, is frequently still more expensive.

That part of the capital of the farmer which is employed in the instruments of agriculture is a fixed; that which is employed in the wages and maintenance of his labouring servants, is a circulating capital. He makes a profit of the one by keeping it in his own possession, and of the other by parting with it. The price or value of his labouring cattle is a fixed capital in the same manner as that of the instruments

得货币以前,不能提供收入或利润;货币在没有重新付出换得货物以前也是一样。商人的资本不断以一个形态支出,而又以另一个形态收进;而且也只有依靠这种流通,或依靠这种持续不断的交换,才有利润可赚。因此,这样的资本可称为流动资本。

第二,资本又可用来改良土地,购买有用的机器和工具,或用来配备无须更换所有权人或无须进一步流通即可提供利润的东西。这样的资本可称为固定资本。

(2)要么通过使用固定资本。

不同行业所必需的固定资本与流动资本之间的比例,差异很大。

不同行业的要求固定与流动资本之间的比例也不同。

例如,商人的资本全部是流动资本。他简直不需要使用机器或工具,除非把商店或货栈也看作是机器或工具。

手工业者和制造者的资本,一部分必须固定在工具上。不过,这部分的大小,各个行业有所不同;有的行业很小,有的行业很大。裁缝业者除了一包针外,不需要其他任何工具。制鞋业者的工具比较值钱一些,但也多得有限。织布者与制鞋业者相比较,工具就贵得多了。但是,这一类手工业者的资本,大部分是流动的,一开始或作为工人工资而流出,或作为原材料价格而流出,然后再从产品价格流入,其中还含有利润。

在其他行业里,就需要数量大得多的固定资本了。比如,一个大铁工厂,要设置熔铁炉、锻造场、截铁场,非有很大数量的经费不可。再加上开采煤矿所需的抽水机以及其他各种机械,所需花费还要多。

就农场主来说,用于购买农具的资本是固定的;用于维持工人与支付工资的资本是流动的。他保管前者在手中从而获取利润,他把后者支付出去从而获取利润。耕畜的价格或价值,和农

of husbandry: Their maintenance is a circulating capital in the same manner as that of the labouring servants. The farmer makes his profit by keeping the labouring cattle, and by parting with their maintenance. Both the price and the maintenance of the cattle which are bought in and fattened, not for labour, but for sale, are a circulating capital. The farmer makes his profit by parting with them. A flock of sheep or a herd of cattle that, in a breeding country, is bought in, neither for labour, nor for sale, but in order to make a profit by their wool, by their milk, and by their increase, is a fixed capital. The profit is made by keeping them. Their maintenance is a circulating capital. The profit is made by parting with it; and it comes back with both its own profit, and the profit upon the whole price of the cattle, in the price of the wool, the milk, and the increase. The whole value of the seed too is properly a fixed capital. Though it goes backwards and forwards between the ground and the granary, it never changes masters, and therefore does not properly circulate. The farmer makes his profit, not by its sale, but by its increase.

<small>The stock of a society is divided in the same way into</small>

The general stock of any country or society is the same with that of all its inhabitants or members, and therefore naturally divides itself into the same three portions, each of which has a distinct function or office.

<small>(1) the portion reserved for immediate consumption,</small>

The First, is that portion which is reserved for immediate consumption, and of which the characteristic is, that it affords no revenue or profit. It consists in the stock of food, clothes, household furniture, &c. , which have been purchased by their proper consumers, but which are not yet entirely consumed. The whole stock of mere dwelling-houses too subsisting at any one time in the country, make a part of this first portion. The stock that is laid out in a house, if it is to be the dwelling-house of the proprietor, ceases from that moment to serve in the function of a capital, or to afford any revenue to its owner. A dwelling-house, as such, contributes nothing to the revenue of its inhabitant; and though it is, no doubt, extremely useful to him, it is as his clothes and household furniture are useful to him, which, however, make a part of his expence, and not of his revenue. If it is to be let to a tenant for rent, as the house itself can produce nothing, 1 the tenant must always pay the rent out of some other revenue which he derives either from labour, or stock, or land. Though a house, therefore, may yield a revenue to its proprietor, and thereby serve in the function of a capital to him, it cannot yield any to the public, nor

具一样，可称为固定资本；饲养牲畜的费用和维持工人的费用一样，可称为流动资本。农场主获取利润的方法，一个是保有耕畜，一个是支付饲养牲畜的费用。但要是以出售为目的，而不是以代耕为目的的牲畜，其购买费和饲养费却都应归入流动资本之中。在这里，农场主靠出卖牲畜来获取利润。在生产牲畜的国家，不是以代耕或贩卖为目的，而是以剪毛、挤乳、繁殖类似获取利润为目的而买入的羊或牛，应当称为固定资本；在这里生利的方法在于保有它们。它们的维持费是流动资本；在这里，生利的方法在于付出维持费。在赚回维持费用时，维持费的利润及牲畜全部价格的利润，都会在羊毛价格、产乳价格、繁种价格上体现出来。种子的全部价值，也可称为固定资本。种子虽然往返于土地与谷仓之间，但没有更换所有权人，所以没有真正地流动过。农场主获取利润，不是靠出售种子，而是靠种子生产产品。

一个国家或一个社会的总财货，也就是其全体居民的财货，所以也就自然分为这三个部分，各自发挥自己的特殊作用。_{社会上的财货以同样的方式分为三部分：}

第一部分是留作目前消费使用，其特性是不提供收入或利润。已经被消费者购买，但还没有被完全消费掉的食品、衣服、家具等物，属于这一类。仅供居住的国内房屋，也是这个部分中的一个部分。投在房屋上的财货，如果该房屋是由其所有者自住，那么，从那时刻起就失去资本的作用；就是说，它对屋主不提供任何收入。这样的住房，虽然与衣服、家具一样对他很有用，但也像衣服、家具一样，不能给他提供收入。它只是费用的一部分，不是收入的一部分。向他人出租房屋，可以获取租金，但房屋本身不能生产任何东西，承租人仍须从劳动、资本或土地上所得的收入来支付租金。所以，对于房屋所有权人，它虽然提供收入，因而有_{（1）留作直接消费的部分。}

serve in the function of a capital to it, and the revenue of the whole body of the people can never be in the smallest degree increased by it. Clothes, and household furniture, in the same manner, sometimes yield a revenue, and thereby serve in the function of a capital to particular persons. In countries where masquerades are common, it is a trade to let out masquerade dresses for a night. Upholsterers frequently let furniture by the month or by the year. Undertakers let the furniture of funerals by the day and by the week. Many people let furnished houses, and get a rent, not only for the use of the house, but for that of the furniture. The revenue, however, which is derived from such things, must always be ultimately drawn from some other source of revenue. Of all parts of the stock, either of an individual, or of a society, reserved for immediate consumption, what s laid out in houses is most slowly consumed. A stock of clothes may last several years: a stock of furniture half a century or a century: but a stock of houses, well built and properly taken care of, may last many centuries. Though the period of their total consumption, however, is more distant, they are still as really a stock reserved for immediate consumption as either clothes or household furniture.

(2) the fixed capital, which consists of

The Second of the three portions into which the general stock of the society divides itself, is the fixed capital; of which the characteristic is, that it affords a revenue or profit without circulating or changing masters. It consists chiefly of the four following articles:

(a) useful machines,

First, of all useful machines and instruments of trade which facilitate and abridge labour:

(b) profitable buildings,

Secondly, of all those profitable buildings which are the means of procuring a revenue, not only to their proprietor who lets them for a rent, but to the person who possesses them and pays that rent for them; such as shops, warehouses, workhouses, farmhouses, with all their necessary buildings; stables, granaries, &c. These are very different from mere dwelling houses. They are a sort of instruments of trade, and may be considered in the same light:

(c) improvements of land,

Thirdly, of the improvements of land, of what has been profitably laid out in clearing, draining, enclosing, manuring, and reducing it into the condition most proper for tillage and culture. An improved farm may very justly be regarded in the same light as those useful machines which facilitate and abridge labour, and by means of which, an equal circulating capital can afford a much greater revenue to its employer. An improved farm is equally advantageous and more dura-

资本作用,但对社会公众,则不提供收入,不能有资本作用。它丝毫不能增加全体人民的收入。同样,衣服和家具有时也可提供收入,从而对特殊个人有资本作用。化装舞会盛行的地方,就有人以出租化装衣服为业,租期为一个夜晚。家具商人常常按月或按年出租家具;殡仪店往往按日按星期出租殡葬用品。还有许多人出租带有家具的房屋,不仅收取房租,还收取家具租金。总之,这种租赁事件到处都有。但由出租此种物品而得来的收入,归根结底总是来自其他收入来源。此外,还有一件事情必须加以注意,即无论就个人来说或就社会来说,在留作目前消费的各种财货中,消费最慢的是投在房屋上的那一部分。衣服可穿用数年,家具可使用 50 年或 100 年,但建筑坚固、保护周全的房屋,却可使用好几百年。不过房屋虽需要很长时间才会消耗掉,但它仍是供作目前消费的财货,与衣服、家具一样。

  第二部分就是固定资本。其特性是不必经过流通,不必更换所有权人,即可提供收入或利润。其中主要包含四项: (2) 固定资本包括:

  第一,所有便利劳动和节省劳动的有用机器与工具。(a) 有用的机器;

  第二,一切可以获取利润的建筑物,如商店、货栈、工场、农屋、厩舍、谷仓等。这类建筑物,不仅对出租房屋的房东提供收入,而且对承租人来说也是获取收入的手段。这种建筑物和房屋大不相同。这是营业上的工具,也应该视为营业上的用具。(b) 营利性建筑;

  第三,用开垦、排水、围墙、施肥等有利可图的方法所投下的、使土地变得更适于耕种的土地改良费。改良的农场好像有用的机器,可以便利劳动,节省劳动;它使投资者投下的等量流动资本能提供大得多的收入。这两者是一样有利的,但机器较易磨损,而改良的土地却比较耐久。农场主除了按照最有利的方法,投下 (c) 土地改良;

ble than any of those machines, frequently requiring no other repairs than the most profitable application of the farmer's capital employed in cultivating it:

<small>and(d) acquiced and useful abilities,</small> Fourthly, of the acquired and useful abilities of all the inhabitants or members of the society. The acquisition of such talents, by the maintenance of the acquirer during his education, study, or apprenticeship, always costs a real expence, which is a capital fixed and realized, as it were, in his person. Those talents, as they make a part of his fortune, so do they likewise of that of the society to which he belongs. The improved dexterity of a workman may be considered in the same light as a machine or instrument of trade which facilitates and abridges labour, and which, though it costs a certain expence, repays that expence with a profit. ①

<small>and (3) the circulating capital, which consists of</small> The Third and last of the three portions into which the general stock of the society naturally divides itself, is the circulating capital; of which the characteristic is, that it affords a revenue only by circulating or changing masters. It is composed likewise of four parts:

<small>(a) the money,</small> First, of the money by means of which all the other three are circulated and distributed to their proper consumers:

<small>(b) the stock of provisions in the possession of the sellers,</small> Secondly, of the stock of provisions which are in the possession of the butcher, the grazier, the farmer, the corn-merchant, the brewer, &c. and from the sale of which they expect to derive a profit:

<small>(c) the materials of clothes, fur. niture, and buildings,</small> Thirdly, of the materials, whether altogether rude, or more or less manufactured, of clothes, furniture and building, which are not yet made up into any of those three shapes, but which remain in the hands of the growers, the manufacturers, the mercers, and drapers, the timber-merchants, the carpenters and joiners, the brick-makers, &c.

<small>and (d) completed work in the hands of the merchant or manufacturer.</small> Fourthly, and lastly, of the work which is made up and completed, but which is still in the hands of the merchant or manufacturer, and not yet disposed of or distributed to the proper consumers; such as the finished work which we frequently find ready-made in the shops of the smith, the cabinet-maker, the goldsmith, the jeweller, the china-merchant, &c. The circulating capital consists in this manner, of the provisions, materials, and finished work of all kinds that are in the hands of their respective dealers, and of the money that is necessary for circulating and distributing them to those who are finally to

---

① [But in bk. i., ch. x., the remuneration of improved dexterity is treated as wages.]

耕种所必须投下的资本以外,对于土地简直用不着什么修缮。

第四,社会上一切人民学到的有用才能。学习一种才能,须受教育,须进学校,须做学徒,所费不少。这样费去的资本,好像已经实现并且固定在学习者的身上。这些才能,对于他个人自然是财产的一部分,对于他所属的社会,也是财产的一部分。工人熟练程度的提高,可和便利劳动、节省劳动的机器和工具同样看作是社会上的固定资本。学习的时候,固然要花一笔费用,但这种费用可以得到偿还,并且赚取①利润。(d) 有用才能的获得。

社会总资本中第三部分也是最后一部分是流动资本。其特性是要依靠流通、要靠变换所有权人而提供收入。它也包含四项:(3) 流动资本包括:

第一,货币。只有依靠货币,其他三项流动资本才能周转而分配给真正的消费者。(a) 货币。

第二,屠户、牧畜业主、农场主、谷物商、酿酒商等人所有的食品;他们从出售这种食品中可以获得利润。(b) 销售者手中的食物。

第三,还在耕种者、制造者、布商、木材商、木匠、瓦匠等人手中的衣服、家具、房屋三者的材料。如果还没有加工制成衣服、家具或房屋的材料,也就属于这一项的范畴。(c) 用来制造衣服、家具和建筑的材料。

第四,已经制成,但仍在制造者或商人手中,还没有出售给或分配给真正消费者的物品,例如锻冶店、木器店、金店、宝石店、瓷器店以及其他各种店铺柜台上陈列着的制成品。这样,流动资本包含各种商家手里的食品、材料、制成品及货币。食品、材料、制成品的流转和分配,都必须要有货币。否则就不能到达最后使用 (d) 商制业者或手人造业成中的制品。

---

① 在第一篇第十章里,熟练技能的报酬被当作工资看待。

use, or to consume them.

Of these four parts three, provisions, materials, and finished work, are, either annually, or in a longer or shorter period, regularly withdrawn from it, and placed either in the fixed capital or in the stock reserved for immediate consumption.

_{The last three parts of the circulating capital are regularly withdrawn from it. Every fixed capital is derived from and supported by a circulating capital, and cannot yield any revenue without it.}

Every fixed capital is both originally derived from, and requires to be continually supported by a circulating capital. All useful machines and instruments of trade are originally derived from a circulating capital, which furnishes the materials of which they are made, and the maintenance of the workmen who make them. They require too a capital of the same kind to keep them in constant repair.

No fixed capital can yield any revenue but by means of a circulating capital. The most useful machines and instruments of trade will produce nothing without the circulating capital which affords the materials they are employed upon, and the maintenance of the workmen who employ them. Land, however improved, will yield no revenue without a circulating capital, which maintains the labourers who cultivate and collect its produce.

_{The end of both fixed and circulating capital is to maintain and augment the other part of the stock.}

To maintain and augment the stock which may be reserved for immediate consumption, is the sole end and purpose both of the fixed and circulating capitals. It is this stock which feeds, clothes, and lodges the people. Their riches or poverty depends upon the abundant or sparing supplies which those two capitals can afford to the stock reserved for immediate consumption.

_{The circulating capital is kept up by the produce of land, mines, and fisheries.}

So great a part of the circulating capital being continually withdrawn from it, in order to be placed in the other two branches of the general stock of the society; it must in its turn require continual supplies, without which it would soon cease to exist. These supplies are principally drawn from three sources, the produce of land, of mines, and of fisheries. These afford continual supplies of provisions and materials, of which part is afterwards wrought up into finished work, and by which are replaced the provisions, materials, and finished work continually withdrawn from the circulating capital. From mines too is drawn what is necessary for maintaining and augmenting that part of it which consists in money. For though, in the ordinary course of busi-

或消费它们的人手中。

在这四项中,有三项即食品、材料、制成品,通常在一年内或在比一年要长或短的时期内,由流动资本变成固定资本,或者变成留作目前消费的财货。

> 流动资本三个部分经常从中退出

固定资本都来源于流动资本,而且要不断地由流动资本来补充。营业上一切有用的机器工具,都出自流动资本。流动资本提供建造机器的材料,提供维持建造机器的工人的费用。机器制成以后,又常常必须由流动资本来修理维护。

> 固定资本来源于流动资本,并得到流动资本的支持,所有资本来源于流动资本

如果没有流动资本,固定资本就不能提供任何收入。工作所使用的材料和工人生存所依赖的食品,都出自流动资本。没有流动资本,即使最有用的机器和工具,也不能生产一点东西。土地无论怎样改良,没有流动资本,也不能提供收入。维持耕种和收获的工人,也非要有流动资本不可。

> 没有流动资本,固定资本就不可能生任何收入。

固定资本和流动资本具有唯一的目的,那就是,使留作目前消费的财货不致缺乏,而且还能够增加。人民的衣食住宅都依靠这种财货。人民的贫富与否,也取决于这两种资本所能够提供的这项财货是丰富还是贫乏。

> 固定资本和流动资本唯一的目的是保住财货其他并有所增加。

为了补充社会上固定资本和用作目前消费的财货,需要不断从流动资本中抽出大部分,所以流动资本也必须不断地补充。如果没有这种补充,流动资本不久就会干竭。这种补充有三个主要来源,即土地产出物品、矿山产出物品和渔业产出物品;这三个来源不断供应食品和材料。其中有一部分通过加工制造为产成品。正是由于有了这种供给,从流动资本里撤离出来的食品、材料和产成品,才有了新的补充。此外,还必须使用矿山开采出来的金属进行铸造货币,用来维持和补充流动资本的货币部分。在普通

> 流动资本由土地、矿业和渔业产出物品供应

ness, this part is not, like the other three, necessarily withdrawn from it, in order to be placed in the other two branches of the general stock of the society, it must, however, like all other things, be wasted and worn out at last, and sometimes too be either lost or sent abroad, and must, therefore, require continual, though, no doubt, much smaller supplies.

<small>which require both fixed and circulating capitals to cultivate them,</small> Land, mines, and fisheries, require all both a fixed and a circulating capital to cultivate them: and their produce replaces with a profit, not only those capitals, but all the others in the society. Thus the farmer annually replaces to the manufacturer the provisions which he had consumed and the materials which he had wrought up the year before; and the manufacturer replaces to the farmer the finished work which he had wasted and worn out in the same time. This is the real exchange that is annually made between those two orders of people, though it seldom happens that the rude produce of the one and the manufactured produce of the other, are directly bartered for one another; because it seldom happens that the farmer sells his corn and his cattle, his flax and his wool, to the very same person of whom he chuses to purchase the clothes, furniture, and instruments of trade which he wants. He sells, therefore, his rude produce for money, with which he can purchase, wherever it is to be had, the manufactured produce he has occasion for. Land even replaces, in part at least, the capitals with which fisheries and mines are cultivated. It is the produce of land which draws the fish from the waters; and it is the produce of the surface of the earth which extracts the minerals from its bowels.

<small>and, when their fertility is equal, yield produce proportionate to the capital employed.</small> The produce of land, mines, and fisheries, when their natural fertility is equal, is in proportion to the extent and proper application of the capitals employed about them. When the capitals are equal and equally well applied, it is in proportion to their natural fertility.

<small>Where there is tolerable security all stock is employed in one or other of the three ways.</small> In all countries where there is tolerable security, every man of common understanding will endeavour to employ whatever stock he can command, in procuring either present enjoyment or future profit. If it is employed in procuring present enjoyment, it is a stock reserved for immediate consumption. If it is employed in procuring future profit, it must procure this profit either by staying with him, or by going from him. In the one ease it is a fixed, in the other it is a circulating capital. A man must be perfectly crazy who, where there is tolerable security, does not employ all the stock which he commands, whether

情况下，货币虽然不需要从流动资本抽出来用作固定资本或目前消费的财货，但像其他东西一样，货币难免磨损，有时难免丢失或被输往外国，所以仍然要不断地加以补充，不过数量上要小得多。

土地、矿山和渔业都需要有固定资本和流动资本来经营。这些行业的产出，不仅要偿还各自投下的资本，还要偿还社会上一切其他投入的资本，并且还带来利润。制造者每年消费的食品和材料由农场主年年来补充；与此同时，农场主每年所消费的工业品则由制造者年年来补充。在这两个阶级之间虽然用制造品和农产品互相直接交换的情况很少发生，但他们之间年年进行交换的实际情况却就是如此进行的。很少直接交换的原因在于，农场主所销售的是谷物、牲畜、亚麻、羊毛；他所要的是衣服、家具和工具。买谷物、牲畜、亚麻、羊毛的人，很少就是要卖衣服、家具、工具的人。所以农场主先用原生产出物品换取货币；有了货币，他就可以随地购买他所需要的制造品。经营渔业和矿业的资本，也至少有一部分由土地来补充。从水里捕鱼和从地里挖掘开采矿产，都离不开地面上的产物。

在自然生产力大小相等的情况下，土地、矿山和渔场的产出数量，都与所使用资本数量的大小与使用得当与否成比例。在资本数量相等，投资使用方法又同样适当的情况下，它们的产出数量就和它们的自然生产力的大小成比例。

在一切生活比较安定的国家里，有常识的人，无不愿用可供他使用的资财来满足目前享乐，或用来赚取未来利润。如是用来满足目前享乐，那它就是留作目前消费的资财。如是用来追求未来利润，那么赚取利润的方法，不是把资财保留在手里，就是把资财花用出去。在前一场合，它是固定资本；在后一场合，它是流动

it be his own or borrowed of other people, in some one or other of those three ways.

<small>But in countries where violence prevails much stock is buried and concealed.</small>   In those unfortunate countries, indeed, where men are continually afraid of the violence of their superiors, they frequently bury and conceal a great part of their stock, in order to have it always at hand to carry with them to some place of safety, in case of their being threatened with any of those disasters to which they consider themselves as at all times exposed. This is said to be a common practice in Turkey, in Indostan, and, I believe, in most other governments of Asia. It seems to have been a common practice among our ancestors during the violence of the feudal government. Treasure-trove was in those times considered as no contemptible part of the revenue of the greatest sovereigns in Europe. It consisted in such treasure as was found concealed in the earth, and to which no particular person could prove any right. This was regarded in those times as so important an object, that it was always considered as belonging to the sovereign, and neither to the finder nor to the proprietor of the land, unless the right to it had been conveyed to the latter by an express clause in his charter. It was put upon the same footing with gold and silver mines, which, without a special clause in the charter, were never supposed to be comprehended in the general grant of the lands, though mines of lead, copper, tin, and coal were, as things of smaller consequence.

资本。在生命财产相当安全的场合,一个人如果不把他所能支配的一切资财(不管是自有的或借入的)用于这些用途之一,说他不是疯狂,我是不能相信的。

在那些不幸的国家里,人民害怕最高统治者随时对他们财产进行侵犯,因此,人民往往把大部分财货埋藏起来;这样做的目的是,一旦他们时时刻刻所提防的灾难降临时,他们就可以随时把财货带往安全地方。据说,在土耳其、在印度,以及我相信在亚洲其他各个国家,都常常发生这种事情。在封建暴政时代,这种情况在我们国家似乎也很普遍。在那个时代里,发掘出土的珍宝被视为欧洲各大国君主的一项重要收入。凡是埋藏地下、无从证明属于谁的物品,一律视为国王所有;除非经过国王特令恩准,否则物品的所有权就既不属于发现者,也不属于土地所有者;这种珍宝在当时极受重视。当时的金银矿产也是同样的政策。如果不是明令特许的话,金银矿产并不包含在普通土地所有权之内;随意开采是不行的。但铅、铜、锡、煤矿由于比较起来不算重要,所以才听任人民自由开采。

> 在那政府暴虐的国家里,许多财货被埋藏和隐匿起来。但这些肆虐国里,